Out of the Shadows, Into the Streets!

Out of the Shadows, Into the Streets!

Transmedia Organizing and the Immigrant Rights Movement

Sasha Costanza-Chock

The MIT Press
Cambridge, Massachusetts
London, England

For information on quantity discounts, please email special_sales@mitpress.mit.edu.

This book was set in ITC Stone Serif and Stone Sans Serif 9/14 by Toppan Best-set Premedia Limited. Printed and bound in the United States of America.

Library of Congress Cataloging-in-Publication Data is available.

Costanza-Chock, Sasha, 1976–
Out of the shadows, into the streets! : transmedia organizing and the immigrant rights movement / Sasha Costanza-Chock ; foreword by Manuel Castells.
    pages   cm
Includes bibliographical references and index.
ISBN 978-0-262-02820-2 (hardcover : alk. paper)
1. United States—Emigration and immigration—Government policy. 2. Immigrants—Civil rights—United States. 3. Mass media—United States. 4. Social justice—United States. 5. Europe—Emigration and immigration—Government policy. 6. Immigrants—Civil rights—Europe. 7. Mass media—Europe. 8. Social justice—Europe.   I. Title.
JV6456.C67   2014
323.3'29120973—dc23
2014013216

10 9 8 7 6 5 4 3 2 1

We are multitudes. *No conocemos las fronteras.*

Contents

Foreword

Manuel Castells

Over the last few years, a wave of social protests has rippled across the world, and in its wake we have witnessed the profile of the social movements of the information age. Yet, because of the novelty of their forms of mobilization and organization, an ideological debate is raging over the interpretation of these movements. Since in most cases they challenge traditional forms of politics and organizations, the political establishment, the media establishment, and the academic establishment have for the most part refused to acknowledge their significance, even after upheavals as important as those represented by the so-called Arab Spring, the Icelandic democratic rebellion, the Spanish "Indignant" movement, the Israeli demonstrations of 2012, Occupy Wall Street, the Brazilian mobilizations of 2013, and the Taksim Square protests, which shook up the entrenched Islamic government of Turkey. Indeed, between 2010 and 2014, thousands of cities in more than one hundred countries have seen significant occupations of public space as activists have challenged the domination of political and financial elites over common citizens, who, according to the protesters, have been disenfranchised and alienated from their democratic rights.

A key issue in this often blurred debate is the role of communication technologies in the formation, organization, and development of the movements. Throughout history, communication has been central to the existence of social movements, which develop beyond the realm of institutionalized channels for the expression of popular demands. It is only by communicating with others that outraged people are able to recognize their collective power before those who control access to the institutions. Institutions are vertical, and social movements always start as horizontal organizations, even if over time they may evolve into vertical organizations for the sake of efficiency. (This evolution is seen by many in the movements as the reproduction of the same power structures that they aim to overthrow.)

If communication is at the heart of social mobilization, and if holding power largely depends on the control of communication and information, it follows that the transformation of communication in a given society deeply affects the structure and dynamics of social movements. This transformation is multidimensional: technological, organizational, institutional, spatial, cultural. We live in a network society in which people and organizations set up their own networks according to their interests and values in all domains of the human experience, from sociability to politics, and from networked individualism to multimodal communities. In the twenty-first century there has been a major shift from mass communication (characterized by the centralized, controlled distribution of messages from one sender to many receivers and involving limited interactivity, as exemplified by television) to mass self-communication (characterized by multimodality and interactivity of messages from many senders to many receivers through the self-selection of messages and interlocutors and through the self-retrieving, remixing, and sharing of content, as exemplified by the Internet, social media, and mobile networks). The appropriation of networked communication technologies by social movements has empowered extraordinary social mobilizations, created communicative autonomy vis-à-vis the mass media, business, and governments, and laid the foundation for organizational and political autonomy. In a world of 2.5 billion Internet users and almost 7 billion mobile phone subscribers, a significant share of communication power has shifted from corporations and state bureaucracies to civil society—a shift well established by research.

However, we have only scant grounded analysis of the technological, organizational, and cultural specificity of new processes of social mobilization and community networking. Too often, there is a naïve interpretation of these important phenomena that boils down to descriptive accounts of the use of the newest communication technologies or applications by social activists. Instead, a complex set of distinct developments is at work. It is simply silly (or ideologically biased) to deny or downplay the empirical observation of the crucial role of networking technologies in the dynamics of networked social movements. On the other hand, it is equally silly to pretend that Twitter, Facebook, or any other technology, for that matter, is the generative force behind the new social movements. (No observer, and certainly no activist, defends this latter position; it is a straw man erected by traditional intellectuals, mainly from the left, as a way to garner support for their belief in the role of "the party"—any party—in leading "the masses," who are deemed unable to organize themselves.) Moreover, my observations of movements around the world reveal that the new social movements are networked in multiple ways, not only online but in the form of urban social networks, interpersonal networks, preexisting social networks, and the networks that form and reform spontaneously in cyberspace and in physical public space. This networking consists of a process of communication that leads to mobilization and is facilitated by organizations emerging from the movement, rather than being imported from the established political system. However, to make progress in understanding these movements, we need scholarly research that goes beyond the cloud of ideology and hype to examine with methodological reliability how communication works in such movements and to understand with precision the interaction between communication and social movements.

From this perspective, the book you hold in your hands represents a fundamental contribution to a rigorous characterization of the new avenues of social change in societies around the world. The concept of transmedia organizing that Sasha Costanza-Chock proposes integrates the variety of modes of communication that exist in the real media practices of social movements. From the activists' point of view, any communication mode that works is adopted, so that the Internet and mobile platforms are used alongside and in interaction with paper leaflets, interpersonal face-to-face communication, bulletins and newspapers, graffiti, pirate radio, street art, public speeches and assemblies in the square. Everything is included in what Costanza-Chock calls the media ecology of the movement. This is the reality of the new movements and the foundation of their communicative autonomy, on which their very existence depends, particularly when repression inevitably falls on them.

Costanza-Chock identified this novel interaction between the shifting media ecology and social movements long before the Arab Spring uprisings or the Occupy movement came to the attention of the mass media. He focused on a most significant social development, the movement for immigrant rights that exploded across the United States in 2006, with its epicenter in Los Angeles. He studied this movement between 2006 and 2013, beginning with his participation in the Border Social Forum, where the new realities of immigration were debated. Through a commitment to methods of participatory research, he partnered with organizers and activists from the immigrant rights movement, and worked with them as codesigners and coinvestigators in a range of popular communication initiatives. This courageous strategy of engaged scholarship allowed him to see the specific, sometimes contradictory effects of different communication processes in the dynamics of the movement. For example, he identified the centrality of critical digital literacy in grassroots social mobilization. In a world in which the fight for one's rights can be shaped decisively by one's ability to use the new means of communication, it is crucial to equalize access to the direct use of communication technologies by grassroots actors. By developing digital literacy, the movement can raise consciousness as well as find better uses for digital tools as they are adapted to movement goals. Otherwise the inevitable professionalization of transmedia organizers leads to the formation of a technical leadership that does not necessarily coincide with the leadership emerging from the grassroots.

The close analysis of these and related processes presented in the pages of this fascinating book is of utmost importance for understanding the new, networked social movements of the Internet age, as well as the potential of new communication technologies to broaden citizen participation in institutional decision making. In the midst of a widespread crisis of legitimacy faced by governments around the world, understanding these processes is crucial for activists, concerned citizens, open-minded officials, and scholars everywhere. This book engages us in a fascinating intellectual and political journey. It raises, and often solves, many of the questions now being asked about networked social movements. It is based on impeccable scholarship, in which the author's commitment to the defense of immigrant rights does not impinge on the integrity of his observation and analysis. This is social research as it best: when normative values are not denied by a detached academic but are served by investigative imagination and theoretical capacity, yielding an accurate assessment of the ways and means of the new world in the making.

Author's Note

The author will donate half of the royalties from the sale of this book to the Mobile Voices project. Mobile Voices (VozMob) is "a platform for immigrant and/or low-wage workers in Los Angeles to create stories about their lives and communities directly from cell phones. VozMob appropriates technology to create power in our communities and achieve greater participation in the digital public sphere." More information can be found at http://vozmob.net.

Acknowledgments

This book owes everything to those who struggle on a daily basis to build beloved community in the immigrant rights movement and beyond. First, *grácias a* María de Lourdes González Reyes, Manuel Mancía, Adolfo Cisneros, Crispín Jimenez, Marcos and Diana, Alma Luz, Ranferi, and the Popular Communication Team of VozMob.net. Your stories continue to travel around the world, providing insight and inspiration to everyone they touch. You are truly *leyendo la realidad para escribir la historia.* Amanda Garces, you taught me so much; it's incredible to look back and see how far we came together. Thanks also to the tireless efforts of Raul Añorve, Marlom Portillo, Neidi Dominguez, Brenda Aguilera, Natalie Arellano, Luis Valentín, Pedro Joel Espinosa, and the whole IDEPSCA extended family. I feel honored to have been able to spend time building community with you. It's been a true journey through difficult times, *pero llena de amor, respeto*, and also delicious food. Thank you for exploring participatory research and design, together with Carmen Gonzales, Melissa Brough, Charlotte Lapsansky, Cara Wallis, Veronica Paredes, Ben Stokes, François Bar, Troy Gabrielson, Mark Burdett, and Squiggy Rubio.

Thanks are also due to Virginia, Cristina, Cruz, Miguel, Consuelo, and everyone who participated in *Radio Tijera*, as well as to Marissa Nuncio, Delia Herrera, Luz Elena Henao, Kimi Lee, simmi gandi, and all the incredible past and present organizers at the Garment Worker Center. Danny Park, Eileen Ma, and Joyce Yang, thank you for hosting the CineBang! screenings and for providing a welcoming space at Koreatown Immigrant Workers Alliance. Odilia and Berta at the Frente Indígena de Organizaciones Binacionales, and Max Mariscal: I still think about the taste of *tamales y atole* during APPO-LA protests and screenings at the Mexican consulate.

To Victor Narro, Saba Waheed, Stefanie Ritoper, Nancy Meza, and everyone at the UCLA Labor Center, I love the community you have created, and I hope to spend more time working, visioning, and playing with you. Nancy, thank you for providing feedback, encouragement, and insightful comments in the margins of my messy draft chapters. Ken Montenegro, Erik Huerta, and Maegan "La Mamita Mala" Ortiz: thanks for helping me sharpen my prose. You made me condense key arguments to 140 characters during our ongoing #twitternovela! Celso Mireles, I hope to see you again soon among red rocks; thanks to you and to the rest of the UndocuTech crew.

A big shoutout to Dorothy Kidd, Evan Henshaw-Plath, Biella Coleman, Mako, Luz y Timo Ruíz, Pablo Ortellado, Gaba, Mark Burdett, Jeff Perlstein, Marisa Jahn, Micha Cárdenas, and all those who I first met in the Indymedia network. You've transformed my life forever. To Bob McChesney, Joe Torres, and Free Press, thank you for supporting me to work with Seán Ó Siochrú, Bruce Girard, and so many other scholar/activists in the campaign for Communication Rights in the Information Society. Big up to Media Justice visionaries Malkia Cyril, Amalia Deloney, Betty Yu, Steven Renderos, Andrea Quijada, Josh Breitbart, Kat Aaron, Shivaani Selvaraj, Adrienne Marie Brown, Pete Tridish, Graciela Sánchez, Myoung Joon Kim, Tammy Ko Robinson, Dalida María Benfield, and so many more. I have massive love for the Allied Media Projects Board: Emi Kane, Chancellor Williams, Hannah Sassaman, and Dani McClain; also for AMP staff Jenny Lee, Diana Nucera, and Mike Medow. You keep me focused on liberation, creativity, and transformative struggle.

Huge thanks are due to Marguerite Avery, my editor at MIT Press, whose vision of open access to knowledge I share. Margy successfully advocated in support of my desire to release this book under a creative commons license. I'm looking forward to the fruits of your plans to guide book publishers into the future—gently, if possible, but kicking and screaming if necessary! Thank you for believing in this project, from our first conversations onward. Let's meet at Voltage soon to plan our next collaboration.

Special thanks to Deborah M. Cantor-Adams and Marjorie Pannell at the MIT Press, who helped shepherd the manuscript to publication with meticulous edits; to Ana and Michael Prosetti, who provided excellent transcription services; and to Naomi Linzer, who prepared the index.

I am thrilled to have found a home at MIT in the Department of Comparative Media Studies/Writing. My colleagues have been deeply supportive, especially T. L. Taylor and Jim Paradis, who have both been unerring guides, mentors, and advocates for an unconventional junior scholar. T. L. and Jim also provided detailed and very valuable feedback on the manuscript, as did Otto Santa Ana, Virginia Eubanks, Nancy Meza, Chris Schweidler, and several anonymous readers from the MIT Press.

CMS/W faculty and staff, including William Uricchio, Vivek Bald, Fox Harrell, Nick Montfort, Ian Condry, Heather Hendershot, Junot Díaz, Helen Elaine Lee, Thomas Levenson, Kenneth Manning, Seth Mnookin, David Thorburn, Jing Wang, and Ed Schiappa, as well as Kurt Fendt, Sarah Wolozin, Scot Osterweil, Philip Tan, Andrew Whitacre, Susan Tresch Fienberg, Jill Janows, Mike Rapa, Becky Shepardson, Jessica Tatlock, Patsy Baudoin, Federico Casalegno, Jessica Dennis, Sarah Smith, Shannon Larkin, and Karinthia Louis, have created a welcoming space for deep discussion and debate around the questions that animate this book.

It was a pleasure to work closely with Rogelio Alejandro Lopez, who conducted a series of interviews with immigrant rights activists for this project and also for his own work. Rogelio's master's thesis, a comparative study of media practices in the farm workers movement and the immigrant youth movement, shaped my thinking about transmedia organizing as an approach that has been used throughout social movement history. I have also greatly enjoyed discussing the dynamics of media, publicity, and hidden resistance with Sun Huan, the history of consensus process and prefigurative politics with Charlie De Tar, networked social movements with Pablo Rey Mazón, and collaborative design with Aditi Mehta.

Dan Schultz egged me on to keep pushing the limits; I still insist he's a dead ringer for Guy Fawkes. Joi Ito had me covered when there was blowback, and I can't say more in public.

Thanks also to the brilliant and hardworking crew at the Center for Civic Media, especially Ethan Zuckerman, whose tweets urged me across the finish line, as well as Lorrie LeJeune, Rahul Bhargava, Ed Platt, Becky Hurwitz, and Andrew Whitacre. I am constantly amazed at the breadth and depth of knowledge across the Civic community. I have only one question for brilliant graduate students and fellows Chelsea Barabas, Willow Brugh, Denise Cheng, Heather Craig, Kate Darling, Rodrigo Davies, Ali Hashmi, Alexis Hope, Catherine d'Ignazio, Nick Grossman, Alexandre

Goncalves, Erhardt Graeff, Nathan Matias, Chris Peterson, Molly Sauter, Sun Huan, Rogelio Alejandro Lopez, Matt Stempeck, Wang Yu, and Jude Mwenda Ntabathia: What does the fox say?

Bex Hurwitz, you've been an excellent partner in crime; it has been truly fabulous to work with you to develop theory and practice around collaborative design. I'm looking forward to many RAD projects to come!

Early stages of work on research that made its way into this book were supported by research assistantships with Manuel Castells, Ernest J. Wilson, François Bar, Holly Willis, and Jonathan Aronson, as well as by grants from the HASTAC/MacArthur Foundation Digital Media and Learning Competition, the USC Graduate School Fellowship in Digital Scholarship, the Social Science Research Council Large Collaborative Grants program, and an Annenberg Center for Communication Graduate Fellowship. More recently, my research has been supported by John Bracken at the Knight Foundation, Archana Sahgal at the Open Society Foundations, and Luna Yasui at the Ford Foundation's Advancing LGBT Rights Initiative.

Manuel Castells guided me during the earliest stages of this project, and continually urged me, with a twinkle in his eye, to struggle for liberation in the institutions, on the net, and in the streets. Ivan Tcherepnin taught me how to listen to the universe, and first turned me on to the political economy of communication. Silke Roth introduced me to social movement studies, Dorothy Kidd gave me hope that scholars could stay linked to movements, and Dee Dee Halleck inspired me with handheld visions. Steve Anderson pushed me to develop a practice of scholarly multimedia. Larry Gross, mentor and friend since we first met at the University of Pennsylvania, encouraged me to take up the path of engaged scholarship. This book would not exist if it weren't for him.

My parents, Carol Chock, Paul Mazzarella, Peter Costanza, and Barbara Zimbel, always inspired me to dream of another possible world, and to take action to make it real. We have to make it happen, not least for my tiny niece, Colette Miele. Larissa, I love you; Grandpa Jack and Grandma Brunni, I miss you.

I could never have completed this book without the love, support, and sharp editorial eye of my partner, Chris Schweidler. Chris helped me shape this book from its earliest incarnation onward. Thank you for helping me finally push it out into the world! Among the boulder piles of Joshua Tree, the otherworldly red rock formations of Sedona, and the limitless skies of

Abiquiú, you have guided me toward a new understanding of love and liberation. I want to walk beside you always.

As this book goes to press, President Obama has deported two million people. The immigrant rights movement is mobilizing across the country to demand an end to deportations and meaningful immigration policy reform. Yet the so-called comprehensive immigration reform bills that Congress is debating begin with $46 billion for the deadly political theater of border militarization: more walls, drones, and Border Patrol agents; more deaths, detentions, and deportations. In the face of such cruel absurdity, I only hope that this book can contribute in some small way to the long struggle for freedom of movement, social justice, and respect for the planet on which we all live and move, born *sin patrón y sin fronteras.*[1]

Introduction: *¡Escucha! ¡Escucha! ¡Estamos en la Lucha!*

"*¡Escucha! ¡Escucha! ¡Estamos en la lucha!*" (Listen! Listen! We are in the struggle!) The sound of tens of thousands of voices chanting in unison booms and echoes down the canyon walls formed by office buildings, worn-down hotels, garment sweatshops, and recently renovated lofts along Broadway in downtown Los Angeles. The date is May 1, 2006, and I am marching as an ally along with more than a million people from working-class immigrant families, mostly Latin@. We are pouring into the streets at the peak of a mobilization wave that began in March and swept rapidly across the United States, grew to massive proportions in major metropolitan areas such as Chicago, New York, L.A., Philadelphia, San Francisco, Las Vegas, and Phoenix, and reached much smaller towns and cities in every state. The trigger was the draconian Sensenbrenner bill, H.R. 4437. The bill would have criminalized more than 11 million undocumented people and those who work with them, including teachers, health care workers, legal advocates, and other service providers.[1] The movement's demands quickly expanded beyond stopping the Sensenbrenner bill and grew to encompass an end to U.S. Immigration and Customs Enforcement (ICE) raids, a fair and just immigration reform, and, more broadly, respect, dignity, and the recognition that immigrants are human beings.

Another chant begins to build: "*¡No somos cinco, no somos cien! ¡Prensa vendida, cuentenos bien!*" (We aren't five, we aren't one hundred! Sold-out press, count us well!) While the Spanish-language media played a crucial role in supporting the mobilizations, the unprecedented magnitude of the marches caught the English-language media by surprise. Major English-language newspapers, television and radio networks, blogs, and online media outlets only belatedly acknowledged the sheer scale of the movement. Some, in particular right-wing talk radio and Fox News, used the marches as an opportunity to launch xenophobic attacks against immigrant workers, filled with vitriolic language about "swarms" of "illegal aliens," "anchor babies," and "diseased Mexicans."[2] A forest of dishes and antennae bristles from the backs of TV network satellite trucks that line the streets near City Hall. As the crowd passes the Fox News truck, the *consigna* (chant) changes again, becoming simple and direct: "*¡Mentirosos! ¡Mentirosos!*" (Liars! Liars!)

Emerging from Broadway into the open area around City Hall, I feel a powerful emotional wave course through the air. As a committed social justice activist as well as an engaged scholar and media-maker, I've been to many protests before. Often, these are composed of the same relatively small group of familiar faces. The wave of historic mobilizations against the Iraq War in 2003 is the last time I can remember being surrounded by literally hundreds of thousands of people, many of them marching in the streets for the first time in their lives, joined in a broad coalition by shared demands.[3] "*¡Se ve, se siente, el Pueblo esta presente!*" (You can see it, you can feel it, the people are here!) For decades, modern social movements have aimed to capture mass media attention as a crucial component of their efforts to transform society.[4] Those who marched over and over again for immigrant rights during the spring of 2006 did so in large part to fight for increased visibility and voice in the political process, and they explicitly demanded that the English-language press accurately convey the movement's size, message, and power. Yet over the course of the last twenty years, widespread changes in our communications system have deeply altered the relationship between social movements and the media. Following the Telecommunications Act of 1996, which eliminated national caps on media ownership and allowed a single company to own multiple stations in the same market, the broadcast industry was swept by a wave of consolidation.[5] Spanish-language radio and TV stations, once localized to individual cities, built significant market share, attracted major corporate advertisers, and were largely integrated into national and transnational conglomerates.[6] This process delinked Spanish-language broadcasters from local programming and advertisers while simultaneously constructing new, shared pan-Latin@ identities.[7]

In the 2006 mobilizations, Spanish-language print media, television, and radio stations provided extensive coverage, and also played a critical role in calling people to the streets. The massive demonstrations underscored not only the power of the Latin@ working class but also the growing clout of commercial Spanish-language media inside the United States.[8] At the same time, the rise of widespread, if still unequal, access to the Internet and to digital media literacy provided new spaces for social movement participants to document and circulate their own struggles.[9] Movements, including the immigrant rights movement, have rapidly taken to blogging, participatory journalism, and social media.[10] Some immigrant rights activists, who recognize these changes while remaining wary of the exclusion of large segments of their communities from the digital public sphere, struggle for expanded access to critical digital media literacy. They also strive to better integrate participatory media into daily movement practices. Others, uncomfortable with the loss of message control, resist the opening of social movement communication to a greater diversity of voices. This book, based on seven years of experience with participatory research, design, and media-making within the immigrant rights movement, explores these transformations in depth.

A Book Born on the Border

This book was born on the southern side of an invisible line in the sand between Texas and Chihuahua. At the Border Social Forum in Ciudad Juárez, Mexico, between October 12 and 15, 2006, almost one thousand activists, organizers, and researchers gathered for three days. We met to build a stronger transnational activist network against the militarization of borders and for freedom of movement and immigrant rights. I traveled to the Border Social Forum to connect with immigrant rights organizers who were enthusiastic about integrating digital media tools and skills into their work. Many were based in L.A., and after the forum was over, we followed up to meet and develop projects together. Over the next few years I worked with organizers from the Los Angeles Garment Worker Center, the Institute of Popular Education of Southern California, the Indigenous Front of Binational Organizations, the Koreatown Immigrant Workers Alliance, and other immigrant rights groups and networks. Together we developed workshops, tools, and strategies to build the media capacity of the immigrant rights movement in L.A.

These movement-based media experiences provided the foundation for my understanding of the core issues addressed in this book. Working with community organizers inspired me to undertake research that might help movement participants, organizers, and scholars better understand the shifting relationship between the media system and social movements. I participated in or led more than one hundred hands-on media workshops using popular education and participatory design approaches, conducted forty formal semistructured interviews, took part in dozens of actions and mobilizations, and assembled an archive of media produced by the movement. Some of the research that led to this book took place in partnership with community-based organizations (CBOs), some did not. A full description of the methods I employed can be found in the appendixes to this book.

In general, my work falls under the rubric of participatory research, a term subsuming a set of methods that emphasize the development of communities of shared inquiry and transformative action.[11] In other words, I consider the groups and individuals I work with to be coresearchers and codesigners, rather than simply subjects of research or test users. As an engaged scholar, media-maker, and technologist, I have used these methods to work with youth organizers, the global justice movement, the Indymedia network, antiwar activists, media justice and communication rights advocates, LGBTQ and Two-Spirit communities, Occupy Wall Street, worker centers, and the immigrant rights movement, among others. In some cases I identify as a movement participant, in others as an ally. I'm a white, male-bodied, queer scholar/media-maker/activist with U.S. citizenship who grew up in Ithaca, New York. In my teen years I lived in Puebla, Mexico, during the Zapatista uprising against NAFTA (the North American Free Trade Agreement) and neoliberalism. I went to Harvard as an undergraduate, organized raves and electronic arts events with the Toneburst Collective, became involved in youth organizing in the Boston area, got connected to the global justice movement through the Indymedia network, produced movement films, and took my first job as a community arts worker in San Juan, Puerto Rico. I went to graduate school at the University of Pennsylvania, then focused on media policy advocacy for several years with Free Press. I then moved to L.A. to pursue a doctorate at the Annenberg School for Communication & Journalism at the University of Southern California and became deeply involved in the immigrant rights movement. I'm now assistant professor of civic media in the Comparative Media Studies/Writing Department at MIT. I work to leverage my race, class, gender, and educational privilege to amplify the voices of communities that have been systematically excluded from the public sphere. To that end, I conduct research, write, teach, organize software development teams, and produce media in partnership with CBOs and movement groups. My deepest and most long-lasting community engagement is as an ally of low-wage immigrant workers, especially those from Latin America and the Spanish-speaking Caribbean.

I wrote this book because I believe that the immigrant rights movement has a great deal to teach us all. Both scholars and activists recognize that media and communications have become increasingly central to social movement formation and activity.[12] However, both scholarship and practice in this field suffer from at least three basic shortcomings. First, in the past, most studies of social movements focused exclusively on the mass media as the arena of public discourse. The ability of a social movement to change the public conversation was often measured by looking at articles in elite newspapers or by counting sound bites in broadcast channels.[13] Second, as movements became increasingly more visible online, a growing spotlight on the latest and greatest communication technologies began to obscure the reality of everyday communication practices.[14] On the ground, social movement media-making tends to be cross-platform, participatory, and linked to action.[15] In other words, as I note throughout this book, social movements engage in what I call *transmedia organizing*. Third, the rise of the Internet as a key space for social movement activity cannot be fully theorized without sustained attention to ongoing digital inequality.[16] Understanding digital inequality means focusing on critical digital media literacy, in addition to basic questions of access to communication tools and connectivity.[17] This book addresses these shortcomings by looking at the broader media ecology rather than focusing exclusively on one or a handful of platforms, by exploring daily movement media practices within a framework of transmedia organizing, and by confronting the challenges of digital inequality in the context of the immigrant rights movement. My aim is to help us better understand how social movement actors engage in transmedia organizing as they seek to strengthen movement identity, win political and economic victories, and transform consciousness. The main site of research is L.A., although I also incorporate examples from Boston and elsewhere in the country, and the focus is the contemporary immigrant rights movement from 2006 to 2013.

The Revolution Will Be Tweeted, but Tweets Alone Do Not the Revolution Make

In 2010, writing against the idea that specific media technologies automatically produce movement outcomes, Malcolm Gladwell argued in a widely debated article that social media fail to produce the strong ties and vertical organizational forms that he considered crucial to the success of the civil rights movement.[18] Gladwell did provide useful pushback against technological determinism, and he reminded us that the key force in social movements has always been strong personal connections. However, he failed to acknowledge that social media are often used to extend and maintain existing face-to-face relationships, including the "strong ties" he values so much, over time and space. There's actually no contradiction between the position that strong personal relationships are the key to social movements and the observation that social media are now important tools for movement activity. More problematic is Gladwell's conflation of strong ties with vertical organizational structure, which led him to argue that powerful social movements require a strong, military-style hierarchy. The idea that only vertically structured movements are effective is both dangerous and wrong. It ignores the theory, practices, processes, and tools of social transformation that have emerged from the last fifty years (at least) of horizontalist organizing and the anti-authoritarian left. Feminists, ecologists, queer organizers, indigenous activists, and anarchists of various stripes have long rejected top-down institutional structures and patriarchal and hierarchical styles of organizing. The turn toward power-sharing, consensus process, horizontalism, and networked movement forms has certainly been aided and enabled by networked information and communication technologies (ICTs). However, there is a much deeper history that underlies this shift. Horizontalism (or *horizontalidad* in the Latin American context, as described so beautifully in Marina Sitrin's book of the same name)[19] surged in popularity from the late 1960s through the 1970s, spread by way of underground cultural scenes during the resurgence of the right in the 1980s, and burst onto the forefront of globalized social movement activity in the mid-1990s with the Zapatista uprising in Chiapas, Mexico. It took off again following the 1999 World Trade Organization protests, dubbed the "Battle of Seattle," when horizontally organized, networked affinity groups (consisting mostly of people who had been friends for a long time beforehand) shut down the WTO's Ministerial Conference and catapulted the global justice movement into high visibility.[20] This mobilization was also the birthplace of Indymedia, a ragtag band of media activists who scooped the major news networks from inside the clouds of tear gas with cheap handheld cameras and an open publishing news site built with Australian free software.[21] Coders from the Indymedia network went on to play key roles in the development of many widely adopted social media platforms, including Twitter.[22]

By 2010, even as Gladwell was repeating the tired claim that we don't see movements like we used to because everyone is too busy with clicktivism, horizontalist movements were laying the foundation for an explosive global cycle of struggles that linked decentralized mobilizations across the planet in what Manuel Castells has called "networks of outrage and hope."[23] It's true that most people in most times and places don't become movement militants, yet "anti-clicktivism" looks downright silly in the face of the current social movement wave. The global protest cycle includes anti-austerity riots in Greece; student protests for the right to education in London, Santiago de Chile, and Quebec; and the uprisings of the so-called Arab Spring that brought the fall of dictators in Tunisia and Egypt (and led to civil war in Libya and Syria). It resonates from Tahrir Square to the Spanish Acampada del Sol, from Gezi Park in Istanbul to Occupy Wall Street and back again to #IdleNoMore. These movements are wildly disparate in their composition, goals, and outcomes; each is based in the specificity of local histories and conditions, but all share certain key components. First, they involve the reclaiming of public space by mass mobilizations. Second, significant groups within each movement reject the formal aspects of representative democracy (political parties, governance based on periodic ballots to elect political leaders, and so on) and enact *prefigurative politics*.[24] In other words, within the self-organized spaces controlled by the movement they attempt to directly build the types of social relationships that they would like to see reflected in broader society.[25] Third, as described by Paolo Gerbaudo, all are characterized by their ability to maintain a presence in both *tweets* and the *streets:* these movements are based on the physical occupation of key urban locations, while they simultaneously capture the imagination of networked publics through extended visibility across social media sites.[26]

This cycle of struggles is also linked to a renewal of intense popular and scholarly debates about the relationship between social media and social movements. Each day brings a broader diffusion of digital technologies, and each day seems also to bring a rush to attribute the latest popular protest to the tools used by the protesters. Iran is the "Twitter Revolution,"[27] the Arab Spring is "powered by Facebook,"[28] and Occupy Wall Street is "driven by iPads and iPhones."[29] However, every activist and organizer I interviewed for this book repeated some version of the idea that "social media should enhance your on-the-ground organizing, not be your only organizing space."[30] Digital media technologies cannot somehow be sprinkled on social movements to produce new, improved mobilizations. On this point, Gladwell had it half right. Further complicating the debate, savvy activists, as well as critical scholars such as Siva Vaidhyanathan, also note the transition of the net from a relatively autonomous communication space to one dominated by the rise of corporate social media platforms, online versions of traditional media firms, and search and advertising companies (Google).[31] The noted Internet skeptic Evgeny Morozov points out that movement participants face increased surveillance when they take their activities online; he has turned attacking social media boosterism into a cottage industry by mixing valuable critiques of net-centric thinking with flashy rants against cyberutopian straw men.[32] My belief is that we can avoid both cyberutopianism and don't-tweet-on-me reactions with a quite simple strategy: learn from social movements about how they use various ICTs to communicate, organize, and mobilize, rather than start by researching ICTs and arguing about whether they are revolutionary. Indeed, careful social movement scholars have done just that, and have begun to develop a more nuanced understanding of the relationships between social media and social movements. For example, we know from the work of Lance Bennett and others that social media are used by protesters to bridge diverse networks during episodes of contentious politics,[33] that coalitions use digital media to personalize collective action, and that digital media enable less rigid forms of affiliation while maintaining high levels of engagement, a focused agenda, and high network strength.[34]

Much in this vein of scholarship resonates with the conclusions I draw here about the ways that immigrant rights activists use social media. At the same time, I believe that an overemphasis on social media, and a failure to engage seriously with movement media across platforms, misses the forest for the trees.[35] Social movement media practices don't take place on digital platforms alone; they are made up of myriad "small media" (to use Annabelle Sreberny's term) that circulate online and off.[36] Graffiti, flyers, and posters; newspapers and broadsheets; community screenings and public projections; pirate radio stations and street theater—these and many other forms of media-making abound within vibrant social movements. Activists also constantly seek and sometimes gain access to much wider visibility through the mass media. Photographs and quotes in print newspapers, speaking slots on commercial FM radio, interviews on mainstream television news and talk shows—all these make up part of the broader media ecology. The majority of people still receive most of their information from the mass media, so social movements still struggle to make their voices and ideas heard in mass media outlets. It is my contention that neither cyberutopians nor technopessimists (if either truly exist) have done a very good job of delving deeply into day-to-day media practices within social movements. This book attempts to do so, and to demonstrate that the revolution will be tweeted—but tweets alone do not the revolution make.

Si, Se Puede: Organized Immigrant Workers in L.A.

It may at first seem strange, when discussing the transnational mobilization wave that has inspired a new conversation about media and social movements, to focus on the immigrant rights movement in Los Angeles. Yet L.A. has long been a key location for new models of social movement organizing, on the one hand, and the globalization of the media system, on the other. For example, innovative worker organizing models have continued to emerge from L.A. even as labor unions across the United States have steadily lost momentum from the 1950s on. In part, this is because Los Angeles is one of the few U.S. cities that still retains a substantial manufacturing industry. L.A. has also been the site of important advances in service-sector organizing. The city is a global hub for immigration and draws many migrants with strong organizing backgrounds, including political refugees who were organizers or revolutionaries in their countries of origin. In their new home, migrants from diverse social movement traditions meet, and so the city has become a crucible of multiracial, cross-cultural organizing.[37]

This was not always the case. Historically, organized labor in L.A. at worst attacked, and at best ignored, new immigrant workers. In addition to low-wage service work, L.A. has the largest remaining concentration of manufacturing in the country,[38] and labor unions for decades focused on waging a losing battle to maintain their existing base in the private manufacturing sector. After the Taft-Hartley Act (1947) hamstrung the U.S. labor movement, regulated strike actions, banned the general strike, and outlawed cross-sector solidarity, the old-guard labor unions, especially the AFL-CIO, shifted vast resources away from organizing new workers into a losing strategy of pouring money into Democratic Party electoral campaigns. They hoped to win new federal labor protections, or simply to maintain existing ones.[39] The largest labor unions continued to follow this strategy, even as the Democratic Party moved ever closer to the business class and repeatedly sold out the labor movement. Union membership steadily declined as free trade became the consensus mantra among both major political parties, and former union jobs in sector after sector were outsourced to cheaper production sites overseas.[40]

Yet starting in the 1990s, L.A. emerged as one of the key centers for the development of new models of labor organizing. This dynamic operated in parallel with the rise of new leadership inside the massive service-sector unions, including the Service Employees International Union (SEIU), the Hotel Employees and Restaurant Employees International Union (HERE), and the Union of Needletrades, Industrial, and Textile Employees (UNITE). These unions, along with the United Farm Workers, United Food and Commercial Workers, and the Laborers' International Union of North America, began to shift resources toward organizing new workers, including recent immigrants.[41] In 2005 they launched the Change to Win Federation, an umbrella campaign designed to link service-sector workers across the country. As a result of organizing new immigrant workers instead of attempting to exclude them, these unions saw a rise in new membership, rather than the steady decline suffered by manufacturing sector unions. SEIU, for example, grew from 625,000 members in 1980 to over 2.2 million in 2013. L.A.'s SEIU Local 1877 pioneered a string of internationally visible campaigns with low-wage immigrant workers in the lead, such as Justice for Janitors, Airport Workers United, and Stand for Security.[42] However, none of the major labor unions, including SEIU and UNITE-HERE, have been willing to devote significant resources to organizing garment workers or day laborers in L.A. They have long seen these workers as unorganizable, based on their assumptions about the high proportion of undocumented workers in these sectors.[43]

Despite the assumption that undocumented workers are unorganizable because they fear deportation, a number of scholars have demonstrated that there is no simple relationship between workers' immigration status and their propensity to unionize.[44] Hector Delgado analyzed unionization campaigns in the light manufacturing sector in L.A. and found that other factors, such as state and federal labor law, organizing strategy, the resources committed to the effort by labor unions, and the resources deployed by the employer to fight unionization, were all far greater determinants of unionization outcomes than workers' immigration status.[45] In fact, in many cases new immigrant workers come from places with much higher rates of unionization, more militant unions, and stronger social movement cultures than their new home; they may arrive with a more concrete class identity than U.S.-born workers, and in some cases may themselves have been trained as organizers. To take one example, day laborers in L.A. have historically been largely unorganized, but this situation has begun to change in recent years. A quarter of day laborers now participate in worker centers, and the number of worker centers is growing. Day laborers in L.A. were the first in the country to organize worker centers, and the model has spread. By 2006 there were sixty-three day laborer centers in cities across the United States, with an additional fifteen CBOs working with the day laborer community.[46] CBOs in L.A., including the Institute of Popular Education of Southern California (IDEPSCA) and the Coalition for Humane Immigrant Rights of Los Angeles (CHIRLA), led the creation of the National Day Laborer Organizing Network, which has now grown to include thirty-six member organizations in cities across the country.[47]

Los Angeles has also been a site for innovative partnerships between the Catholic Church and labor, as well as for models of organizing that focus not only on the workplace but also on building community more broadly. Faith-based organizing in L.A. is closely tied to the history of U.S. imperial adventures in Latin America. In the 1980s, many priests and laity who were active in Central American popular movements against U.S.-backed military dictatorships were forced to flee their countries of origin. Many came to the United States and ended up in L.A., where they have continued to organize their communities through the practice of liberation theology.[48] Diverse histories have thus shaped the immigrant rights movement in L.A. as it has spread through community centers, worker centers, faith-based coalitions, multiethnic organizing alliances, and other innovative forms of community organizing. During the last two decades, there has also been a shift away from "turf war" unionism and towards attempts to organize entire sectors of the workforce at once, through networks of unions, CBOs, churches, and universities.[49] L.A.'s racial, ethnic, and cultural diversity has also generated innovative organizing forms. Aside from the labor movement and the churches, the immigrant rights movement includes a vast and diverse array of less visible but highly active CBOs, student groups, cultural activists, media- and filmmakers, progressive law firms, radical scholars, musicians, punks, and anarchists, hip-hop artists, mural painters and graffiti writers, indigenous rights activists, queer collectives, and many others. The rich history of intersecting social movements in L.A.—described by Laura Pulido as "Black, Brown, Yellow, and Left"—has been extensively documented by many scholars and activists, and I encourage interested readers to explore that literature further on their own.[50]

At the same time, L.A. has long been a key site for the development and growth of the globalized cultural industries. Hollywood remains both the symbolic and material center of global film production, despite trends toward transnational coproduction networks, recentralization in cheaper sites of production, and the rise of studios in New York, Toronto, and New Zealand, not to mention the steady growth of competitive regional film export industries in India (Bollywood), Nigeria (Nollywood), South Korea, and China.[51] Besides film, native media industries in L.A. include television, music, games, and, most recently, transmedia production companies. The city looms large in wave after wave of transformation in the broader media ecology. L.A. occupies a unique location in the global imagination: it is a city of dreams, image making, and myths. It symbolizes both the promise and the deception of the American project, and it remains an important site of popular resistance, radical imagination, and concrete movement-building work.

The immigrant rights movement in L.A. is thus a rich, complex, multilayered world. It lies at the fertile confluence of the cross-platform power of the globalized cultural industries and the innovative, intersectional organizing models of multiracial, feminist, queer, and working-class social movements. Immigrant rights organizers in L.A. have a great deal to teach anyone who studies or takes part in social movements today, as well as media-makers, scholars, and activists. It is my hope that this book can provide, at the very least, a window into this world.

Chapter Overview

The chapters that follow are organized around key events and core concepts that emerged from interviews, workshops, and media organizing projects that I took part in between 2006 and 2013. Each chapter describes important moments in the immigrant rights movement, clarifies and develops terms, draws on relevant literature and research material to deepen the analysis, and concludes with a summary of the main insights. A more in-depth discussion of my research methods is available in the appendixes.

Following this introduction, chapter 1, "A Day Without an Immigrant: Social Movements and the Media Ecology," examines the 2006 protests against the Sensenbrenner bill (H.R. 4437). This protest wave culminated in the historic "Day Without an Immigrant," a nationwide immigrant strike and march on May 1, 2006. This event was the largest mass mobilization in U.S. history. The scale of the protests was due largely to the active participation of commercial Spanish-language broadcasters, which have gained power and reach over the last two decades, and partly to the integration of social media into daily life, which savvy organizers use to great effect. I describe the relationship between the movement and the broader media ecology and explore how the immigrant rights movement is able to leverage not only the Internet (in particular social media) but also Spanish-language radio, TV, and print newspapers. A cross-platform analysis centers the reality that social movements enjoy differential access to opportunities in an increasingly complex and diversified media ecology. To some degree, my argument in this chapter contrasts with the platform-centric analysis that seems so attractive to (some) journalists, funders, scholars, CBOs, and activists. Although a focus on the latest and greatest media technology can be exciting, it can also make it difficult to understand how social movement media practices actually work. It can also obscure innovative new cross-platform strategies that movements develop to gain access to broader visibility in a complex media ecology.

Chapter 2, "Walkout Warriors: Transmedia Organizing," is an in-depth study of the media practices of the college, high school, and middle school students who organized the largest wave of student walkouts since the Chican@ Blowouts in the 1970s. They did this through a combination of face-to-face organizing, especially by way of long-established student groups, and the abundant use of new media tools and platforms, in particular text messaging and MySpace. They also leveraged culturally relevant protest tactics. School walkouts, already part of what social movement scholars call the "repertoire of contention"[52] of Chican@ student activism, were made especially salient by the production process of the HBO film *Walkout,* released in 2006. Produced by Edward James Olmos and Moctezuma Esparza (one of the organizers of the dramatized events), the film used East L.A. high schools as sets and hundreds of students as extras. Like Spanish-language broadcasters and social network sites, as discussed in the first chapter, the film mediated and promoted specific movement tactics. At the same time, walkout participants produced and circulated their own media across multiple platforms, linked media directly to action, and did so in ways accountable to the social base of their movement. In other words, they took part in what I have termed *transmedia organizing.* The term builds on media scholar Henry Jenkins's concept of transmedia storytelling,[53] as well as on transmedia producer Lina Srivastava's transmedia activism framework,[54] while shifting the emphasis from professional media producers to grassroots, everyday social movement media practices. I argue that transmedia organizing is the key emergent social movement media practice in a converged media ecology shaped by the broader political economy of communication.[55]

Chapter 3, "'MacArthur Park Melee': From Spokespeople to Amplifiers," explores the transition of allied media-makers from spokespeople for social movements to aggregators and amplifiers of diverse voices from the movement base. On May Day of 2007, the Los Angeles Police Department (LAPD) brutally attacked a peaceful crowd of thousands of immigrant rights marchers in L.A.'s MacArthur Park. Using batons, rubber bullets, and motorcycles, nearly 450 officers in full riot gear injured dozens of people and sent several to the hospital, including reporters from Fox News, Telemundo, KPCC, KPFK, and L.A. Indymedia. The police were later found by the courts to be at fault for unnecessary violence against the protesters. LAPD Chief Bratton apologized, the commanding officer was demoted, seventeen other officers faced penalties, and the LAPD paid more than $13 million in damages. However, in the immediate aftermath of the event, the police, nonprofit organizations, and an ad hoc network of grassroots media-makers fought an intense battle over media attention and framing. This took place in a context in which national TV networks that once covered the civil rights movement in sympathetic terms have increasingly turned toward a "violent conflict" framing of domestic political protest, when they cover it at all. Some professional nonprofit organizations attempted to act as movement spokespeople and reproduced the "violent conflict" frame as a strategy to gain access to broadcast media. At the same time, transmedia organizers challenged the dominant narrative by working to gather, curate, remix, and amplify the voices of marchers who had been attacked. Ultimately, professional movement organizations face growing pressure to shift from speaking for the movement to amplifying the voices of an increasingly media-literate base. Those who make this shift will benefit greatly, while those who attempt to retain control of the conversation will lose credibility.

Chapter 4, "APPO-LA: Translocal Media Practices," follows a series of protests by the Asociación Popular de los Pueblos de Oaxaca, Los Angeles (the Popular Association of the Oaxacan Peoples, L.A., or APPO-LA). In June 2006, the southern Mexican state of Oaxaca was convulsed by a general strike against the corrupt (and questionably elected) governor Ulises Ruiz Ortíz. Teachers, indigenous peoples, women, students, and workers joined forces in a popular assembly that occupied city plazas for months, took over radio and TV stations, demanded the governor's resignation, and called for a constituent assembly to rewrite the state constitution. Oaxacan migrants in L.A. organized a powerful series of solidarity actions, raised thousands of dollars to support the general strike, and generated attention for the situation in Oaxaca both online and in Spanish-language mass media. This chapter traces the ways that translocal media practices, deployed by Oaxacan migrants on a daily basis to strengthen connections between their places of origin and their new communities abroad, are often used in times of crisis to build social movement visibility and power.

Fluency with digital media appears to be a precondition for effective transmedia organizing. Digital media literacy provides opportunities to take advantage of the changed media ecology, but low-wage immigrant workers face persistent digital inequality. They have less access to digital media literacy, tools, and skills than any other group in the United States. What is the immigrant rights movement doing to ensure that its social base gains access to digital media tools and skills? Many activists, organizers, and educators wrestle with this question. In chapter 5, "Worker Centers, Popular Education, and Critical Digital Media Literacy," I describe how CBOs at the epicenter of the immigrant rights movement struggle to support their communities by setting up computer labs and organizing courses in computing skills. Some go further and use popular education methods to link digital media literacy directly to movement building. I discuss the mobile media project VozMob and the community radio workshop *Radio Tijera* to illustrate the ways that immigrant rights organizers are creating popular education workshops that combine critical media analysis, media-making, participatory design, cross-platform production, leadership development, and more. I argue that these organizers are developing a *praxis of critical digital media literacy* within the immigrant rights movement. They have a great deal to teach organizers in other social movements. Educators who are concerned about digital media and learning would do well to learn from their example.

Chapter 6, "Out of the Closets, Out of the Shadows, and Into the Streets: Pathways to Participation in DREAM Activist Networks," follows the diverse paths people take as they become politicized, connect to others, and make their way into social movement worlds. In this chapter I focus on DREAMers: undocumented youth who were brought to the country as young children and who are increasingly stepping to the forefront of the immigrant rights movement. The term comes from the proposed Development, Relief and Education for Alien Minors Act, which offers a streamlined path to citizenship for youth brought to the United States by their parents. Among other pathways to participation, I find that making media often builds social movement identity; in many cases, media-making projects have a long-term impact on activist's lives. DREAM activists, often young queer people of color, have developed innovative transmedia tactics as they battle anti-immigrant forces, the political establishment, and sometimes mainstream immigrant rights nonprofit organizations in their struggle to be heard, to be taken seriously, and to win concrete policy victories at both the state and federal levels.

Chapter 7, "Define American, the Dream is Now, and FWD.us: Professionalization and Accountability in Transmedia Organizing," explores the mainstreaming of transmedia organizing. As comprehensive immigration reform made its way through both houses of the U.S. Congress in 2013, three professional transmedia campaigns unfolded. Pulitzer Prize–winning journalist and undocumented activist Jose Antonio Vargas developed Define American, a participatory video campaign linked to a feature-length documentary film. Laurene Powell Jobs, the widow of Apple founder Steve Jobs, funded Davis Guggenheim, producer of *An Inconvenient Truth*, to create a transmedia campaign called The Dream is Now, which culminated in a high-production-value short film that was screened at the White House. In addition, a group of Silicon Valley executives, including Facebook's Mark Zuckerberg, launched FWD.us, a sophisticated media campaign that uses cutting-edge online organizing tools to build support for comprehensive immigration reform, with a primary goal of increasing the number of visas available for high-skill information workers. In this chapter I explore these three transmedia organizing campaigns, each better resourced but less accountable to the immigrant rights movement than the last. I locate this transition period for transmedia organizing within the longer history of the professionalization of social movements, and argue for the importance of strong accountability mechanisms in movement media work.

Finally, in the concluding chapter I summarize the key points of the book, then end with a discussion of the future of transmedia organizing in the immigrant rights movement and beyond. I remain focused throughout on the question of how social movements use transmedia organizing to strengthen movement identity, win political and economic victories, and transform consciousness.

Conclusion

Los Angeles is a hub for immigrant workers, who come to the city from across the globe but especially from Mexico and Central America. Many find employment in light manufacturing or garment work; in the service sector, especially in hotel and restaurant service, health care, and household work; and in construction and gardening, often as day laborers. They face widespread wage and safety violations, as well as abuse from employers, police, and the English-language media. After many decades of antagonistic relations with labor unions, the situation has begun to shift:

immigrant workers now make up a growing proportion of new union members and organizers, especially in the service-sector unions. They are also increasingly active in the fight for immigration reform, as well as in other social struggles, and constitute a large and growing political force both in L.A. and nationwide.

However, even as the Internet steadily gains importance as a communication platform, a workplace, a site of play, a location for political debate, a mobilization tool, and indeed as a necessity in all spheres of daily life, low-wage immigrant workers are largely excluded from the digital public sphere. Many are not online, and less than a third have broadband access in the home. While most do have access to basic mobile phones or feature phones with cameras, few have smartphones. Yet at the same time, the immigrant rights movement is one of the most powerful social movements in the United States today. During the last decade the movement has repeatedly produced major episodes of mobilization, blocked key legislative attacks at both state and federal levels, forced the Republican Party to abandon the Sensenbrenner bill, compelled the Obama administration to implement the Deferred Action for Childhood Arrivals program, won state-by-state victories and fought hard against state-level defeats, and in 2013 moved comprehensive immigration reform to the top of the national agenda. How? In this book, I explore this question, guided by insights gained from my own participation as a movement ally, as well as from interviews, workshops, media archives, and more.

I wrote this book in part because I believe there are some big analytical gaps in how we think about the relationship between social movements and the media. I don't believe it's productive to try to prove or disprove a causal relationship between technology use and social movement outcomes. Rather than think of technology use as an independent variable that can predict movement outcomes—a claim that may or may not be true, and one that I'm not making and am not in a position to empirically test—I'm encouraging social movement and media scholars, as well as movement participants, to stop treating the media as either primarily an environmental element, something external to the movement dynamic, or a dependent variable, something to be "influenced" by effective movement actions. Instead, I hope to demonstrate in depth the ways in which media-making is actually part and parcel of movement building. I believe that this has always been true, but that it's more obvious now because we can see it unfolding online. Social movements have always engaged in transmedia organizing; organizers bring the battle to the arena of ideas by any media necessary.

I hope this book can help us move past the current round of debates about social movements and social media. It is past time to challenge narrow conceptions of the movement-media relationship. Let's replace both paeans to the revolutionary power of the latest digital platform and reductive denunciations of "clicktivism" with an appreciation of the rich texture of social movement media practices. Along the way, I hope that this book also may provide useful lessons for activists as they attempt to navigate a rapidly changing media ecology while organizing to transform our world.

Figure 1.1
May Day 2006: A Day Without an Immigrant.
Source: Photo by Jonathan McIntosh, posted to Wikimedia.org at http://commons
.wikimedia.org/wiki/File:May_Day_Immigration_March_LA03.jpg (licensed CC-BY-
2.5).

1 A Day Without an Immigrant: Social Movements and the Media Ecology

The image in figure 1.1 depicts the streets of downtown Los Angeles on May 1, 2006. This scene was mirrored in cities across the country as millions of new immigrants, their families, and their allies joined the largest protest in U.S. history.[1] They left their homes, schools, and workplaces, gathered for rallies and mass marches, and took part in an economic boycott for immigrant rights. This chapter explores the May Day 2006 mobilization, known as A Day Without an Immigrant, through the lens of the changing media ecology.[2]

Our media are in the midst of rapid transformation. On the one hand, mass media companies continue to consolidate, more and more journalists are losing their jobs to corporate downsizing, and long-form, investigative journalism is steadily being replaced by less costly recycled press releases and entertainment news.[3] Public broadcasters remain one of the most trusted information sources, but their funding is under attack. As audiences fragment across an infinite-channel universe, the agenda-setting power of even the largest media outlets wanes. On the other hand, regional consolidation has produced new channels that speak from the former peripheries. For example, Latin American media firms now reach across the United States, and Spanish-language print and broadcast media draw larger audiences and wield more influence than ever before.[4] At the same time, widespread (though still unequal) access to personal computers, broadband Internet, and mobile telephony, as well as the mass adoption of social media, have in some ways democratized the media ecology even as they increase our exposure to new forms of state and corporate surveillance.

Social movements, which have always struggled to make their voices heard across all available platforms, are taking advantage of these changes. The immigrant rights movement in the United States faces mostly indifferent, occasionally hostile, English-language mass media. The movement also enjoys growing support from Spanish-language print newspapers and broadcasters. At the same time, commercial Spanish-language mass media constrain immigrant rights discourse within the framework of neoliberal citizenship. Community media outlets that serve new immigrant communities, such as local newspapers and radio stations, continue to provide important platforms for immigrant rights activists. Increasingly, social movement groups also self-document: they engage their base in participatory media-making, and they circulate news, information, and culture across many platforms, especially through social media. In the spring of 2006, the immigrant rights movement was able to take advantage of opportunities in the changing media ecology to help challenge and defeat an anti-immigrant bill in the U.S. Congress.

Immigration policy, border militarization, domestic surveillance, raids, detentions, and deportations are all key tools of control over low-wage immigrant workers in the United States. These tools are not new. They have been developed over the course of more than 130 years, at least since the Chinese Exclusion Act of 1882, the first major law to restrict immigration. This law, the culmination of decades of organizing by white supremacists, barred Chinese laborers from entering the United States and from naturalization.[5] Immigration policy, surveillance, detention, and deportation have long been used to target "undesirable" (especially brown, yellow, black, left, and/or queer) immigrants[6] and thereby to maintain whiteness, heteropatriarchy (the dominance of heterosexual males in society),[7] and capitalism.[8] The past decade, however, has been particularly dark for many immigrant communities. After the September 11, 2001, attacks, the consolidation of Immigration and Naturalization Services into the Department of Homeland Security was followed by the "special registration" program, then by a new wave of detentions, deportations, and "rendering" of "suspected terrorists" to Guantánamo and to a network of secret military prisons for indefinite incarceration and torture without trial.[9] In 2006, Immigration and Customs Enforcement (ICE) increased the number of beds for detainees to 27,500, opened a new 500-bed detention center for families with children in Williamson County, Texas, and set a new agency record of 187,513 "alien removals."[10] By the spring of that year, it had become politically feasible for the Republican-controlled House of Representatives to pass H.R. 4437, better known as the Sensenbrenner bill.

Sensenbrenner would have criminalized 11 million unauthorized immigrants by making lack of documentation a felony rather than a civil infraction. It would also have criminalized the act of providing shelter or aid to an undocumented person, thus making felons of millions of undocumented folks, their families and friends, and service workers, including clergy, social service workers, health care providers, and educators.[11] The Republican Party used the bill and the debates it provoked to play on white racial fears in an attempt to gain political support from the nativist element of their base. The Sensenbrenner bill abandoned market logic: a Cato Institute analysis found that reducing the number of low-wage immigrant workers by even a third would cost the U.S. economy about $80 billion. By contrast, the same study found that legalizing undocumented workers would grow the U.S. economy by more than 1 percent of GDP, or $180 billion.[12]

The response to the Sensenbrenner bill was the largest wave of mass mobilizations in U.S. history. A rally led by the National Capital Immigration Coalition on March 7 brought 30,000 protesters to Washington, D.C.; soon after, on March 10, 100,000 attended a protest in downtown Chicago.[13] Yet these events were only the tip of the iceberg. March, April, and May 2006 saw mass marches in every U.S. metropolis, as well as in countless smaller cities and towns. In the run-up to May Day (May 1), a date still celebrated in most of the world as International Workers' Day, immigrant rights organizers called for a widespread boycott of shopping and work. The economic boycott, also a de facto general strike, was promoted as "A Day Without an Immigrant," a direct reference to the 2004 film *A Day Without a Mexican*. The film (a mockumentary by director Sergio Arau) portrays the fallout when immigrant Latin@s disappear from California en masse, leaving nonimmigrants to do the difficult agricultural, manufacturing, service-sector, and household work that is largely invisible, but provides the foundations for the rest of the economy. Participation in the Day Without an Immigrant mobilizations was immense: half a million people took to the streets in Chicago, a million in Los Angeles, and hundreds of thousands more in New York, Houston, San Diego, Miami, Atlanta, and other cities across the country. In many places, these marches were the largest on record.[14]

What produced such a powerful wave of mobilization? The surging strength of the immigrant rights movement was built through the hard work of hundreds of organizations, including grassroots groups, nonprofit organizations, regional and national networks, and policy-focused Beltway groups.[15] At the same time, the rapidly changing media ecology provided crucial opportunities for the movement to grow, attract new participants, reach an unprecedented size, and achieve significant mobilization, cultural, and policy outcomes.[16]

A Day Without an Immigrant

English-language TV news channels have long played important roles in the information war that swirls around human migration. However, in the spring of 2006, all major English-language media outlets completely failed to anticipate the strength of the movement and the scale of the mobilizations. By contrast, Spanish-language commercial broadcasters, including the nationally syndicated networks Telemundo and Univision, provided constant coverage of the movement. Spanish-language newspapers, TV, and radio stations not only covered the protests but also played a significant role in mobilizing people to participate.[17] This was widely reported on in the English-language press after the fact.[18] Indeed, by most accounts, commercial Spanish-language radio was the key to the massive turnout in city after city. In L.A., Spanish-language radio personalities, or *locutores*, momentarily put competition aside in order to present a unified message: they urged the city's Latin@ population to take to the streets against the Sensenbrenner bill. Media scholar Carmen Gonzalez describes a historic meeting and press conference held by the *locutores*:

On March 20th all of the popular Spanish-language radio personalities gathered at the Los Angeles City Hall to demonstrate their support for the rally and committed to doing everything possible to encourage their listeners to attend. Those in attendance included: Eduardo Sotelo "El Piolín" & Marcela Luevanos from KSCA "La Nueva" 101.9FM; Ricardo Sanchez "El Mandril" and Pepe Garza from KBUE "La Que Buena" 105.5FM; Omar Velasco from KLVE "K-Love" 107.5FM; Renan Almendarez Coello "El Cucuy" & Mayra Berenice from 97.7 "La Raza"; Humberto Luna from "La Ranchera" 930AM; Colo Barrera and Nestor "Pato" Rocha from KSEE "Super Estrella" 107.1FM.[19]

These and other *locutores* across the country had a combined listener base in the millions. They ran a series of collaborative broadcasts during which they joined each other physically in studios and called in to one another's shows. They focused steadily on the dangers of H.R. 4437, the need to take to the streets, and the demand for just and comprehensive immigration reform. Gonzalez surveyed mobilization participants in the streets of L.A. and found that, after face-to-face conversations, Spanish-language commercial radio was the most important platform in terms of motivating march turnout (friends and family were the primary source of protest information, followed by radio).[20] One of the community organizers I later interviewed reiterated this point:

We saw it with the 2006 marches, where the radios had, some would say ... most of the push. Not the organizations that were organizing. They've been doing their work for a long time, but that whole thing of being able to be on the radio in front of millions of people really motivated the majority of people to participate in the economic boycott, and in the walkouts.[21]

While immigrant rights groups in L.A. organize yearly May Day marches that tend to turn out several thousand people, in the spring of 2006 the marches were ten to a hundred times larger than usual. The threat of the Sensenbrenner bill, combined with the involvement of the commercial *locutores*, produced this massive shift.[22]

The Walkouts

Figure 1.2
Silver Lake area students walk out for immigrant rights on March 29, 2006.
Source: Photo by pseudonymous poster "jlr-builder123," posted to L.A. Indymedia at http://la.indymedia.org/news/2006/03/152082_comment.php.

While the mass marches were largely organized through broadcast media, especially Spanish-language talk radio, text messages and social networking sites (SNS) were the key media platforms for the student walkouts that swept Los Angeles and some other cities during the same time period.[23] As the anti-Sensenbrenner mobilizations provided fuel for the fires of the (mostly Anglo, middle-class) blogosphere, walkout organizers enthusiastically turned to MySpace and YouTube to circulate information, report on their own actions, and urge others to join the movement. At the same time, text messaging (also called SMS, or short messaging service) was used as a tool for real-time tactical communication. Student organizers I interviewed made it clear that both text messaging and MySpace played important but not decisive roles in the walkouts.[24] Pre-existing networks of students organized the walkouts for weeks beforehand by preparing flyers, meeting with student organizations, doing the legwork, and spreading the word. Some said that text messages and posts to MySpace served not to "organize" the walkouts but to provide real-time confirmation that actions were really taking place. For example, one student activist told me about checking her MySpace page during a break between classes. She said that it was when she saw a photograph posted to her wall from a walkout at another school that she realized her own school's walkout was "really going to happen."[25] That gave her the courage to gather a group of students, whom she already knew through face-to-face organizing, and convince them that it was time to take action.[26] Another high school student activist explained:

It was organized, there was flyers, there was also people on the Internet, on chat lines and MySpace, people were sending flyers also. So that's also one of the ways that it was organized. The thing is that students just wanted their voice to be heard. Since they can't vote, they're at least trying to affect the vote of others, by saying their opinion towards H.R. 4437 affecting their schools and their parents or their family.[27]

This student activist, like many of those I worked with and interviewed, emphasized the pervasive and cross-platform nature of movement media practices during the spring of 2006. Staff at community-based organizations repeatedly described radio as the most important media platform for mobilizing the immigrant worker base. By contrast, student activists often mentioned SNS (specifically MySpace, the most popular SNS at the time) as a key communication tool during the walkouts. A few also mentioned email (especially mailing lists) and blogs, but most emphasized that organizing took place through a combination of face-to-face communication with friends, family, and organized student groups, printed flyers, text messages, and MySpace. I discuss the walkouts in more detail in chapter 2; for now it is enough to say that media organizing during the walkouts involved pervasive all-channel messaging, as young people urged one another to take action to defeat Sensenbrenner and stand up for their rights.

Analyzing A Day Without an Immigrant and the student walkouts side by side, we can see the contours of the overall media ecology for the immigrant rights movement in 2006. Although ignored, if not attacked, by English-language mass media and bloggers, the movement against the Sensenbrenner bill was able to grow rapidly by leveraging other platforms. Commercial Spanish-language broadcast media reported on the movement in detail, and, in the case of Spanish-language radio hosts, actively participated in mobilizing millions. At the same time, middle school, high school, and university students combined face-to-face organizing and DIY media-making, and used commercial SNS and mobile phones to circulate real-time information about the movement, coordinate actions, and develop new forms of symbolic protest. As these practices spread rapidly from city to city, the mobilizations continued to grow in scope and intensity. The vast scale of the movement was reflected in the slogan, "The sleeping giant is now awake!" The movement's power briefly caught the opposition off guard, and the Sensenbrenner bill died, crushed by the *gigante* (giant) of popular mobilization.

Movements and the Media Ecology: Looking across Platforms

We've seen, briefly, how the changing media ecology presented opportunities for the immigrant rights movement during the 2006 mass mobilization wave. Next, we will explore how immigrant rights activists engage across all available media platforms, including English-language mass media, Spanish-language mass media, community media (especially radio), and social media. The immigrant rights movement can teach us a great deal about how social movement media strategy today extends across platforms, despite the recent turn in the press, the academy, and activist circles toward a nearly exclusive emphasis on the latest and greatest social media platforms. At the same time, cross-platform analysis helps us understand what is really new in social movement media practices. For example, in the past, the main mechanism for advancing movement visibility, frames, and ideas was through individual spokespeople who represented the movement in interviews with print or broadcast journalists working for English-language mass media. This mechanism is now undergoing radical transformation. For the immigrant rights movement, increasingly powerful Spanish-language radio and TV networks provide important openings. At the same time, social media have gained ground as a crucial space for the circulation of movement voices, as the tools and skills of media creation spread more broadly among the population. I begin, however, by looking at the tense relationship between the movement and what activists call "mainstream media."

English-Language Mass Media

Many immigrant rights organizers express frustration with "mainstream media." By mainstream media they usually mean English-language newspapers and TV networks, especially those with national reach. Their feelings about unfair coverage are supported by the scholarly literature. For example, a recent meta-analysis of peer-reviewed studies of immigration framing in English-language mass media (by Larsen and colleagues) found that when immigrants are covered at all, they are usually talked about in terms that portray them as dangerous, threatening, "out of control," or "contaminated."[28] Despite some recent gains, such as the Drop the I-Word campaign that, in 2013, convinced both the Associated Press and the *Los Angeles Times* to stop using the terms "illegal immigrant" and "illegal alien," professional journalists generally continue to use dehumanizing language to refer to immigrants who lack proper documentation.[29] Indeed, a 2013 study by the Pew Research Center found that, despite some recent shifts toward the use of "undocumented immigrant" and away from "illegal alien," "illegal immigrant" remains by far the most common term used in the English-language press.[30]

Nonetheless, by focusing on lifting up the voices of immigrants and portraying them as full human beings, the immigrant rights movement has sometimes been able to shift public discourse. For example, immediately after the 2006 mobilizations, a research group led by Otto Santa Ana at UCLA conducted a critical discourse analysis of mainstream newspaper reporting on immigration policy, immigration, and immigrants. The group gathered one hundred key newspaper articles from two time periods: first, immediately after the May 2006 mobilizations, and second, in October 2006, after public attention had moved on. The authors found and categorized approximately two thousand conceptual metaphors used to refer to immigrants in English-language newspaper coverage during these time periods. They determined that the discursive core of the immigration debate is about the nature of unauthorized immigrants: on one side, there is a narrative of the immigrant as a criminal or animal, and on the other there is a narrative of the immigrant as a worker or a human being. Through a quantitative analysis of metaphor frequency, they found that, during coverage of the mass mobilizations in the spring of 2006, newspapers did shift toward a balance between the use of humanizing (43 percent) and dehumanizing (57 percent) metaphors about immigrants. However, by October, after the mobilizations had faded from public memory, newspapers switched back to employ dehumanizing metaphors more than twice as frequently as humanizing ones (67 percent of the time).[31] The discursive battle in English-language mass media is thus a long, slow, and painful process for immigrant rights organizers and for the communities they work with.

Many organizers say they occasionally do manage to gain coverage in mainstream media, but only in exceptional circumstances. One, who works with indigenous migrant communities, put it this way: "It's rare that we get the attention of the mainstream media unless there's blood or something. Then they'll come to us if it's related to indigenous people."[32] She feels that she is called on to speak as an expert about indigenous immigrants, but only in order to add color to negative stories about her community. She also mentioned that the difficulty seemed specific to L.A., and to the *Los Angeles Times* in particular; she feels that local partners of her organization in some other Californian cities have more luck with mainstream media. Many also express frustration that movement victories in particular are almost never covered. They find it especially galling that the mass media flock to cover the activities of tiny anti-immigrant groups while ignoring the hard day-to-day work done by thousands of immigrant rights advocates. One said, "I feel like a lot of the great work that's going on with organizations, say day laborers won a huge settlement or claim, you're not going to hear about it in the mass media. What we do hear about immigrant rights is anti-immigrant rights and anti-immigrant sentiment. That's pretty [much] across the board, that's how it's presented."[33] A few feel that anti-immigrant rights activists get more coverage because they are more savvy about pitching their actions to journalists, and that the immigrant rights movement could do a much better job of placing its stories and frames in English-language mass media.[34] Others feel that mainstream outlets consistently reject even their best media strategies.[35]

A few activists, mostly those who participate in more radical social movement groups, shared an explicit analysis of the mass media as a powerful enemy. One said, "We have an understanding that the media is not on our side. The corporate media is not on the side of the people, and they're actually an extension of the state, of these corporations."[36] The same activist, however, also talked about how the corporate media can occasionally be used to the movement's advantage:

We know they can reach way more people than we can at this point. Until we take over their TV stations, we're not going to be able to trust them. But around specific cases of police murder, for example an incident that happened in East L.A. recently was Salvador Cepeda, who was an eighteen-year-old, [who was] murdered by the sheriffs in the Lopez Maravilla neighborhood. We put out a press release and they came out to the vigil that we had. We try to encourage the families to speak out, to get it out there, but we're not going to be dependent on them.[37]

Whether they believe mass media to be actively antagonistic to the immigrant rights movement or not, most are frustrated by the way that they feel the media either ignore them or twist their words. Both activists' experiential knowledge and qualitative and quantitative scholarly studies demonstrate the systematic difficulties immigrant rights organizers face as they try to shape public discourse. Yet most continue to engage the mass media. Only two activists I interviewed, both from a collective called Revolutionary Autonomous Communities (RAC), said they had moved beyond anger and frustration and decided to stop speaking to "the corporate media:" "RAC has the position that as RAC, we're not going to rely on the corporate media at all. We're not going to speak to them. Anything we do, it's not going to be popularized through the corporate media. Because they're going to try to tell our stories their way."[38] One of the reasons RAC decided to stop speaking to corporate media was to avoid what they described as the problem of media "creating movement leaders" through selective decisions about whom to interview for the movement's perspective, a dynamic I return to below.

Most immigrant rights organizers, however, desire more and better coverage from English-language print and broadcast media. To achieve this, they emphasize the importance of personal relationships with reporters.

Some talked about specific reporters with whom they had developed a rapport. For example, one online organizer with a national group described how journalists who have a personal connection to immigration, especially those who come from immigrant families themselves, are easier to work with and more likely to report on the movement in a positive light:

It's a lot easier to get your message across through someone who has a personal connection to it.... I have a relationship with a writer from the Associated Press, he's of Mexican descent, he loves us. I pitched him this piece about us going to donate blood as undocumented students, and he wrote an article about it.... It was really well written and just put us in a really positive light, there's these students going out all across the nation, and going to donate blood around Christmas time, and so it was kind of like, is their blood illegal or something?[39]

Despite occasional examples of excellent coverage in English-language mass media outlets, often based on the long-term cultivation of connections with reporters and sometimes facilitated by the relative ease of contacting journalists through social media (especially Twitter), immigrant rights activists generally find themselves turning to other outlets that are more receptive: Spanish-language mass media, community radio, and the "ethnic press."

Spanish-Language Mass Media

Spanish-language mass media, especially commercial radio *locutores* (or announcers), played a key role in supporting the 2006 mobilizations against the Sensenbrenner bill. This was by no means a new development. Spanish-language media in Los Angeles have historically provided support for the immigrant rights movement, as Elena Shore has extensively documented.[40] More broadly, Juan Gonzales and Joe Torres have recently written a detailed popular history of the U.S. media that traces the role of the black press, the Spanish-language press, and the Chinese American press in the long struggle toward racial justice.[41] These accounts provide important context for the experiences of many in today's movement, who intimately understand the importance of Spanish-language mass media to their organizing efforts. For example, savvy immigrant rights organizers recognize that Facebook and Twitter are crucial for reaching immigrant youth, but they also know that to reach the broader Latin@ immigrant community, Univision and Telemundo are the most important channels to target:

When talking about immigrant youth, definitely, I would say [email, Facebook, and Twitter are] probably the biggest mediums. But when you're talking about the immigrant community broadly, Univision and Telemundo are huge. They're some of the most watched TV channels in this country.[42]

Immigrant rights organizers across the spectrum share this opinion. Students, labor organizers, indigenous community activists, staff at independent worker centers, and members of radical collectives all agree that commercial Spanish-language media frequently provide coverage where English-language media are nowhere to be found.[43] When they talk about the media used by the communities they organize, some mention not only the largest Spanish-language newspapers (*La Opinión*) and television channels (Univision, Telemundo) but also outlets focused on migrant workers' city, state, or community of origin. For example, many Oaxacans follow the major pan-Latin@ media but also read the Oaxacan newspapers *El Oaxaqueño* or *El Impulso de Oaxaca*[44] (I return to this dynamic, also known as *translocal media practices*, in chapter 4.) These patterns are also generational: younger indigenous people, especially those born in L.A., are more likely to "go to MySpace, listen to Rage Against the Machine, everything else."[45] Media use, in particular the adoption of SNS, is also related to how long the person has been a resident of the United States, although this is changing as SNS use rates increase in the home countries of migrant workers.[46]

The Spanish-language press is not the only important media ally for immigrant rights activists in L.A. To some degree, similar dynamics apply across all immigrant communities. For example, organizers from the Koreatown Immigrant Workers Alliance (KIWA) discussed gaining coverage in Korean-language media outlets during their supermarket workers' campaign, which ultimately secured a living-wage agreement in five different supermarkets in L.A.'s Koreatown.[47] Strategies for gaining newspaper coverage, whether the newspaper is in English, Spanish, Korean, or any other language, include building relationships with individual reporters, calling in favors from high-status allies, and the use of timely or familiar frames.[48] In the case of KIWA's Koreatown supermarket campaign, these strategies were highly effective in generating attention from Korean-language media, which covered the campaign "every step of the way."[49] KIWA's experience of positive coverage by Korean-language media thus mirrors many Latin@ activists' experience with the Spanish-language press. However, there are important differences. Spanish-language media in the United States have grown into nationwide, and in some cases transnational, networks that now reach a massive pan-Latin@ market.[50] The reach and power of Spanish-language mass media thus dwarf that of other minority-language outlets.

Leveraging this power does not come without complications. While commercial Spanish-language radio stations provide important opportunities, many activists feel that these stations are also sensationalist, materialistic, sexist, racist, and homophobic.

Those are very commercial outlets. They're in favor of immigrant rights but in kind of a very general way. And then sometimes they'll talk about raids and things like that, which is a big concern in the immigrant community and in the immigrant rights community. But they don't do what I would want them to do, which would be very proactive about warning people, having people call in when they see ICE vans, warning people where they see them, that's what I would really like to see those media outlets do.... They're as bad or worse as the mainstream media in English.[51]

Many immigrant rights organizers have mixed feelings about the role of Spanish-language mass media. Their experiential knowledge is again supported by critical scholarship, such as work by Beth Baker-Cristales, who analyzed the role of Spanish-language mass media in the 2006 marches.[52] Baker-Cristales provides rich detail about the key media personalities and networks involved in supporting the protests. She argues that, even as they played an important role in mobilizing Spanish-speaking immigrants to participate, print newspapers, TV, and radio networks also shaped the protests in ways that reproduced the dominant post-9/11 ideology of neoliberal citizenship. In other words, Spanish-language mass media successfully shaped protesters' ideas, language, and protest tactics to conform to the narrative of immigrants as ideal citizens, hard workers, and consumers who primarily desire cultural and political assimilation into mainstream, 'all-American' (Anglo, middle-class, heteronormative, U.S. nationalist) values.[53] Protesters were encouraged to portray themselves as "good immigrants," as opposed to the negative (and racially coded) categories "criminals" and "terrorists." Additionally, Baker-Cristales shows how the media chastised those who engaged in nonsanctioned forms of protest, such as the high school (and middle school) walkouts. Spanish-language broadcasters also heavily discouraged protesters' attempts to assert their own cultural or national identities alongside their desire for immigration policy reform. Most visibly, this took place through repeated calls for immigrant rights protesters to abandon flags from their own countries of origin and replace them with U.S. flags. This was meant to demonstrate "undivided" loyalty, despite the reality that many migrants do feel connected both to their communities of origin and to their new homes, and do participate meaningfully in binational or translocal citizenship.[54]

Community Radio

While Spanish-language commercial radio *locutores* with daily audiences of millions played the most important role in catalyzing the marches of 2006, their support for the immigrant rights movement overall has been sporadic. Community radio stations, on the other hand, reach fewer people at any one time but play an ongoing role in covering, supporting, and strengthening the movement. This should not be surprising. From Bolivian miners' radio[55] to the first pirate station in the United States, linked to the black power movement,[56] from the struggle for civil rights in the U.S. South[57] to the international feminist radio collective FIRE, community radio has long been a core tool of social movement communication.[58] Movement-based radio played a key role in the Algerian national liberation struggle,[59] the rise of the antiwar counterculture in the United States during the Vietnam War, and the Italian labor and social struggles of the 1970s, to name a few examples among many.[60] Today, the number of community radio stations continues to climb, even as the number of firms that control hundreds (or thousands) of full-power stations shrinks. Since the reregulation of radio in the United States in 1996, the radio giant Clear Channel has snapped up more than 1,200 stations. At the same time, however, the World Association of Community Radio Broadcasters counts 3,000 member stations across 106 countries.[61] In the United States, community radio activists such as Philadelphia's Prometheus Radio Project have struggled for, and won, expanded access to legal low-power FM licenses.[62] These and other battles have led some to theorize community radio as a social movement in and of itself.[63] Indeed, despite the recent wave of enthusiasm for social media as the key strategic tool for social movements, there is little doubt that community radio continues to play a critical role. In general, radio remains the primary news source for many of the world's poorest people. This is true everywhere, but it is most marked in parts of Latin America, Africa, and Asia, particularly where illiteracy rates are high and where there are communities of indigenous language speakers who are marginalized from national-language media.⁶⁴ These conditions describe low-wage immigrant workers on the margins of global cities everywhere, including Los Angeles.

In L.A., a number of community radio stations support social movements on a daily basis. These stations include the Pacifica affiliate KPFK, which carries Spanish-language movement programming such as *Mujeres Insurgentes* (Insurgent Women), *Voces de Libertad* (Voices of Freedom), and others; the streaming Internet station Killradio.org, originally a project of L.A. Indymedia; an unlicensed station run by Proyecto Jardín (Garden Project), an unlicensed station run by La Otra Campaña del Otro Lado (the Zapatista-affiliated Other Campaign from the Other Side); and *Radio Sombra* (Radio Shadow) in East L.A. Other radio stations linked to the immigrant rights movement include Radio Campesina, the network of local stations run by the United Farm Workers, which started in 1983 with KUFW in Visalia and now includes stations in Bakersfield, Fresno, Lake Havasu (Arizona), Phoenix, Salinas, Tri-Cities (Washington), and Yuma (Arizona). Many, if not all, of these radio stations and networks participated extensively in immigrant rights organizing in 2006. A study by Graciela Orozco for the Social Science Research Council analyzed coverage of the 2006 mobilization wave by Radio Bilingue (Bilingual Radio), a more than two-decades-old nonprofit network of Latin@ community radio stations with six affiliates in California and satellite distribution to over one hundred communities in the United States, Puerto Rico, and Mexico. She found that the nonprofit network played an important role in circulating information and encouraging people to join the mobilizations.⁶⁵

Some immigrant rights organizations have developed relationships with specific community radio outlets over time. For example, the Frente Indígena de Organizaciones Binacionales (Indigenous Front of Binational Organizations, FIOB) has a long-standing relationship with Radio Bilingue. The network will often air audio content, interviews, and public service announcements (PSAs) provided by FIOB. For a time, FIOB ran a regular public affairs show called *Nuestro Foro* (Our Forum).⁶⁶ In similar fashion, KIWA was able to secure a monthly hourlong radio show called *Home Sweet Home* on Radio Seoul, a Korean-language radio station that broadcasts in Koreatown.⁶⁷ Similar dynamics play out in many locales; for example, one immigrant rights organizer in Boston described community radio as an important outreach avenue: "Radio's huge for a lot of different types of immigrant communities. I'm working not only with the Spanish-speaking immigrant community, but there's Haitian radio, there's Brazilian radio, that's the way people get a lot of their news."[68] Community-based, minority-language radio thus remains a key part of the media ecology for many in the immigrant rights movement.

Streaming Radio and Internet-Enabled Distribution

As I note throughout this book, the most dynamic social movement media practices often take place across platforms. By 2006, at the time of the mass mobilizations against the Sensenbrenner bill, many movement-based radio stations were operating live streams over the Internet. Activists use streaming radio to transmit audio to remote listeners, who may listen via a computer linked to speakers, a mobile phone with a data connection, a stereo in the home, or a portable music player. Movement radio producers throughout the world also use the net to share and distribute both audio files and streams, which are picked up by community radio stations for local transmission on AM or FM bands. Examples in Los Angeles include Kill Radio, Radio Sombra, and Radio Insurgente, the EZLN station in Chiapas that is rebroadcast locally by pirate radios throughout the Americas (http://radioinsurgente.org). Several activists I worked with and interviewed were involved in movement radio projects, and all were quite familiar with live streaming radio over the net.

We have a show on killradio.org.... We're able to do our own reporting, interviews with people that are in different cities, organizing around ICE raids, immigration, indigenous rights, police brutality, other things that are happening, which is a good thing. Eventually I think we want to maybe even do it where—I know one of our members from Copwatch, he has raisethfist.org, where he has an Internet news show and then it's through FM dial. He's going to rebroadcast some of our shows, too. It's heard throughout Compton, Long Beach, Southeast L.A.[69]

As this activist describes, pirate radio stations now operate their studios in one location, then stream live over the Internet to a radio transmitter (or to multiple transmitters) for FM broadcast. This is known as a streaming studio-to-transmitter link (STL). The increasingly common use of this approach in the United States is confirmed by FCC reports, which indicate that in the majority of FCC raids on pirate broadcasters, the seized transmitters are remotely controlled.[70]

Movement-based audio production and distribution networks include the Latin American Association of Radiophonic Education (http://aler.org), which distributes programming across the hemisphere via satellite and Internet, with eight uplinks, 187 satellite receivers, and 117 affiliates. Free Speech Radio News (FSRN, http://fsrn.org) counts over two hundred journalists from fifty-seven countries around the world and is broadcast on the five Pacifica Network stations and more than fifty community stations in the United States, as well as in 120 countries via the Internet, shortwave, and community radio stations.[71] Workers' Independent News Service (WINS, http://laborradio.org) produces syndicated daily headline news segments, in-depth features and stories, economic reports, and raw audio archives that are used by radio stations and print publications. The content is created by local unions and allied activists, gathered together, edited, and repackaged, then distributed by audio streaming and podcast. The Internet has thus facilitated the growth of distribution networks that gather audio material from movement-based radio producers, package it, and amplify its impact through online streaming and delivery to network affiliates for AM or FM broadcast.

Community Media

Commercial Spanish-language media, including large-circulation newspapers and major TV networks, are key allies of the immigrant rights movement. They regularly report on immigration as an issue, follow immigration policy debates, and send reporters to cover immigrant rights activism. Sometimes, as in the spring of 2006, they also participate in efforts to mobilize the Latin@ community to take political action. At the same time, Spanish-language commercial media shape and constrain the language, strategy, and tactics of the immigrant rights movement. In addition, not every immigrant community is Spanish-speaking, and so not every immigrant community can count on access to the same kind of amplification. However, to some degree, every immigrant community does have access to community media, sometimes in its mother tongue, sometimes in English, and often bi- or multilingual. Indeed, the history of the U.S. media system is largely a history of newspapers and radio stations founded to serve the needs of new immigrant communities. This field is sometimes referred to as the ethnic press. Although the term is used by many immigrant rights activists, I avoid it, since it tends to mask the ethnicity of the Anglo (white) press.[72] In any case, ethnic/community media outlets such as newspapers, radio stations, and, increasingly, websites continue to play a crucial role in the immigrant rights movement. Many immigrant rights organizers see a presence in these media as essential:

> Ethnic media has been one of our biggest resources. *El Mundo, El Planeta,* the *Brazilian Times,* and all the Brazilian media outlets, because they get the narrative out there. And they usually use the narrative that we want them to use, which is different from the American media.[73]

Print newspapers especially still provide legitimacy for activists. For example, student organizers in Boston mentioned that newspaper coverage produces credibility in working-class immigrant communities:

> It makes people trust us. When they see us in *El Planeta,* they're like, "Oh, I saw you in *El Planeta,* so that's why I want to be involved," or "I saw you in the *Brazilian Times* and I heard so much about you guys, here's a hundred dollars, I want to donate to the campaign." So in terms of getting more support from your own community, it's a good resource, 'cause it almost makes you more legit, you know. Even though it's your community, when they see you in the paper they're like, "Oh, these kids are real."[74]

Community media thus act as legitimators of immigrant rights activists, and cover them far more frequently than mainstream English-language papers. Although community media have far less reach than either English- or Spanish-language mass media, the content they publish circulates across outlets through both formal and informal distribution networks. In particular, some activists cited the community media content network New American Media as a key media ally.[75]

The strength of local community media outlets has direct impacts on the strength of local organizing efforts. One activist who works as an online organizer for a national immigrant rights organization noted that the movement in Wisconsin has been consistently able to turn out large numbers of people for marches and mass mobilizations. He attributed the high turnout to the presence of a number of community media outlets, including newspapers and radio shows, produced by the immigrant community.[76] In the Boston area, the same organizer mentioned an AM radio station that sells hourly time slots. Organizations such as Centro Presente and Better Youth Boston take advantage of this and help members produce their own radio programs.

There is a long history in the United States of new immigrants creating media for their community of national origin, published in their mother tongue. However, many immigrant rights activists point to a shift in the past decade toward increased access to these outlets. For example, one described how what she termed "ethnic media" have emerged over the past decade as a key space for community-based organizations to gain coverage, where previously English-language print journalists and broadcasters ignored them:

> For us, we always have to stop and think, "What's the best way?"... And even till now, we still hit that mainstream newspaper, and then we realize other things that work because the mainstream doesn't show up, but the ethnic does. So for us ethnic media was this huge opening.... We eventually learned how to navigate ethnic press—really, pretty soon the mainstream were going to the ethnic press to get the information.[77]

The ethnic press is thus important not only because it covers stories that mainstream media ignore but also because it has become a source of stories for the mainstream press. This closely mirrors the more widely heard argument that the mass media now regularly draw stories from blogs and social media. The same organizer described the press strategy around a campaign to gain increased fares for taxi workers in New York:

> So I worked on a project in New York, with Taxi Workers, and pitched it to the *New York Times*.... The reporter bought it, and he was totally down with it, had the cover of the local news, you know, "Taxi drivers can't support their families." And we're like, "Could it have been more perfect?" That morning that it came out is when we sent out the press release for the wider "report comes out today." We got thirty media, local radio, TV, newspaper, tons of ethnic press, and that led to both *New York Daily News* and the *New Yorker*, the two smaller, the weeklies, to actually write editorials that support[ed] taxi workers in getting a fare increase. They never, ever, ever, ever say anything nice about the drivers. Which led to the fare increase victory.[78]

This story reveals the continued importance of the mainstream print media (the *New York Times*). At the same time, it illustrates how coverage by a major media outlet is situated within a changed media ecology that savvy organizers have learned to exploit. The initial story in the *Times* provided important momentum and credibility to the campaign, which organizers then leveraged to increase visibility for a report release about conditions in the industry, thereby generating a flurry of coverage across local and community media and ultimately securing a fare increase for immigrant taxi drivers.

Social Media

In the current media ecology, the immigrant rights movement is generally denied access to the English-language mass media, but is able to find openings in Spanish-language commercial media, as well as in community media outlets. In addition, despite deeply unequal levels of digital media access,[79] many grassroots media activists, immigrant rights organizers, and movement participants do use the Internet extensively to promote, document, and frame their activities. By 2006, the time of the Sensenbrenner mobilizations, social movements everywhere, including the immigrant rights movement, had widely adopted SNS. The first SNS to gain significant visibility was Friendster, soon followed by MySpace, then Facebook and Twitter (as well as a host of other, nationally specific SNS, such as Orkut in Brazil, Cyworld in Korea, and Sina Weibo in China). Social movements have used each of these SNS to advance their goals. For example, MySpace was originally marketed as a site for independent musicians to promote their music and connect with fans, but it soon became the most popular SNS for young people in the United States.[80] By 2006, a wide spectrum of activist networks and social movement groups, including anarchists, environmentalists, and feminists, all had MySpace profiles.[81] Activists use SNS as tools to announce meetings, actions, and events, distribute movement media, and reach out to Internet-savvy demographics.[82] Some SNS focus explicitly on facilitating face-to-face meetings based on shared interests. For example, in 2004, Howard Dean's campaign recognized that MeetUp could help the candidate's base self-organize during Dean's bid for the Democratic Party presidential nomination.[83] The use of MeetUp emerged first from the base of Dean supporters and was then encouraged and fostered by campaign leadership.[84] This case, and the social media–savvy strategy of the Obama campaign in 2008 and again in 2012, illustrate how participatory media practices have been used to revitalize vertical political organizational forms. Movement appropriation of SNS takes place even while these sites are also spaces where users replicate gender, class, and race divisions—for example, see danah boyd on how Indian Orkut users replicated the caste system, and on teens' class- and race-based discourse about MySpace versus Facebook.[85]

Movements extensively use the Internet and mobile phones as tactical mobilization tools. For example, we have seen how students in the L.A. Unified School District used MySpace and SMS to help coordinate walkouts that saw 15,000 to 40,000 students take the streets during the week follow-ing the March 25, 2006, marches.[86] I return to the walkouts in chapter 2.

Almost all the immigrant rights activists I worked with and interviewed said that social media are important organizing tools that can be used to connect with and inspire new activists, even as they repeatedly emphasized that the core work of movement building takes place through face-to-face connection. Movements are about relationships, and in-person communi-cation is essential.[87] At the same time, many organizers also note that social media can be used to develop or extend relationships not only with the networks of other activists but also with reporters. Personal relationships with reporters, in turn, are essential to garner positive coverage in print and broadcast media. For example, several DREAM activists talked about developing Twitter relationships with reporters. They found that Twitter produces higher response rates and faster response times from reporters than traditional press releases: "I could send a Twitter message to a reporter and that reporter will respond ten times faster than if I send a press release. And it's ten times less work."[88]

Mobile phones are also key. Many organizers who talk about Facebook, Twitter, and email lists as important tools for connecting with immigrant youth emphasize that mobile phones are a crucial platform in new immi-grant communities:[89]

Folks that grew up in this country mostly, they use a lot of the newer tools, like Facebook and Twitter, and e-mail lists is a way a lot of people communicate. But I work in a community [which] broadly uses cell phones a lot more. So for instance I just sent out this tweet to ask people to sign a mobile petition to stop deportation, and I actually tried to get them to send me their emails, to get them to formally sign the petition. Also, I'll hopefully follow up with them through email so I can explain the case more broadly; it's a little bit hard to do it with 140 characters. A lot of people signed, or wanted to sign, the petition and not as many sent the email. I mean, it shows that more people use mobile phones than emails,... so that's where I think the future is for our community.[90]

Widespread access to mobile phones has also produced an important shift over the last few years, from the use of the web to document past actions and mobilizations to real-time social media practices. As one interviewee stated,

I think right now we're at this point where suddenly we're kind of moving into this ... different area of real-time web.... I mean I'm finding with video, for example, how feasible it is to make a video and put it up the day that it happens.... In the past, I think in 2006, we wouldn't really have thought like that.[91]

He said that a few years earlier, activists would have mostly relied on commercial TV stations to provide video coverage of an action or mobilization,
then recorded the TV broadcast and perhaps used it later to point to evidence
of successful organizing. Today, by contrast, social movements are increasingly able to provide real-time or near real-time coverage of their own
actions. It is not uncommon, for example, for movement media-makers to
document a day's action, then post the video to the web within a few hours.
Increasingly, movement media-makers also broadcast their own actions via
commercial live-streaming sites. For example, DREAM activists used UStream
to provide real-time feeds from sit-ins at Department of Homeland Security
(DHS) offices, congressional offices, and Obama campaign headquarters in
2012. Most famously, media activists with Occupy Wall Street used UStream,
Livestream, and other services to broadcast everything from General Assemblies to the violent displacement of protest camps by riot police.[92]

Some immigrant rights activists feel that the assumption that social
media makes organizing easier is not necessarily true. For example, one
online organizer who works for a national media-savvy organization
described both positive and negative aspects of what he calls "new media"
in the context of community organizing. On the "good side," he felt that
social media allow rapid list building and getting in touch with many
people quickly, and he offered the example of Occupy Wall Street. He also
pointed to the ability to "control and tell your own story, which is extremely
powerful. The power of narrative, public narrative is amazing.... It's huge
to be able to say now, they don't have to tell our story, we're going to tell
our own story."[93] On the other hand, he described social media as having
three main drawbacks. First, it produces a mode of activism that he calls
"reactionary as opposed to intentional"; in other words, activists end up
responding to online debates about various events rather than "sitting
down and figuring out what you're going for." Second, it blurs the boundaries of public and private, which he sees as potentially harmful. Organizers
who default to public by posting everything on social media end up making
mistakes and "putting out all these fires that you don't necessarily want to
be putting out." Third, he is concerned about social media's ability to
produce the illusion of making a difference. His example of this dynamic:
"Someone puts out a Facebook status update 'Call your senator,' and then
you click 'Like,' and you're like 'Ah, I just did something good today.' If you
click 'Like' and you didn't call a senator, you just did absolutely nothing."[94]

Immigrant rights activists also see great potential for the amplification of their voices in digital space but are frustrated by the current lack of realization of that possibility. For example, many feel that progressive English-language bloggers don't spend a lot of time engaging immigration issues.[95] They see this as a crucial problem, especially since right-wing and anti-immigrant frames and language are widespread across the blogosphere. One interviewee noted that phrases like "What part of illegal don't you understand?" often dominate the comment sections of articles, blog posts, and other online spaces.[96] At the same time, he noted that the relatively small but highly motivated group of older white racists who systematically post negative comments are more familiar with "older technology like forums, but they're not good at using some of the newer tools that we have."[97] Some online platforms are thus seen (if only temporarily) as friendlier to immigrant rights advocates than others.

Activists also note that social media can be used to reinforce power inequality. For example, one online organizer observed that although revolutionary uses of social media have been widely covered and discussed in the wake of the so-called Arab Spring, social media are primarily used by elites. Those who have greater access to digital media tools and skills tend to be those who have class or educational privilege. He gave an example from Guatemala, where an elite lawyer recorded a YouTube video critical of the left-leaning president just before committing suicide. The video was circulated widely via SNS and then amplified by right-leaning news websites, in a context in which only the wealthy have broadband Internet access. Elites used the video as a rallying tool against the democratically elected president, almost to the point of constitutional crisis.[98] Ultimately, none of my interviewees argued that social media or the Internet per se have a transformational impact on organizing or social movements. Instead, they see them as tools that can be applied to organizing but are currently underutilized by their communities.

The Power of Fox News: "We Know the Law's Racist But We Still Support It Anyway"

Changes in the media ecology provide important new opportunities for the immigrant rights movement. However, these changes should not be overestimated. Even as the movement gains visibility, as activists develop new relationships with journalists, and as movement participants increasingly self-document their struggles, the media system remains dominated overall by language, frames, and metaphors that systematically dehumanize immigrants.[99] Many activists also emphasize that they still face daunting opposition in the form of powerful right-wing broadcast media. Even as the immigrant rights movement wins certain kinds of victories, both symbolic and political, it can be very difficult to withstand concerted attacks from the anti-immigrant media machine:

> When we get the full force of the media outlets, we generally get our asses kicked. I think a good example of that is [Arizona State Bill] SB-1070. We came out very strong, framing that through our story of racial profiling and oppression.... The best image I had was the image of the Phoenix Suns wearing the "Los Suns" jersey, 'cause they were saying "solidarity with the Latino community." But you know, after Fox News and all these folks started going after us, the polling changed on it. It was the worst polling ever, 'cause they were like, "We know the law's racist but we still support it anyway."[100]

In the fight against Arizona's SB 1070 (key components of which have now been struck down as unconstitutional), even support from a major sports team was not enough to counter the force of a sustained attack from Fox News and right-wing talk radio. The changed media ecology, while it provides many important opportunities, is still often hostile terrain for the immigrant rights movement.

The Immigrant Rights Movement and the Media Ecology: Conclusions

In the spring of 2006, the immigrant rights movement burst out of the shadows and into the streets. The Sensenbrenner bill was crushed by a massive protest wave, the largest in U.S. history. Organizers were successful in part because they leveraged new opportunities in a changing media ecology.

The dominant component of the media ecology, English-language mass media, remains challenging terrain for the immigrant rights movement. When activists do receive coverage in English-language print and broadcast media, they are often framed in ways that do not help them achieve their goals. Occasionally, however, the English-language press does tell immigration stories in ways that humanize immigrants. Organizers feel that cultivating relationships with individual sympathetic reporters is key to increasing the frequency of favorable frames. They also note that this can sometimes be more easily achieved with reporters who have a personal connection to immigration.

In general, the movement enjoys better access to commercial Spanish-language radio and television, even as these outlets grow in reach and political power. Yet commercial Spanish-language media constrain the immigrant rights movement within "safe," and often deeply problematic, assimilationist narratives of neoliberal citizenship: "good" versus "bad" protesters and "hard workers" versus "criminals" and "terrorists." Over the past few years, organizers have become more savvy about how to generate coverage in community media (the ethnic press), and how to further push such coverage until it bubbles up to wider circulation via the mainstream media. Community media also provide access to more recent immigrants, and help legitimize immigrant rights activists within their own communities. As we shall discuss in chapter 4, translocal media practices also facilitate movement building, as migrants increasingly access and sometimes create content for media outlets in their hometowns, cities, or communities of origin.

At the same time, the explosion of access to social media helps organizers more directly involve movement participants, allies, and supporters in the production and circulation of their own rich media texts. The rise of Spanish-language commercial media and the spread of social media both provide important openings for the insertion of movement narratives into public consciousness. In addition, English-language mass media outlets sometimes pick up and amplify stories that begin in social media, community media, or Spanish-language mass media. More recently, movement participants have begun to produce real-time or near real-time self-documentation of their struggles. Yet even as social media have steadily grown in importance, according to organizers, nothing displaces the power of face-to-face communication.

Overall, the media ecology is evolving: where once there were only a few pathways to public visibility, there are now more, and more flexible, routes. However, activists can effectively leverage this flexibility only if they recognize the opportunities available in the new media ecology rather than remain focused solely on gaining access to English-language print and broadcast media. The next chapter describes how the immigrant rights movement uses what I call *transmedia organizing* strategies to become visible across platforms, to open up the movement narrative to participatory media-making, to link attention to action, and to do all this in ways that remain accountable to the movement's social base.

Figure 2.1
Walkout Warriors sticker, April 2006.
Source: Unknown photographer, image widely circulated as a wall post on MySpace.

2 Walkout Warriors: Transmedia Organizing

In the previous chapter, we explored the transformation of the media ecology and the implications for the immigrant rights movement. Despite continued lack of access to English-language mass media, the growing power of the Spanish-language press, together with the rise of social and mobile media, provides a clear opening for organizers. In this chapter I develop the concept of *transmedia organizing*. I use this term to talk about how savvy community organizers engage their movement's social base in participatory media-making practices. Organizers can push participatory media into wider circulation across platforms, creating public narratives that reach and involve diverse audiences. When people are invited to contribute to a broader narrative, it strengthens their identification with the movement, and over the long run increases the likelihood of successful outcomes. Yet many organizations continue to find transmedia organizing risky. In part, this is because it requires opening up to diverse voices rather than relying primarily on experienced movement leaders to frame the narrative by speaking to broadcast reporters during press conferences. Those who embrace the decentralization of the movement's story can reap great rewards, while those who attempt to maintain top-down control risk losing credibility.

Transmedia Organizing: A Working Definition

The term "transmedia organizing" is a mash-up of the concept of transmedia storytelling, as elaborated by media studies scholars, and ideas from social movement studies. In the early 1990s the scholar Marsha Kinder developed the idea of transmedia intertextuality to refer to the flow of branded and gendered commodities across television, films, and toys. Kinder was interested in stories and brands that unfolded across platforms, and took care to analyze them in the context of broader systemic transformation of the media industries. She focused especially on the deregulation of children's television during the Reagan years. Throughout the 1970s, Action for Children's Television, a grassroots nonprofit organization with 20,000 members, organized for higher-quality children's TV and against advertising within children's programming, with some success.[1] However, by the early 1980s both the Federal Communications Commission and the National Association of Broadcasters were pushing aggressively to abandon limits on advertising to children and product-based programming. It was during this shift that Kinder conducted a series of media ethnographies with children. She was interested in better understanding young people's relationships to franchises such as Teenage Mutant Ninja Turtles, which children experienced across platforms as a comic magazine, an animated TV series, a line of toys, a videogame, and so on. She found that cross-platform stories and branded commodities not only increased both toy and ad sales but also produced highly gendered consumer subjectivity in children.[2] In 2003, Henry Jenkins reworked the concept for an era of horizontally integrated transnational media conglomerates, and defined transmedia storytelling as follows:

Transmedia storytelling represents a process where integral elements of a fiction get dispersed systematically across multiple delivery channels for the purpose of creating a unified and coordinated entertainment experience. Ideally, each medium makes its own unique contribution to the unfolding of the story.[3]

He went on to articulate the key points of transmedia storytelling in the context of a converged media system. Chief among them are the following: transmedia storytelling is the ideal form for media conglomerates to circulate their franchises across platforms; transmedia storytelling involves "world building" rather than closed plots and individual characters; it involves multiple entry points for varied audience segments; it requires co-creation and collaboration by different divisions of a company; it provides roles for readers to take on in their daily lives; it is open to participation by fans; and it is "the ideal aesthetic form for an era of collective intelligence."[4]

In the decade since Jenkins's 2003 explanation of these key elements, the media industries have increasingly adopted transmedia storytelling as a core strategy. The term *transmedia* is now regularly used to describe the work of professional producers who create cross-platform stories with participatory media components.[5] Individuals, consultancies, and firms, initially small boutique shops but increasingly also units within larger media companies, have positioned themselves as transmedia producers. In 2010 the Producers Guild of America announced the inclusion of "transmedia producer" in the Guild's Producers Code of Credits for the first time.[6] More recently, institutions such as the Sundance Institute and the Tribeca Film Festival have begun to recognize, fund, curate, and promote transmedia projects.[7]

In 2009 the media strategist Lina Srivastava proposed that activists and media artists might apply the ideas of transmedia storytelling to social change, through what she termed transmedia activism: "There is a real and distinct opportunity for activists to influence action and raise cause awareness by distributing content through a multiplatform approach, particularly in which people participate in media creation."[8] Several firms now explicitly describe themselves as working on transmedia activism. In 2008 the Mexican film star Gael Garcia Bernál and the director Marc Silver (with Srivastava as a strategy consultant) launched the transmedia activism production company Resist Network.[9] New examples of transmedia storytelling for social change emerge on a regular basis.[10] Many of these projects are honest attempts to translate the lessons of transmedia storytelling from entertainment and advertising into strategies that could be used for activism and advocacy. Others seem more ambiguous, as transmedia producers who primarily work with corporate clients identify opportunities to win contracts with social issue filmmakers, nonprofit organizations, and NGOs. In any case, by 2013 there were several high-profile, professionally produced transmedia campaigns focused specifically on immigrant rights. Jose Antonio Vargas's project Define American, Laurene Powell Jobs–backed (and Davis Guggenheim–produced) film *The Dream is Now*, and the Silicon Valley campaign FWD.us (spearheaded by Facebook founder Mark Zuckerberg) are probably the three best known, and I return to them in chapter 7.

I am excited by the growing interest in transmedia storytelling for social change among media professionals. However, in this book the term *transmedia organizing* does not center on the emerging professionalization of transmedia strategy, whether for entertainment, advertising, or activism. Instead of carefully managed media initiatives, I primarily emphasize organic, bottom-up processes. More broadly, I suggest that social movements have always engaged in transmedia organizing, and the process has become more visible as key aspects of movement media-making come online. This is not to suggest that nothing new is taking place. However, I believe that the recent emphasis on technological transformation is misplaced, to the degree that it blinds us to a comprehensive analysis of social movement media practices. In addition, while movements do already engage in transmedia organizing, they can be more effective if they are intentional about this approach. To that end, I suggest the following definition:

Transmedia organizing includes the creation of a narrative of social transformation across multiple media platforms, involving the movement's base in participatory media making, and linking attention directly to concrete opportunities for action. Effective transmedia organizing is also accountable to the needs of the movement's base.

I contend that transmedia organizing involves the construction of social movement identity, beyond individual campaign messaging; it requires co-creation and collaboration across multiple social movement groups; it provides roles and actions for movement participants to take on in their daily life; it is open to participation by the social base of the movement; and it is the key strategic media form for social movements in the current media ecology. While the end goal of corporate transmedia storytelling is to generate profits, the end goal of transmedia organizing is to strengthen social movement identity, win political and economic victories, and transform the consciousness of broader publics. Effective transmedia organizing also includes accountability mechanisms so that the narrative and the actions it promotes remain grounded in the experience and needs of the social movement's base. A concrete case study will better illustrate what I mean by "bottom-up" transmedia organizing. To this end, I now turn to the student walkouts of 2006.

Transmedia Organizing: Walkouts

In chapter 1, we saw that students in Los Angeles used MySpace as an organizing tool during the 2006 walkouts in protest of the Sensenbrenner bill. Here I look much more closely at the fine-grained texture of movement media practices in the midst of the mobilization. Some commentators at the time believed that immigrant rights organizations used social networking sites (SNS) to push their organizing efforts out, from the top down, to a new youth constituency. However, for the most part my experience, the interviews I conducted with protesters, and media archives suggest a different story. For example, almost none of the flyers that were circulated on MySpace were created by established immigrant rights organizations. Instead, they were produced and spread by students themselves:

Figure 2.2
Spring 2006 walkout flyer.
Source: Original source unknown, reposted to multiple MySpace walls.

Students created a wide range of these virtual flyers using graphical styles and techniques ranging from hand-drawn art to scanned paintings, from remix and photo-collage to text-heavy flyers with varied fonts, colors, and clip art. I found very few examples of MySpace flyers created by existing political organizations; the vast majority were made by students and circulated through their friendship networks in the form of wall posts and bulletins. MySpace also functioned as a kind of digital public sphere (if commercial, surveilled, and circumscribed) for students to debate the broader issues of immigration, as well as the specific tactic of the walkouts. One activist from Watsonville High recalled that after the first day of the walkouts, another student posted anti-immigrant commentary on MySpace, which was then printed out and posted up around her school. The printed anti-immigrant MySpace bulletin generated a firestorm of anger among immigrant students and prompted a second day of walkouts.[11]

After the first round of walkouts took place, in early March, students used MySpace posts, bulletins, chats, and forums to document their actions, post and circulate photos and videos, and debate tactics:

BIGGEST WALKOUT IN STUDENT HISTORY ON MARCH 31, 2006

ON FRIDAY MARCH 31, 2006 ALL MEXICANS/LATINOS/HISPANICS/CHICANOS ARE TO WALK OUT OF CAMPUS AFTER 1ST PERIOD AND ARE TO MARCH TO EVERY POLITICAL BUILDING THEY CAN REACH. IF YOU GOT FRIENDS THAT AREN'T MEXICANS INVITE THEM TO PROTEST TOO TELL EM THEY COULD BE LOSING FRIENDS/GIRLFRIENDS ECT ... WEATHER THEY BLACK, WHITE, JAP., ECT ... TELL EM TO HELP OUT THIS FRIDAY IS GONNA BE THE BIGGEST STUDENT PROTEST THE GOVERNMENT HAS SEEN BUT THERE IS TO BE NO WALKOUTS (WEDNESDAY AND THURSDAY) LET THE SCHOOL AND THE GOVERNMENT THINK WE HAVE STOPED PROTESTING AND THIS WAY THEY WON'T PUT SCHOOLS ON LOCKDOWN ... WE GONNA MAKE HISTORY THIS MONTH[12]

MySpace became a venue not only to discuss tactics but also to contextualize the walkouts within the larger histories of colonization, indigenous rights, and the ongoing wars in Iraq and Afghanistan:

The senate has just approved that bill enforcing ... the immigration law ... this is bullshit ... cuz there is no real american in this country ... the real americans were those natives, and they even immigrated,... we can't have our liscenses but yet they want us to go fight a war that isn't ours ... fuck this shit.... WEDNESDAY WALKOUT[13]

In addition to posting comments and images to friends' walls, creating and sending bulletins, and using forums, students also created numerous MySpace groups with names such as NO on HR4437, FUCK THA HR-4437, UNITED MEXICANS, !~PrOuD BeAnErs~!, Indigenous Resistance, Protest Bill HR4437!, undocumented immigrants' rights, Say No to HR 4437, and the like. Student activists also found ways to appropriate technical affordances originally designed for individual expression and repurpose them for collective expressions of political engagement and group solidarity. For example, many changed their profile pictures to "No on HR4437" images or flyers and changed their display names to walkout-related terms, such as "nohr4437," "walkout," or "4 A Reason."

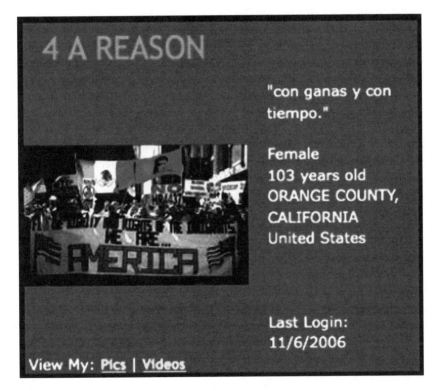

Figure 2.3
MySpace profile picture and display name changed in political protest.
Source: Screen capture from MySpace.com.

They also used real-time tools such as AIM and other chat clients to discuss past and upcoming walkouts, share experiences and tactics, and spread the word about future actions, as in this instant message exchange:

kooky(7:44:47 p.m.): IT WAS SOO MUCH FUN!
kooky(7:44:48 p.m.): <3
wiggle2(7:44:57 p.m.): HELLZ YEAH
wiggle2(7:45:22 p.m.): like 500 students left the school
wiggle2(7:45:39 p.m.): thats like half. lmaoo.
kooky(7:53:59 p.m.): shit was CRAZY
kooky(7:54:08 p.m.): ohh mann
kooky(7:54:13 p.m.): I cant wait till next yearr
kooky(7:54:15 p.m.): xD
wiggle2(7:54:59 p.m.): werrd me either what i find funny is that u started from the middle of the crowd nd ended up leading
kooky(7:55:48 p.m.): werrdd[14]

MySpace user wiggle2 (whose username I changed to preserve privacy) not only employed AIM to discuss the walkout with other students but documented this practice and then circulated it through wall posts to MySpace.

In moments of mass mobilization, movement participants seize new media platforms for tactical communication, and simultaneously use them to document, share, and strategize around movement activity. Student activists documented their own walkouts with still and video cameras as well as mobile phones, and also learned new media skills. For example, several people told me that in the immediate wake of the walkouts, friends showed them how to transfer documentation from cameras and phones to computers, edit photos and video, and upload content to the web. Others described spending extensive amounts of time online during the mobilization wave, not only posting and sharing movement media across SNS but also learning new photo and video editing skills, "profile pimping" for the cause, and so on.[15]

Middle school students as well as high school students participated in the walkouts. One organizer, a middle school teacher at the time, told me about daily conversations she had with her students about their own plans to participate. She noted that there was wide disparity in access to mobile phones among middle and high school students, based on income as well as age. For example, most of her younger middle school students did not have access to mobile phones or digital cameras. They heard about the walkouts through their parents, elder siblings, or existing chapters of student organizations such as MEChA (Movimiento Estudiantil Chicano/ a de Aztlán). Their lack of access to digital cameras and mobile phones meant that police repression of middle school walkouts went largely undocumented and unreported.[16]

The Sensenbrenner crisis and the walkouts produced a generative moment, as young people appropriated social media tools to circulate information about the struggle in (nearly) real time. Simultaneously, the crisis provided a crucible for the development and diffusion of emergent sociotechnical practices such as modifying display names or profile pictures to articulate political demands.[17] These practices, created organically by the students themselves and only later adopted by formal political organizations, networks, nonprofit organizations, and policy advocates, take advantage of the changed media ecology to generate collective consciousness, enhance movement identity, and circulate knowledge of key processes, actions, and events.

The Walkouts: Beyond Social Media

High school and middle school students effectively used MySpace as a platform to circulate calls for walkouts, document their experiences, and discuss strategies for political action. They also used SNS to reflect publicly on the emotional power of mass mobilization. Yet it would be a mistake to assume that SNS were the primary generative space for the success of the walkouts as a tactic. Rather, walkouts are a long-standing part of what Doug McAdam, Sydney Tarrow, and Charles Tilly have called the *repertoire of contention* of Latin@ high school students in Los Angeles.[18] In 1968, more than 20,000 Latin@ (mostly Chican@) high school students across L.A. walked out of their schools to demand educational justice. They protested the racism they suffered at the hands of administrators and teachers and called for equal treatment, the inclusion of non-European cultural history in the curriculum, new investment in crumbling infrastructure, and an end to 50 percent dropout rates.[19] These events, also known as the Blowout, were a defining moment in Chican@ movement history. They set the stage for the emergence of a new generation of social movement leaders, organizations, and networks, as well as for the rise of influential Latin@ politicians and public officials.[20] High school students took up the same tactic in 1994 during the battle against California's Proposition 187, a referendum designed to exclude undocumented immigrants from access to public services and benefits. Thousands of students across the state walked out of their schools in protest in the weeks leading up to the Prop 187 vote.[21] Even after Prop 187 passed, resistance continued until the proposition was declared unconstitutional by the courts. Michelle Holling has described how struggles against Prop 187 mixed street actions such as walkouts with online protest—although at the time, access to the Internet was mostly limited to academics, and online protest participation primarily involved posting to email lists, such the CHICLE Chican@ Studies listserv.[22]

Not only have walkouts been an important tactic throughout Chican@ and immigrant rights movement history in Los Angeles, that history was also recirculated and pushed back into popular consciousness through the mass media immediately before the 2006 wave of walkouts. In March 2006, HBO aired the film *Walkout*. This docudrama, directed by Edward James Olmos, tells the story of the Chicano high school teacher Sal Castro and the student activist Paula Crisostomo, both key actors in the 1968 student movement.

Although the broadcast of the film did not take place until the March 2006 cycle of walkouts was already under way, prerelease versions of the film were seen by groups of high school student activists across L.A. in December and January.[23] Beginning in December 2006, student groups around the city (some, like the Brown Berets, first established in the late 1960s) organized prerelease screenings and discussions of the HBO film. One article about the making of the film put it this way:

The persistent educational problems faced by Latino students is one reason [director Edward James Olmos] wanted to make this film—scheduled to air March 18—about events that for most people remain lost in L.A. history. "The dropout rate is higher than it was when these walkouts took place," says Olmos, citing recent (and disputed) statistics that have stirred new debates about the quality of education here, especially for ethnic minorities. "That's why we're making this movie. We're hoping that the kids will walk out again."[24]

Perhaps most important, hundreds of students took part in the film's production, acting as extras in scenes of *Walkout*. The film production process linked present-day student struggles even more tightly to the cultural memory of the walkouts as a powerful movement tactic and provided a space for literally rehearsing mass mobilization. The film—in its

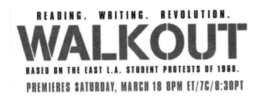

Figure 2.4
Still from the HBO film *Walkout.*
Source: Screen capture from HBO.com.

production process, in prerelease screenings organized by student activists, and in student conversations on MySpace—contributed to the broader circulation of tactics during the run-up to the mobilization against the Sensenbrenner bill. For example, one post on the wall of a MySpace user put it this way: "[I] saw the movie walkout its really good it got me all emotional. actually i saw it exactly one day before the RHS walkout it inspired me i guess. i will try to go to the screening in reedley it really is a good movie."[25]

Walkout was not the only film that contributed to the political atmosphere during the spring of 2006. The fictional feature *A Day Without a*

Mexican was also widely referenced prior to May Day 2006. Many organizers promoted May Day either under the rubric *Gran Boicott* (The Great Boycott) or, in a direct reference to the film, as "A Day Without an Immigrant."[26] For example, a MySpace protest text (posted to http://groups.myspace.com/NoOnHR4437, ellipsis at end inserted) read as follows:

If HR4437 is passed NO WORK or SCHOOL
Body: Subject: May 1st will be the DAY WITHOUT LATINOS
wear white tuesday!!!!!!!
If HR 4437 is passed:
no school or work on May 1st
tell everyone you not to attend school and tell your parents not to work
the movie "A Day Without a Mexican" will become real ... spread the word!

Films thus provided inspiration for real-life protest tactics. In turn, the real-life mobilizations served as sites for film production. Both amateur and professional media producers actively sought to weave video created by immigrant rights marchers into music videos, documentaries, and fiction films. Examples include the music videos for the songs "Cazador" by the band Pistolera and "Marcha" by MC Malverde, film compilations such as *Gigante Despierta* (Giant Awake), and feature-length documentary films, including *Undocumented*.

For the most part, the larger, vertically structured social movement organizations noticed the organic appropriation of SNS as a result of the walkouts. A few then attempted to strategically adopt SNS as a distribution platform for their preexisting messaging, with varying degrees of success, but none were able to effectively drive future mass mobilizations by students. In informal conversations with activists as well as in formal interviews, immigrant rights nonprofit organizations noted that they began to set up or more actively promote their own MySpace accounts only after the success of the 2006 walkouts, based on what they had seen of students' tactical innovation.[27] An organization called BAMN (By Any Means Necessary) was perhaps most successful in this strategy, but it was never able to mobilize more than a few hundred students. In some cases nonprofits were even attacked in MySpace posts by students denouncing them as "opportunists" and *gabachos* (whites) attempting to capitalize on the Latin@ student movement in order to advance their own political ends.

This provides an example of how organizations that attempt to adopt social media tools pioneered by movement participants or ad hoc networks run the risk that the tactic will backfire. This can happen if the existing online community, in this case students, perceive it as inauthentic, forced, or opportunistic. Simply having a presence on the latest SNS is not an effective transmedia organizing strategy. The use of participatory media in this case was most effective for the loosely linked, informal network of student walkout participants, in combination with other media texts across platforms.

Transmedia Organizing Practices

So far in this chapter I have described transmedia organizing as a process whereby activists develop a narrative of social transformation across multiple media platforms, involve their movement's base in participatory media practices, amplify movement voices by way of the mass media, and provide concrete opportunities for action. I introduced a case study of the student walkouts for immigrant rights in 2006 to illustrate organic transmedia organizing. The next section zooms out to a broader set of interviews and examples that illustrate transmedia organizing across the immigrant rights movement.

Basta Dobbs: Presente.org's Cross-Platform Strategy
Making and circulating media across platforms was crucial to the success of Presente.org's Basta Dobbs campaign. In 2009, immigrant rights groups, Latin@ civil rights organizations, celebrities, and local community-based groups across the country came together in a national campaign to remove anti-immigrant commentator Lou Dobbs from CNN. The campaign was coordinated by Presente.org, at the time a project of Citizen Engagement Labs. It was designed to use online organizing methods developed by MoveOn.org, but applied to the Latin@ community. The Basta Dobbs campaign deployed a sophisticated transmedia strategy across the web, mobile phones, and broadcast radio, and rapidly built a database of tens of thousands of email addresses and phone numbers. Participants were encouraged to write and call network executives, and they did so by the thousands.[28]

One activist I interviewed felt that the campaign's success was largely based on the combination of broadcast radio, mobile phones, and social media:

The Basta Dobbs Campaign, I think that was one of the first times. I mean we had organizations or groups like Move On, and all these different groups that were doing advocacy and very successful, Moms Rising, all these groups that have huge Internet power bases. But the immigrant community wasn't really involved in that, and neither were their supporters. So what we saw in Basta Dobbs was this, kind of this new model.[29]

The Basta Dobbs campaign was built to engage Latin@ activists first, and the Latin@ community more broadly. Campaign organizers appeared on Spanish-language radio and television and asked listeners and viewers to sign up for the campaign by sending an SMS (text message) to a shortcode. This was combined with regular radio and TV appearances by organizers:

They had a text messaging hub, through their web site. So they wanted everybody to sign up on that…. Jet Blue was offering $600 flights, and you could travel anywhere you wanted to in the country, wherever they flew for a month as many times as you wanted for the $600. So they took advantage of that and they did this country tour. And they went on all the radio spots, all the TV shows, and they were able to build up a list within a little bit over a month, maybe two months, about a hundred thousand people to join Basta Dobbs.[30]

The Basta Dobbs campaign illustrates the importance of the relationship between broadcast media and social media. It was through a nationwide speaking tour, organized in partnership with local community-based organizations and broadcast by local radio stations, that Basta Dobbs organizers were able to quickly build a critical mass of tens of thousands of people willing to sign up to receive SMS action alerts for the campaign. SMS alerts were used not only to ask people to sign petitions, call CNN headquarters, or write letters to the editor but also to invite them to physical protests at CNN offices around the country. The campaign itself, because of the rapid growth of its SMS list, the high number of views on its professionally produced videos, and the real-world mobilizations coordinated by local grassroots groups, augmented by SMS action alerts from the national campaign, quickly became a story that both Spanish-language and English-language mass media outlets were interested in covering. As organizers unrolled a public campaign to target Dobbs's advertisers, network executives felt rising pressure to take action. The campaign ended in November 2009,

when Lou Dobbs announced the early end of his CNN contract and organizers declared victory.

Effective transmedia organizers thus built a narrative around the
momentum of the movement itself, even while providing multiple points
of connection for further engagement. In this case, most people initially
became aware of the Basta Dobbs campaign from local radio stories or SMS
messages, later through social networking sites, and, once the campaign
was growing, through the mass media. The most effective use of social
media for social transformation occurs when it is coordinated with print
and broadcast strategies, as well as with real-world actions.

Cross-Platform Approach

I have explained that transmedia organizing takes place across multiple
platforms, and indeed, many immigrant rights organizers have explicit
cross-platform media strategies. Most of those whom I interviewed insisted
that different platforms are crucial for reaching different constituents
within the broader immigrant rights movement. Many said that social
media are useful tools for reaching younger people and students, while
radio and newspapers remain key for reaching parents and working-class
communities. For example, in one interview, an activist with Dream Team
LA described the process her group uses to develop media strategy. They
begin with a group brainstorming effort to identify shared values, and from
there develop key points and sound bites to use during a specific campaign.
Based on this shared messaging strategy, developed through a participatory
process, the group then conducts training sessions and works with the
movement base to circulate messages across multiple platforms. This activist described using print newspapers and Spanish-language TV news to
reach the older generation ("the moms, the dads") while connecting with
the younger generation via social media:

For example, whenever we have a rally, an event, we make sure that we have key
networks there, like Univision, Telemundo, Teleflash, Channel 2, Channel 7. But
when the news stories come out, we always post those news stories on our Twitter
and our Facebook, because we know that's the way, the only way that younger folks,
and I would say, 80 percent of people get their news from, so we are very intentional
about connecting the two.[31]

In another interview, a group of DREAM activists described the importance of blogs and SNS for reaching younger audiences, while also

mentioning the continued power of print and broadcast media to shape reputation and increase visibility. They emphasized that social media campaigns are often most effective "when people are already hearing about the DREAM movement through TV or newspapers."[32] In addition, they pointed to the spreadability of social media in the context of their campaigns, both in terms of participatory content creation and in terms of sharing via personal networks. They also felt that the videos they made were much more likely to be shared, and trusted, once their organization began to receive coverage in the mass media: "It's been effective because of the reputation that we [had] already built, and the personal connections we [had] already made."[33]

This is not to say that transmedia organizing is simple, or that strategic platform selection is always obvious. Immigrant rights organizers, like anyone, sometimes find the proliferation of media platforms bewildering. Some attempt to strategically choose platforms based on their campaign goals and targets. For example, one organizer described the need to focus on the *New York Times* to reach most elected officials but emphasized the importance of Spanish-language TV networks when trying to target Cecilia Muñoz, an immigrant rights advocate who became an Obama administration official and an apologist for the controversial federal surveillance and deportation program known as Secure Communities. In other cases, and when unable to secure mass media coverage, this organizer fell back to distributing media via his own blog, YouTube channel, Twitter, and Facebook accounts.[34]

Media Bridging Work

In the heat of large-scale protests, movement media and information often spread across platforms, including online, print, and broadcast. During peak mobilization times, the immigrant rights movement also often receives solidarity and support from other movements. At these moments, activists from other movements circulate immigrant rights media more widely through their own social networks. Some people and organizations dedicate themselves to ensuring that this takes place. Those who focus on transferring media and information across media platforms and between movement networks perform what Ethan Zuckerman calls media bridging work.[35] Bridging work has become increasingly important, and some interviewees described it as part of day-to-day communication practices within the immigrant rights movement. For example, a participant in L.A. Indymedia (Los Angeles Independent Media Center) explained that posting news stories and calendar events to la.indymedia.org is the main activity of his collective. However, for him, work on the Indymedia site is tightly connected to his ongoing participation in multiple channels of movement communication, including email, radio, print, and telephone. He also finds SNS to be a key venue for the circulation of movement media. This interviewee stated that he systematically uses both MySpace and Facebook to distribute links to protest reports, articles, action alerts, and upcoming events:

MySpace, everything I do, every time I write an article I'll put it as a bulletin. And on Facebook, too, I'll put a link to it. And any event, any actions going on, I'll always bulletin those. A lot of times people will repost my bulletins. I'll even compile lists of events that are going on and I usually post them on Fridays 'cause people want to know what's going on for the weekend. So Friday I'll have, when I'm reading the paper, when I'm reading my listservs, when I'm listening to the radio, everything that's coming up I'll put it on my calendar. Then I'll take my calendar, make a list of the stuff going on that week, and Friday post it as a bulletin, and then a lot of people repost those.[36]

Transmedia organizers thus engage in daily practices of media bridging work by taking information from one channel, reformatting it for another, and pushing it out into broader circulation across new networks. Certain individuals and groups spend more time focused on media bridging work, but in transmedia organizing, all movement participants are able to participate in this work to some degree. Movements can also take steps to make this kind of activity as easy as possible. In the social media space, Henry Jenkins and colleagues call this principle spreadability.[37] I found that some of the most interesting media bridging work is done, and the greatest spreadability achieved, by organizers who understand the importance of linking broadcast and social media strategies together.

Finally, many interviewees talked about the continued importance of face-to-face organizing. For example, one activist described media practices in the Garment Worker Center campaign against the clothing label Forever 21. Like other younger people, she had learned about the campaign through an email list, but face-to-face organizing was the key means of reaching garment workers themselves. Social movements often contain people from a mix of backgrounds, and transmedia organizers must provide forms of connectivity and points of entry for all of them:

> I was involved in [the Forever 21 campaign] back in 2001. And we were a pretty small group.... I remember the first protest, the first anti-sweatshop protest against Forever 21. I found out through the internet, and I was like, "I have no idea where Alhambra is. But I guess I'm gonna drive out there."[38]

This activist learned about a protest via email, from a list called the Fair Trade Network that she had joined in 2000 during protests at the Democratic National Convention in Los Angeles. She then followed an invitation to attend a protest action in an unfamiliar part of town. She later went on to get deeply involved in a successful campaign targeting the Forever 21 clothing label for wage theft and abuse of immigrant workers.

Transmedia Organizing 101: Relationships with Reporters and Media Hotlists

Mass media continue to be a crucial arena of struggle, and activists develop a range of specific strategies as they attempt to gain access to the mainstream press.[39] For example, many of those I interviewed brought up the importance of cultivating relationships with reporters. "People think about mainstream media as a big monolithic thing," said one interviewee, "but generally, it's all about relationships."[40] This activist, who had experience working in a newsroom, described the various pressures that go into determining whether reporters choose to cover a particular event or not. He emphasized the importance of personal relationships to this decision-making process, as well as to the kinds of frames that are deployed when the story is written. Others mentioned developing and sharing media hotlists and circulating message memos within movement networks. For example, Dream Team L.A. has a media hotlist of about eighty journalists, including traditional reporters, bloggers, and people with large numbers of followers on Twitter. People on this list are known to show up for actions, write stories, and circulate stories. Dream Team L.A. uses this list to promote actions, events, and campaign communications.[41]

Dream Team L.A. also develops internal memos based on message brainstorming and on testing their framing ideas in focus groups. These memos lay out the group consensus on message framing, and are used for messaging training as well as for "refreshing" prior to interviews. Activists with Dream Team L.A. are quite clear about the structure of stories in traditional media and intentionally develop short, one- and two-sentence sound bites that they practice and rehearse in order to get their points across during interviews with reporters: "In traditional media you have very little space to get your point across. So, for example, a news clip will be two minutes long, and that'll include most bites, so then, you basically have thirty seconds to make your point."[42]

Many activists find Twitter and Facebook to be very effective tools in terms of generating support and getting messages out, but they also point out that traditional print and broadcast news outlets remain important because those are the platforms that reach the broader immigrant community. They describe this dynamic in terms of age and as a generational difference, as well as in terms of Internet access inequality. For example, the parents of DREAMers often don't have access to Internet, or if they do, they are not users of social media. Some also mention a divide between those who use the Internet on their mobile phones and those who do not. To reach their parents' generation, DREAMers emphasize the importance of visibility in Spanish-language print press ("[they read] *La Opinion* every morning") and evening television news ("they're going to turn on Univision at 6 and at 11").[43]

The collapsed category of "social media," while useful in some ways, also masks important differences in the affordances of different tools. For example, one organizer described Twitter as "the quickest," email as the best space for dialogue ("that's when more people start figuring out what's going on"), and finally, articles in newspapers or coverage on television as the indicator that the issue or campaign has reached larger significance.[44] Additionally, traditional activist media practices, such as phone banking, remain important. One interviewee described using email and SNS as tools to gather activists in a physical location in order to spend time together, face to face, making phone calls.[45] This is yet another example of the continued importance of copresent communication for core activists. Although regular communication with broader lists of members and participants is often done through one-to-many email blasts or systematic Facebook outreach, core activists in the immigrant rights movement continue to coordinate through regular face-to-face interactions.[46]

Transmedia Organizing: Conclusions

In chapter 1, we saw that the changing media ecology sometimes provides important openings for movement organizers. In this chapter, we explored specific forms of transmedia organizing within the immigrant rights movement in L.A. A closer look at the student walkouts against the Sensenbrenner bill provided further insight into the dynamics of transmedia organizing. Rather than attribute the success of the 2006 walkouts solely to MySpace and SMS, it is possible to locate the protests within the historical repertoire of contention of the Chican@ movement in Los Angeles. The walkouts also functioned as part of a larger transmedia story that has been told, retold, remixed, and recirculated by movement participants across broadcast and social media platforms. In this case, transmedia organizing serves to represent and strengthen social movement identity, as well as to reproduce and encourage participation in specific movement tactics. The student walkouts in protest of the Sensenbrenner bill were organized in a horizontal, ad hoc network with citywide participation. Student activists used social media (especially SMS and MySpace) to circulate calls to action, file near real-time reports from the streets, and generate multimedia documentation of protests. Their actions were rooted in the larger wave of street mobilizations against the bill, circulated through new participatory spaces in the changing media ecology, informed by the tactical repertoire of the Chican@ movement, and facilitated by the students' fluency in the skills, tools, and practices of network culture.

Zooming out to explore other examples of transmedia organizing, we found that many activists intentionally think about how to circulate media across platforms, while engaging their base in media-making that strengthens movement identity. Many emphasize the importance of using multiple communication platforms to reach various audiences, as well as the fundamental and irreplaceable importance of face-to-face communication in community organizing and movement building. We also saw that certain activists or groups serve as nodes within broader networks, transporting movement media from one platform, location, or modality to another. This media bridging work has become increasingly important as movement participants and audiences fragment across hypersegmented media markets. In addition, effective transmedia organizers in the immigrant rights movement work across broadcast platforms, especially radio, to build participation through social media and SMS, as we saw in the Basta Dobbs campaign. At its most powerful, transmedia organizing engages media-makers across many platforms in generating a shared narrative about the movement while providing concrete actions and entry points for diverse audiences. However, some organizations in the immigrant rights movement continue to operate with a firewall between their participatory media practice, if they have one, and their formal communication strategy. Communication strategy is often still based on top-down PR tactics designed for a time when English-language mass media were the only game in town. The following chapter explores this dynamic more closely. Through a case study of the 2007 "MacArthur Park melee," in which the Los Angeles Police Department brutally attacked a crowd of immigrant rights protesters, we will focus on the tensions between acting as a spokesperson for the movement and becoming an amplifier for voices from the movement base.

Figure 3.1
MacArthur Park May Day images posted to L.A. Indymedia.
Source: Original images by various pseudonymous posters to la.indymedia.org; collage by author.

3   "MacArthur Park Melee": From Spokespeople to Amplifiers

People were getting their cameras smashed by the batons.... We had to get those images because one, that's what we were there to do, and two, we knew that the media wasn't going to show that.

—KB, community organizer

Quickly reorganizing after the defeat of the Sensenbrenner bill, anti-immigrant forces launched a new wave of ICE raids across the country during the fall of 2006.[1] Simultaneously, there was an explosion of right-wing information warfare, stretching from the mass base of talk radio up through the national news networks and spearheaded by a parade of racist, anti-immigrant talking heads on Fox News and by Lou Dobbs on CNN.[2] The renewed attack from the Right generated a baseline of tension for immigrant rights activists in the run-up to May Day 2007. On the anniversary of the historic 2006 May Day marches, hundreds of thousands of people again took the streets across the country. This time, though, the Los Angeles Police Department (LAPD) dealt a crushing blow to protesters in Los Angeles. In this chapter I describe the events of May Day 2007 and analyze how savvy immigrant rights movement communicators are shifting from spokespeople to amplifiers.

Changes in the broader media ecology simultaneously produce new challenges and new opportunities for social movements. On the one hand, local and national TV networks have largely abandoned close, sympathetic, and humanizing coverage of domestic nonviolent protests. Especially where there is police violence, English-language TV news tends to adopt a narrative of violent conflict that distances viewers from identification with protesters as human beings and fails to closely cover movement demands. On the other hand, movements no longer need to rely entirely on broadcast media to circulate their stories, and they no longer need to rely primarily on professional movement spokespeople. In the changed media ecology, effective transmedia organizers shift from speaking *for* movements to speaking *with* them. Transmedia organizing marks a transition in the role of movement communicators from content creation to aggregation, curation, remixing, and recirculation of media texts across platforms.

MacArthur Park, only a few city blocks west of L.A.'s main business district, was built in the 1880s as a white, middle-class vacation destination surrounded by luxury hotels.[3] The area around the park became a working-class African American neighborhood during the 1960s, and once this transition took place, the city withdrew park maintenance resources.[4] By the 1980s the park had gained a reputation as a dangerous and violent place. In the 1990s the area became a working-class Latin@ neighborhood. Gerardo Sandoval has written that Mesoamerican immigrants to the MacArthur Park area continue to build a strong local community even as top-down development plans, including a multi-million-dollar subway stop, have recently transformed the area.[5] Despite fears that this development would displace low-income residents, Sandoval argues that instead, the community has remained strong, while working people have gained increased access to labor markets and mobility. This process was based on a complex set of interactions among city agencies, developers, the business community, the police, and community-based organizations. Sandoval also describes the role of the LAPD, and claims that the Rampart Division (which operates in the area that includes MacArthur Park), once notorious for brutal treatment of immigrant youth and for widespread corruption,[6] shifted from a "warrior police" mentality during the 1990s to a new strategy of community policing under Chief William Bratton.[7] However, MacArthur Park is still represented in the English-language press as a racialized danger zone of "gangbangers," drug dealers, sex workers, and general urban chaos. It is especially infamous as an area where fake identification cards can easily be purchased. This portrayal of MacArthur Park persists despite the actual decline in crime in the area[8] and the park's daily use by Latin@ immigrant families, especially by children, teens, and young adults on the soccer field, picnickers with food and blankets, and couples relaxing under the park's shade trees.

On the afternoon of May 1, 2007, I found myself in MacArthur Park, where the usual crowd of hundreds was multiplied tenfold as people streamed in for a post-march rally organized by the Multi-ethnic Immigrant Worker Organizing Network (MIWON). The rally was cosponsored by a coalition that included the Garment Worker Center (GWC), the Koreatown Immigrant Workers Alliance (KIWA), the Pilipino Workers Center (PWC), the Institute of Popular Education of Southern California (Instituto de Educación Popular del Sur de California, or IDEPSCA), and the Coalition for Humane Immigrant Rights of Los Angeles (CHIRLA), with participation by the South Asian Network (SAN) and other organizations. White-clad families, including many small children and elderly folks, were relaxing in the park. The sound of ice cream vendors' bells rang in the air, and the smell of bacon-wrapped hot dogs wafted on the breeze. The atmosphere was festive, as speakers alternated with musicians, and the soccer field was soon transformed into a dance floor as bands performed from the MIWON sound truck. I was there that day to support the march and rally by performing live music with Fósforo, a reggae-dub-cumbia-jungle band in which I played keyboard, melodica, and sampler. Soon it was our turn to play. As we set up our equipment on the stage, I noticed several friends in the crowd.[9] We introduced ourselves over the PA system, and began our set. As we launched into our second song, a Spanish-language cover of the Bob Marley classic "War," heads began to nod, and sunlight reflected off the mostly white shirts on dancing bodies.[10] Suddenly, I looked up to see thousands of people running en masse from the other end of the park. A wall of riot police marched behind them, and two helicopters swooped low over the crowd, hovering like dark mechanical vultures. People screamed and ran in panic as nearly 450 officers, many in full riot gear, used batons and rubber bullets to attack the peaceful crowd, injuring dozens and hospitalizing several.[11] Members of the media, including Christina Gonzalez of Fox News affiliate KTTV 11, Pedro Sevcec of Telemundo, Patricia Nazario of KPCC, Ernesto Arce from KPFK, and reporters from L.A. Indymedia were also attacked and injured by police.[12] The fact that reporters from mass media outlets were attacked resulted in broadcast TV coverage of police brutality. Footage from these TV news reports was then widely circulated on YouTube:

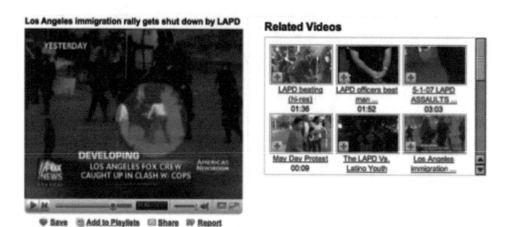

Figure 3.2
Fox News coverage of May Day 2007, reposted to YouTube.
Source: Screen capture from YouTube (http://youtube.com/watch?v=v7xO-GKmH2c).

The LAPD moved quickly (and, at first, successfully) to reframe the brutal attack as a "melee," with the official line from Chief William Bratton being that a communication breakdown in the chain of command had led to a "significant use of force while attempting to address the illegal and disruptive actions of 50 to 100 agitators who were not a part of the larger group of thousands of peaceful demonstrators."[13] The Police Commission's own report later found that the use of force was inappropriate, dispersal orders were not given correctly, and the chain of command had broken down at multiple points, resulting in an incorrect decision to clear the park by force, as well as the unnecessary use of less-lethal weapons, including rubber bullets and batons.[14] However, the report did maintain the justification that the police action was an "overbroad response" to "agitators," despite extensive documentation from police, news, and protester cameras that revealed no aggression by protesters toward police until after the LAPD rode motorcycles into the peaceful crowd.[15] Many witnesses whom I interviewed, including two National Lawyers Guild members who were present as legal observers, also questioned the early deployment of a riot squad on the edge of the park, a move that demonstrated a decision by LAPD commanders to treat the event as one that might need to be dispersed by force.[16] Sandoval argues that the brutal events of May Day 2007 were perpetrated primarily not by officers from the local Ramparts Division but by a riot squad from downtown L.A.[17] Regardless of whether the police attack on the peaceful crowd and reporters was a breakdown of communication, the product of a broader culture of aggression against immigrant populations within certain units of the LAPD, or a calculated tactic to challenge the growing strength of the immigrant rights movement, the result was the same: images of the brutal police riot filled TV screens in L.A. for days, sending a clear message that it was time for the *gigante* to sit down, shut up, and get back to work. The repressive atmosphere continued to escalate nationwide for the rest of the summer of 2007.

Despite the facts about the LAPD's responsibility for the violence that occurred that day (facts that would later emerge in both the LAPD's own report and in the courts), in the immediate aftermath the LAPD's narrative strategy was largely successful at shaping the story. Otto Santa Ana, Layza López, and Edgar Munguía have written the definitive analysis of TV news coverage of the incident.[18] They compared key events as narrated in the LAPD's own report with local and national network TV coverage produced before, immediately after, and the following day. Using frame analysis, visual coding, and critical spoken discourse analysis to examine fifty-one news reports, they found that TV news systematically produced negative or dehumanizing portrayals of peaceful protesters, failed to portray those who were present at the march as full human beings, failed to convey the purpose or demands of the marchers, and framed the events in the park as a clash between two violent groups, police and unruly protesters. Only journalists who were injured by police received coverage that highlighted their humanity, depicted their injuries, and allowed them to speak directly to viewers by making eye contact with the camera. Protesters were described using violent metaphors, were not visually shown in the close to medium shots that most effectively humanize subjects, and were not provided the opportunity to speak complete sentences on camera. The authors also found that local TV news coverage was critical of the police actions in the hours immediately after the attacks but that by the following day, both local and national TV news had shifted to a "violent conflict" frame that implied similar levels of violence by both protesters and police. These findings were consistent across the three methods the research team employed. The authors suggest that the coverage of the May Day events is consistent with a broader, deeply troubling shift in TV news coverage of nonviolent protest in the United States. They point out that the Civil Rights movement succeeded in mobilizing broad support for voting rights and an end to legal segregation largely through nonviolent civil disobedience, which was covered by TV news in a way that emphasized civil rights protesters as full human beings, worthy of empathy. National TV networks that commanded the attention of the entire country represented protesters as occupying the moral high ground against physical violence from multiple actors. This swayed public opinion and created strong pressure on legislators to act. If national TV news networks reframe unprovoked police violence against peaceful protesters as "violent conflict," and if reporters fail to depict the full humanity of protesters or to cover their actual demands, then one of the most powerful avenues by which social movements shape public opinion is blocked.[19]

This broader shift in network TV news, away from the close coverage of social movements and toward a simplified conflict narrative of violent clashes between police and protesters, is deeply troubling. In the case of the immigrant rights movement, it is only partially mitigated by the rise of more sympathetic coverage in Spanish-language print and broadcast media. However, immigrant rights activists should not be thought of simply as "victims" of a mass media framing battle over which they have no control. Instead, they are often active participants. Activists take part in shaping media narratives by participating in news production processes: they hold press conferences, create press releases, provide interviews with journalists, and sometimes pass images and video footage to broadcasters. This type of activity is frequently structured around the activities of movement spokespeople, who work to represent and speak for the broader movement. Sometimes movement spokespeople participate in creating and maintaining discursive frames (versions of the story) that mirror the conflict frame increasingly used by police and broadcast news to cover domestic social movements. I return to this point below.

At the same time, immigrant rights activists also produce and circulate their own media. Indeed, immigrant rights groups engaged in a wide range of media practices immediately after the May Day 2007 police attack. For example, I interviewed members of the Cop Watch L.A. Guerrilla Chapter and asked them to describe communication practices during a recent mass mobilization. One focused on the MacArthur Park events:

I always think about May Day, 2007. Because there was a lot of—you could call it chaos. It was a police riot. There was bullets flying, there was tear gas, there was batons flying everywhere, and Cop Watch L.A., we were asked to observe, right? So we were there observing, and it was hard because we were trying to get our people out of the way. Our children were there.... A lot of our folks were getting hit with batons while observing the police. People were getting their cameras smashed.... We had to get those images because one, that's what we were there to do, and two, we knew that the media wasn't going to show that. Even though they showed a little bit of what happened, because they got the worst end of it too, but they ended up changing their story.[20]

Movement communicators such as those involved in Cop Watch, who work daily to document abuses of power by the police in low-income communities of color, take on a special role during mass mobilizations. They come hoping for the best but prepared to document the worst: violent repression of peaceful protest. In this case, Cop Watch activists gathered a great deal of video footage of the police attack on the crowd. However, and crucially in the context of our discussion of the changed media ecology, they immediately recognized that protest participants had themselves documented the police from nearly every angle, and that gathering this material together would be critical both to creating a narrative of what had happened and to the longer-term legal strategy against police brutality.

From Spokesperson to Amplifier

Whereas in the past, movement documentarians may have seen their primary role as shooting and editing footage, by 2007 even an organization dedicated to documentation, one that counted many trained videographers within its ranks, recognized the importance of compiling video documentation produced by the multitude. The same activist quoted above, KB, described how Cop Watch had "put out a call for people to send us their video," a call he felt was successful since it resulted in anonymous uploads of several hours of original footage.[21] He mentioned that between uploads to the Cop Watch site and to L.A. Indymedia, a great deal of raw footage was made available to both movement filmmakers and to the protesters' legal team. Cop Watch ultimately worked with other antiauthoritarian activists to create a full-length documentary about the events of May Day 2007, titled *We're Still Here, We Never Left*. The film tells the story from the viewpoint of mobilization participants by gathering footage

from over a dozen cameras, and also focuses on disrupting the frame introduced by the LAPD.

We were able to put together the people's side of what happened, through the help
of the People's Network in Defense of Human Rights that was created after May
Day. I guess we took the initiative to put that together, interview folks; we got the
stories from the people in the community.... It meant a lot for our organization,
because we were getting blamed for it, you know? The police were saying it was the
anarchists, and so were some of the organizations. So it was important for us to get
it out there.[22]

Much of the popular media work that Cop Watch and other movement
activists did in the aftermath of May Day took place through the ad hoc
People's Network in Defense of Human Rights (PNDHR). The network
emerged out of a popular assembly held at the PWC within days of the
police riot. Activists gathered video through the Cop Watch L.A. site,
through L.A. Indymedia, from social media sites, and through the extended
network of immigrant rights groups throughout the city. This process was
coordinated not by an individual organization but through a loose working
committee of PNDHR. I participated on the PNDHR communications committee for several weeks. One of our key tasks was to systematically comb
through videos from the MacArthur Park May Day events that people were
posting to YouTube and MySpace, then contact the videographers to see if
they would be willing to share higher-quality versions of their footage, as
well as full access to their source tapes and files. All but one of the many
videographers we contacted were happy to contribute copies of their
footage to the legal team, and several of them joined the working committee. Besides locating footage and videographers, the group also logged and
tagged clips to make them more useful to the legal team. During this
process, group members shared video capture, logging, and transcoding
skills, as well as concrete knowledge about how to use video in court. A
moment of great crisis thus provided, in this case, a hands-on, peer-to-peer
learning opportunity for movement participants to share new media
knowledge and production skills.

Within the PNDHR committee, there were explicit internal debates
about whether and how to relate to the mass media during a time of crisis.
While logging and tagging footage, we came across many shots that were
compelling examples of police brutality. In one of the most memorable,
an officer in full riot gear chops at the legs of a ten- to twelve-year old boy
with his baton until the boy falls to the ground, then waits for him to

stand before shoving him away violently. We discussed whether to send clips like these to the mass media for broader distribution. This kind of conversation is common among horizontalist and autonomist factions of the immigrant rights movement, as in many social movements. One independent media-maker I interviewed, a student who participates in the immigrant rights movement, put it this way:

The better resourced nonprofits, the huge nonprofits that have huge funding and bigger ties to the state, the mayor, these huge corporations, the ones that are non-threatening, they're the ones that have a little bit more connections to the media. It seems like anytime the corporate media is out there, they want to be in front of them.... They used their connections to take the side of the police. To say the same things the police were saying, which to us was like, wow. I guess it showed what side people stand on.[23]

Cop Watch debated whether to set up its own press conference, but in the end made a conscious decision to avoid the mass media. Instead, the group chose to focus on what it called a "grassroots communication" strategy of aggregating video, photographs, audio files, and other documentation of the police attack. The group engaged in systematic outreach to people who posted media to YouTube and MySpace, to L.A. Indymedia, and to local blogs. The members decided to focus all their energy on this strategy, even though it meant turning down opportunities to increase their visibility in broadcast television. They reviewed the aggregated media and acted as curators, remixing the most compelling media elements into new texts, which could then be circulated more widely on social network sites. Eventually, they used this material to develop a feature-length documentary that was screened for audiences in Mexico, Argentina, Venezuela, and South Africa, as well as in the United States.[24]

By contrast, one of L.A.'s larger immigrant rights nonprofits, an organization with a staff of about 40, worked hard in the hours, days, and weeks after the police attack to implement a more traditional, top-down media strategy. The group's communication staff attempted to control, or at least influence, the mass media framing of the event. They did this by holding press conferences and distributing press releases to broadcast and print reporters. Perhaps in an attempt to anticipate the typical police strategy of blaming police violence on protesters, this organization made repeated statements to journalists denouncing the violence but also taking care to distance the majority of "peaceful protesters" from the "violent anarchists" who had "provoked" police violence:

First and foremost, over 25,000 people gathered in the evening to demand their rights and to demand legalization, a path to citizenship, and to peacefully assemble to ensure that their families have a better future in this country. And I want to make sure that their efforts are highlighted. It was unfortunate, and we are indignant at the manner in which the police decided to deal with a group of people who were causing disturbances. These were young anarchists who often join our marches.[25]

These remarks, and others like them, caused intense controversy within the movement. Face-to-face meetings of organizers, as well as discussions on email lists, forums, and other online spaces, were marked by heated debates. Some attacked this organization and demanded that they apologize for repeating what ultimately turned out to be a police lie, while others defended their statements either because they believed them to be true or (more often) because they respected the long history of the organization's work to support immigrant communities. While the organization never issued a public apology for laying the blame on anarchist youth of color, after a month of internal debate other groups, such as the MIWON network coordinators, did change the way they represented the May Day events in public. Subsequent public statements and press releases on the MIWON website, for example, as well as on movement listservs, emphasized that the LAPD had instigated the violence and needed to be held accountable for the May Day attack:

LAPD must take Responsibility as the only instigators of the violence on May Day

Chief Bratton's Report does not address the systemic and cultural changes needed in the LAPD to counter racist and anti-immigrant sentiment plaguing the department.[26]

In this press release, MIWON emphasized the demand for a full review of LAPD internal procedures, described "blatant racism and anti-immigrant sentiment" within the police force, and argued that the LAPD's preliminary report indicated unwillingness to take responsibility for an unnecessary and violent attack against a peaceful crowd.[27] Indeed, MIWON website administrators even made the phrase "LAPD must take responsibility as the only instigators of the violence of May Day 2007" into a stream of red text that followed site visitors' mouse arrow around the page.[28] However, even a year later, spokespeople for the larger immigrant rights nonprofit continued to publicly repeat the story that the police had been provoked by a band of youth agitators:

There was a small group of people that started kind of taunting the police.... The organizers approached the police and asked them, why not separate this small group, isolate them, because they're disturbing everybody else that's having this, you know, peaceful event.... And then, suddenly, you know, there were rubber bullets flying.[29]

While relatively professionalized, top-down nonprofit organizations spent time and energy trying to control the frame by acting as movement spokespeople on broadcast media outlets, horizontalist networks took advantage of the new media ecology to draw attention to images and videos produced by everyday participants, and thereby to shape a different frame. Participatory media practices of aggregation, remix, and circulation amplified this alternative frame to the point that it became possible to challenge the official narratives repeated by the LAPD, broadcast media, and some nonprofit spokespeople. Photographs, videos, and interviews of mobilization participants all showed a peaceful crowd attacked by riot police. By 2009, once the internal police review and legal proceedings had been completed, the verdict was clear: the police use of force was completely unwarranted, and the demonstrators' rights had been deeply violated. Based on LAPD's internal review, extensive grassroots organizing, and the outcome of multiple legal cases, Chief Bratton apologized, demoted the commanding officer, and imposed penalties on seventeen of the officers who had participated in the violence against the protesters. The LAPD settled a massive class action suit for $13 million, and other lawsuits for undisclosed amounts.[30]

Spokesperson or Amplifier? Tensions

The incidents just discussed exemplify the failure of English-language broadcasters to effectively cover domestic protest, and the reproduction of a narrative of violent conflict by the police, the mass media, and some nonprofit organizations. This discussion also revealed grassroots media production practices, including aggregation and remix by movement media-makers, whom we might call "amplifiers" rather than spokespeople. These dynamics were all highly visible in the events around the MacArthur Park incident and its aftermath. Many of the immigrant rights activists I worked with and interviewed described similar dynamics not only during crisis moments, but also in terms of an ongoing transformation of movement media practices. Movement communicators are shifting from being spokespeople to being amplifiers, although few use these exact terms. This transition, however, is controversial. It means that movement groups lose tight control of the message, and this makes many seasoned activists deeply uncomfortable. Media-makers who pride themselves on advanced production skills feel this tension as well, and also worry about the potential loss of creative control.

For example, some media activists who in the past saw themselves as movement documentarians increasingly feel the need to shift to content aggregation, curation, and amplification functions. One interviewee, a professional community organizer and media-maker, described a conversation between organizers discussing how to deal with media during an upcoming mobilization of about 10,000 people:

> In the whole process of being like, "Oh, my God, tomorrow 10,000 people are coming," we came up with the idea of creating these flyers. You know, if you're putting your video up this way, tag it, send it here, or send it to this email or whatever, tag your photo or photography this way. We made I think about a thousand of those flyers, and we pretty much handed them all out, 'cause it was probably that many people filming and taking video.... Then for the next few days, all we were doing was compiling all those videos and photography that people had individually put up on the Internet.... It definitely forced us to be like, how do we deal with the situation of having a thousand people producing media for us?[31]

Transmedia organizers thus develop concrete practices to encourage popular participation in movement media-making. In this case, they promoted particular mobilization tags across social media platforms by printing out and distributing flyers during the mobilization itself. Later they gathered, aggregated, curated, and remixed media made by a large number of people into a short, tightly edited video that served to amplify the voices of the social movement's base.

Movement media-makers are not the only ones turning to social media platforms to gather material. During the past decade, larger media outlets have increasingly institutionalized practices of systematic search through social media for original story ideas, eyewitness photographs and videos, and contacts who can be interviewed to provide additional depth and context. Professional news operations have always included some content produced by "everyday people," but many now regularly use and repackage material they find posted on blogs or social media sites. One interviewee described his reaction to the plagiarism of one of his stories by a major media outlet in this way:

If one of our independent media stories gets into the mainstream media, even if they don't give us credit it's good because at least word is getting out. So I think there's a little bit of exploitation going on. I think that mainstream media and mass media exploit us a little bit. All of our volunteer efforts and our labor.[32]

Another organizer mentioned that the most effective way to get commercial television coverage of movement activity is to provide journalists with sensational video footage, especially footage of police or protester violence.[33] Some media activists find it relatively easy to insert violent video footage of protest activity into broadcast or network TV coverage, but difficult or impossible to effectively frame such clips in ways that would support their goals. When collaborating with broadcast media firms, transmedia organizers often struggle to find an effective balance in the trade-off between increased visibility and the loss of frame control.

The combination of participatory media, which allows grassroots voices to be heard in their own words, and broadcast media, which can amplify those voices to much larger audiences, may be the most effective form of media organizing. However, many groups, if they devote resources to a communications strategy at all, still focus on traditional PR approaches. For example, one organizer felt that the immigrant rights movement was increasingly sophisticated at using digital media for top-down communications, but saw far less activity in the sphere of participatory media-making:

There's definitely a lot of the other stuff, press conferences and all the PR stuff, and creating videos about the message, and putting it out there.... You're more likely to have a communications person in your staff that does all of this, than to have a popular media or multimedia coordinator.... They're treated like two different things, but I think it will be really powerful to see what could they look like when they come together.[34]

Many organizations that do include participatory media-making tend to set it apart from their traditional communication strategy. In other words, most immigrant rights movement groups are not taking full advantage of the possibilities of transmedia organizing. Instead, they use the new tools of networked communication primarily to augment existing top-down media practices. This tension is discussed further in chapter 7.

In general, many professional nonprofit organizations fear social media because it is a space in which they are less able to control the message. Of course, controlling the message is a difficult task in the broadcast media space as well. When asked about organizational fears of letting people from the base speak for themselves, one interviewee described the following scene. At a DREAM Act rally, the executive director of a well-known immigrant rights nonprofit organization took the stage to speak about immigration reform. The interviewee described what happened next:

> She stayed on message about immigration reform. Right now the question is, should we push at least one thing forward, and use it as a victory to build momentum, or really just go for the whole thing and end up getting nothing, and continue to crush the movement? But then right after her a worker spoke, and the worker's message was "if Obama doesn't pass immigration reform, he will not count with our vote." He was immediately sort of pushed to the side, and [the executive director], you could see her face right away was just like, "Oh, I cannot believe he just said that."[35]

This activist went on to describe how the PR staff of the lead organization then approached broadcast media reporters and encouraged them to edit the worker's "off message" statement out of their reports. The PR staff were also deeply worried that citizen journalists, bloggers, or everyday movement participants present at the event would distribute the statement. For organizations that have spent years to decades learning how to stay on message, shape frames through personal relationships with reporters, insert choice quotations into the mass media, and push forward campaigns with a unified voice, social media are a threatening, messy arena in which keeping "message discipline" becomes all but impossible.

Individual cultural workers also experience profound tensions in the changing media ecology. For example, some filmmakers have moved quickly to incorporate participatory media elements into long-form narrative and documentary works. They gather media elements produced by movement participants, then weave them into coherent stories, while providing higher production value, color correction, tight editing, audio, intertitles, animation, and so on. This is not a new practice in a social movement context; indeed, there is a long history of movement documentarians remixing media produced by everyday participants into longer-form works. The award-winning civil rights movement documentary *Eyes on the Prize* is a good example. Producer Judy Richardson has described how, as she transitioned from her role as community organizer with the Student Nonviolent Coordinating Committee to documentary film producer with *Eyes on the Prize,* a key part of her work was to gather Super 8 reels and photographs from the closets and basements of small civil rights organizations and everyday movement participants, then work that material into the series.[36] It is possible, in other words, to open up movement narratives to participatory media made by the base while still making high-quality, high-production-value, beautiful and creative works. However, not everyone sees it that way. Nonprofit PR staff, traditional filmmakers, and many other media-makers who take part in social movement messaging are often unfamiliar with, made uncomfortable by, and feel threatened by participatory media. Individual creative workers sometimes feel the need to assert the value of strong, single-authored narrative and tight creative control in order to produce high-production-value works that broader audiences will find compelling. They argue against "documentary by committee."[37]

Finally, it is worth noting that many organizers find value simply in including the faces and voices of their communities in multimedia movement texts. They point out that this is especially true for immigrant communities, so often ignored or misrepresented by the mass media, but it may also apply to any group that feels excluded from broader visibility. Community-based organizations within the immigrant rights movement regularly use digital media tools to help generate feelings of group identity and solidarity. For example, one KIWA staff member talked about the power of visual media in connecting people to the movement. He described using the organization's website to highlight photographs and slide shows featuring members taking part in actions and campaigns. He felt that when people saw their own face, or their friends' faces, reflected on the website it helped them to identify with the organization. When asked whether this kind of inclusive media practice was something new, or simply the latest incarnation of existing practices, he answered, "It is very new. Nowadays those clips can be taken even with camera or telephone."[38] By contrast, in the past, most video, audio, and photographs recorded on analog media simply sat in boxes, unused. When asked whether KIWA had ever screened older VHS tapes recorded with a camcorder owned by the organization, he replied, "Never."

Before digital camera came in, it was just paper photos. We have probably four to five large boxes of those photos, but it just sits in there. One of our projects with a volunteer is to scan all those so it can be digitized and used.[39]

Digital photography and digital video offer small organizations huge advantages over their analog equivalents in terms of time, money, and equipment. Over the past decade, the affordability of digital recording devices has increased greatly, as has the usability of multimedia production software. The skills needed to transform the raw material of recorded actions into compelling media texts are now more widely distributed across the population, although still unequally so (as I discuss in more detail in chapter 5). Broader participation in movement media production helps strengthen shared memory, feelings of belonging, and social movement identity.

The "MacArthur Park Melee": From Spokespeople to Amplifiers: Conclusions

This chapter has explored the shift in function from spokesperson to amplifier that many social movement media-makers experienced over the past decade. The main case study was the "MacArthur Park melee," or the LAPD riot of May Day 2007. Although the courts ultimately found the police responsible for gross misconduct and massive violation of protesters' rights, in the immediate aftermath of the event the more top-down (vertical) nonprofits focused on disseminating a frame of police "overreaction" to an "anarchist threat" via the mass (broadcast) media. This approach capitalized on the extensive broadcast coverage by both English- and Spanish-language television news, based on the fact that broadcast television reporters were among those who suffered police brutality. At the same time, an ad hoc network composed of horizontalist collectives and organizations worked to aggregate, curate, remix, and amplify media produced by people who had themselves been attacked. Rather than claim that one of these approaches was more successful, we can say that online audiences, especially young immigrant rights activists in Los Angeles, were more likely to have seen one version of events, while those watching broadcast media saw another. For television viewers, police violence did receive extensive coverage during the first day, but by the time the story reached a national broadcast TV audience in the form of short sound bites and clips, it typically carried the headline "MacArthur Park Melee" and implicated youth and anarchist protesters as violent provocateurs. Members of larger nonprofit organizations, following a traditional media strategy, acted as movement spokespeople. By aligning their frame with the police frame, they were able to gain standing and have their voices carried widely in broadcast media. Ad hoc networks such as PNDHR, which advanced a more radical frame while aggregating and circulating video produced by the social base of the movement, were marginalized from broadcast spaces, as they had expected and in some cases chose. Yet their framing persisted and arguably prevailed among activist networks within the immigrant rights movement in Los Angeles. In the changed media ecology, professionalized nonprofit organizations faced intense pressure from an ad hoc network to modify their frame, and ultimately some of them, such as MIWON, did so.

Soon after the events described in this chapter, many of the anti-immigrant aspects of the 2006 Sensenbrenner bill were proposed again in the Secure Borders, Economic Opportunity, and Immigration Reform Act of 2007 (S. 1348). This time the bill was portrayed as a "compromise," but continued to focus on border militarization and policing: it included funding for 300 miles of vehicle barriers, 105 camera and radar towers, and 20,000 more Border Patrol agents, while simultaneously restructuring visa criteria around "high skill" workers for the so-called knowledge economy.[40] It fell apart by June, but in July 2007, $3 billion in new "border security" funding was approved.[41] The transition to the Obama administration initially raised hopes among many in the immigrant rights movement for a progressive restructuring of immigration policy. However, it was soon clear that under President Obama, border militarization would continue, as would raids, detentions, and deportations, and at even greater rates than during the Bush administration.[42] There was no comprehensive immigration reform in Obama's first term. In 2013, at the beginning of Obama's second term, immigration reform was once again placed squarely on the national agenda. The legislative proposal launched in 2013 was largely identical to the bill proposed in 2007: its main components included increased border enforcement; extension of the E-Verify system, which requires employers to check employee status with a federal database and increases the penalties levied against noncompliant employers; and a "pathway to citizenship." This proposed pathway involved payment of back taxes, fines, an application fee, and a background check, followed by a work permit and the possibility of naturalization after "going to the back of the line." Overall, some analysts estimated the process might take thirteen to twenty-three years to complete and would exclude the majority of undocumented immigrants.[43] To date, there has been a complete, and completely unsurprising, failure of the mass media to discuss either the root causes of migration or the possibility of true long-term solutions, such as a human right to migration in an age of unrestricted cross-border capital flows. Chapter 7 further explores the 2013 comprehensive immigration reform bill and transmedia organizing efforts around it. For now, I turn to a close analysis of mobilizations by Oaxacan migrants living in Los Angeles, to better understand the role of translocal social movement media practices.

Figure 4.1
APPO occupies Oaxacan state TV.
Source: Screen capture from *La Toma de Los Medios en Oaxaca* (http://vimeo
.com/6729709).

4 APPO-LA: Translocal Media Practices

In chapters 1 and 2, I explored how Spanish-language mass media, in particular radio, as well as social media, specifically MySpace, transformed the media ecology in Los Angeles. Changes in the media ecology opened new avenues for the public narrative of the immigrant rights movement. Chapter 3 explored the shift from top-down to participatory media practices by immigrant rights advocates. Movement media-makers are rethinking their roles, with some intentionally making a change from spokespeople to amplifiers. At the same time, the media ecology itself is also undergoing a radical transformation in terms of geographic scale. From a top-down perspective, Latin American media companies are now part of transnationally converged media conglomerates. Spanish-language newspapers and broadcasters in the United States are linked in nationwide and transnational networks. Simultaneously, bottom-up processes are also reshaping the media ecology as community media play an increasingly important role in maintaining connections between migrants and their places of origin. The Latin American communication scholar Jesús Martín-Barbero has written extensively about the transnationalization of the media system, emphasizing hybridity, cultural flows across national boundaries, and local appropriation of media texts, while maintaining a critical stance toward the erasure of local forms of cultural production by globalized capitalist cultural industries.[1] As mass media go global and community media move online, both serve to link diasporic communities and to heighten practices of translocal citizenship. Social movements can take advantage of translocal media practices to circulate their struggles and to leverage support from their geographically dispersed but increasingly connected allies. This chapter explores translocal media practices through a case study of indigenous Oaxacan migrant workers and the powerful social movements they have formed across great distances.

The Frente Indígena de Organizaciones Binacionales

The Frente Indígena de Organizaciones Binacionales (Indigenous Front of Binational Organizations, FIOB) provides vivid examples of how translocal media practices have strengthened the immigrant rights movement in Los Angeles. Indigenous immigrants to the United States from the southern Mexican state of Oaxaca founded the FIOB in 1991. Starting in the 1970s, thousands of indigenous Oaxacans migrated to northern Mexico and the United States in search of work; currently, about 500,000 of the 3.5 million Oaxacan-born people live outside their home state.[2] The FIOB was created to provide a transnational structure for indigenous communities, split between Oaxaca and the United States, to better organize around their needs and advocate for resources. As FIOB communications director, Berta Rodríguez Santos, states:

FIOB has approximately 5,000 accredited members in both Mexico and the United States. FIOB members come from various ethnic groups including Mixtecos from Oaxaca and Guerrero, Zapotecos, Triquis, Mixes, Chatinos, Zoques from Oaxaca, and Purépechas from Michoacán. The members are organized into community committees in the Mixteca, Central Valleys, and Isthmus regions of Oaxaca as well as in Mexico City, Estado de México, and Baja California. FIOB is also present in Los Angeles, Fresno, Santa María, Greenfield, Hollister, San Diego, Santa Rosa, and Merced, California. Support groups can be found in the states of Oregon, New York, Arizona, and Washington as well.[3]

Jonathan Fox and Gaspar Rivera-Salgado, indigenous Mexican academics who work with the FIOB, have done extensive work on emergent transnational civil society among indigenous migrants. They have also described the importance of translocal media. For example, the newspaper *El Oaxaqueño*, first published in 1999, is produced and distributed binationally, in both Oaxaca and Los Angeles, with a twice weekly print run of 35,000 copies. The paper reports on everything from "local village conflicts and the campaign to block construction of a McDonald's on the main square in Oaxaca City, to the binational activities of hometown associations (HTAs) and California-focused coalition building for immigrants' right to obtain driver licenses and against cutbacks in health services."[4]

Fox and Rivera-Salgado also write about the radio program produced by FIOB, *Nuestro Foro* (Our Forum), which aired for a time on KFCF 88.1FM in Fresno, and they highlight *El Tequio* magazine, which carries stories of activism across the U.S.-Mexico border. They show that "migrant-run mass media also report systematically on other community initiatives [and] they promote 'virtuous circles' of institution building within indigenous migrant civil society."[5] Migrant-run mass media help sustain what Fox and Rivera-Salgado call cultural citizenship, or citizenship beyond the nation-state. Cultural citizenship may be centered on cultural, ethnic, gender, or class identities. Fox and Rivera-Salgado also emphasize the importance of transnational community, which for them means binational identity sustained over time, and focus intensely on translocal community citizenship, or "the process through which indigenous migrants are becoming active members of both their communities of settlement and their communities of origin."[6]

The dynamics they describe operate in many migrant communities, not only the Oaxacan indigenous migrant groups they work most closely with. Migration scholars in recent years have emphasized that cheaper air travel and increased access to communications allow migrants to remain better connected to their communities of origin.[7] Financial remittances sent home by migrant workers have become increasingly important to local, regional, and national economies. Ideas, practices, and norms also circulate more quickly and extensively than ever before within dispersed communities, in a process that sociologists refer to as social remittances.[8]

Overall, transnational dynamics in the immigrant rights movement are quite complex. On the one hand, migrant workers are by definition transnational (or translocal). They often participate in transnational civic engagement through self-organized social processes such as hometown associations (HTAs).[9] HTAs organize community-based development projects, and to do so they readily adopt new information and communication technologies (ICTs) for ongoing discussion, decision making, and persistent contact. For example, many HTAs take advantage of the Sprint-Nextel network's push-to-talk feature, which allows low-cost real-time audio streaming between the United States and Mexico during transnational HTA assemblies.[10] At the same time, undocumented immigrants face constraints on transnational forms of social and political participation because it is difficult for them to move back and forth across borders. While those with legal status are sometimes able to travel between places, those without the appropriate papers are able to visit their hometowns far less frequently than they desire (although some do make the voyage occasionally).[11] In addition, increased border enforcement since the 1990s has made it more difficult for migrant workers to move back and forth. This has disrupted previous patterns of translocal citizenship. At the same time, local hometown newspapers, radio stations, and TV outlets have come online, while social media have become more widespread. This produces new possibilities for migrant workers to maintain continual connection to family, political, and cultural life in their hometowns.[12] The growing popularity of live videochat services, especially Skype and Oovoo (and, more recently, Google Hangouts), also modifies the dynamics of family separation and translocal community.

As an example of how media practices are used to support translocal community citizenship, Fox and Rivera-Salgado recount how Nahua migrants from the Mexican state of Guerrero organized a successful campaign to block the construction of a hydroelectric dam in 1991. The dam would have resulted in the destruction of their villages, the displacement of 40,000 people, submersion of an important ecosystem, and the loss of a major archaeological site in the Alto Balsas Valley. The campaign capitalized on the upcoming quincentennial of the Spanish Conquest to mobilize funds, social networks, and media attention. Protest participants purchased video cameras (at the time, bulky shoulder-mounted VHS cameras) to document their direct actions. As Fox and Rivera-Salgado describe the scene,

This tactic not only served to inform *paisanos* [countrymen] in the United States, it also inaugurated what became the Mexican indigenous movement's now widespread use of video to deter police violence. Migrant protests in California also drew the attention of Spanish-language television, which led to the first TV coverage of the Alto Balsas movement within Mexico itself.[13]

The FIOB's use of video technology in the early 1990s contributed to an important policy outcome. It also demonstrated the feasibility of gaining increased visibility for movement-produced media on commercial TV networks. This case also illustrates how movement media texts sometimes serve multiple functions: when picked up for broadcast, they can reach larger audiences; at the same time, they circulate among family, friendship, and hometown networks in ongoing practices of translocal community citizenship.

Alongside video activism, the FIOB has a long history of media production across multiple platforms. In 1991 the FIOB began publication of a newspaper called *Puya Mixteca*, and in 1995 the organization inaugurated a radio show, *La Hora Mixteca* (The Mixteca Hour), which was broadcast across the San Joaquin Valley. Soon after it began to coproduce another show, *Nuestro Foro* (Our Forum), on KFCF 88.1.[14] The FIOB also helped set up two community radio stations in the Mixteca region of Oaxaca.[15] As early as 1997, the FIOB had a web presence at http://fiob.org, established with help from La Neta, a Mexican NGO that is part of the international Association for Progressive Communications. La Neta also helped network the Zapatista communities during the 1990s.[16]

Despite its strong history of media and technology use, as an explicitly binational organization that organizes indigenous migrant workers, both in Los Angeles and in their communities of origin, the FIOB faces severe digital access challenges. ICT access levels in rural Oaxaca, where many of the HTAs operate, are much lower than among even the most excluded populations of urban Los Angeles. As one FIOB staff member emphasized, many of the communities they work with have no electricity.[17] In this context, FIOB organizers see the Internet primarily as a resource for movement leadership and allies rather than for members:

Definitely the leaders and people that aren't at the base, because unfortunately, Oaxaca is the third poorest state in Mexico, so it's hard in a village up in the Sierras to have access to Internet. But sometimes when they come to the local city there, the FIOB members show them, hey, this is what we have. They might not be able to fully access it all the time, but they know it's out there because when they come to our meetings, when we have a binational meeting, we show them the Internet: this is how it works, this is where everything is at. But not everyone has access to it; it's actually for others, friends and allies of the Frente, to know our work. And also to make a political stand that we are here as indigenous people, there's an indigenous organization that does all this work.[18]

For FIOB staff, the fact that their membership is not online does not diminish the importance of the Internet as a tool for information circulation and mobilization. Like many organizations, they use the Internet extensively in their work. FIOB staff spend much of each day online, communicating across their network, circulating key information, and working on strategy and campaigns. At the same time, they have developed other forms of media to reach their digitally excluded base. For example, in 2000 the FIOB began production of a TV show called *El Despertar Indigena* (Indigenous Awakening) for Fresno's KNXT. In 2003 it began a coproduction partnership with filmmaker Yolanda Cruz, who made the documentaries *Mujeres Que Se Organizan Avanzan* (Women Who Organize Make Progress), *Sueños Binacionales* (Binational Dreams), and *2501 Migrants: A Journey* (figure 4.2). Cruz continues to create documentaries about the FIOB and the indigenous communities that constitute its base, using participatory video methods to involve the communities in the filmmaking process.[19]

Figure 4.2
Promotional image for the film *2,501 Migrants*, by Yolanda Cruz.
Source: Photo by Johnny Simmons for Petate.org.

The FIOB and its allies, who have a long history of using VHS for social movement ends, are now turning to web video for new translocal movement media practices. They deploy a broad range of media, including web videos, theatrical documentary releases, and community screenings, as well as radio, print, popular theater, and other media, to create a movement media "world" with space for participation by their social base.[20] In other words, the FIOB engages in transmedia organizing. These daily communication practices help inscribe indigenous identities across media platforms and articulate translocal community citizenship.

Of course, migrant indigenous communities also use digital media tools more casually and personally, to share records of daily life and cultural events with friends, family, and people in their home towns. One interviewee, a staff member at FIOB, remarked that Oaxacan HTA members communicate extensively through YouTube by uploading videos of musical events, celebrations of saints' days, funerals, and other cultural activities, then sending links by email to family and friends:

In my community, it started probably in what, 2004, 2003? We started seeing all these events, whatever was happening back home. Somebody's funeral, they would put it there, you could go see it. Or if something happened here, a patron saint's party or celebration, they would put it on the YouTube and the people back home would, you kind of know now that you go on YouTube and you find it. My mom, she doesn't know how to read and write. So she says, hey, can you go to the computer and put the *pueblo* stuff on there? And I say, "Sure, let's put it on!" So she'll have other *comadres* call and say, hey, can you tell [your daughter] to teach me how to get into our webpage? So it's really interesting that YouTube is a way to maintain, to inform and gossip on your HTA.

Q *When was the first time you saw something like that? Or, what was the first thing that you saw?*
Oh, the parties!... Well, I shouldn't call them parties. They're celebrations of the saint. So if someone donated a cow to feed the community, a certain band showed up to do their *guelaguetza* [celebration of indigenous culture] in the community, it would be put on the YouTube.[21]

As can be seen in this interview, migrant communities often use social media to reproduce binational and translocal identities. However, it would be an oversimplification to suggest that the social web has introduced radically new tools, or has completely transformed the communication practices of the FIOB and the HTAs. The same interviewee noted that essentially the same practice—videotaping and sharing recordings of key family and cultural events across borders—was formerly done using VHS camcorders and sending tapes through the mail. In fact, this practice still exists, alongside video sharing via the Internet:

I remember those huge video cameras when they first came out. Everybody had one to document all their events, all of the meetings.

Q   At that time would they send the tapes to each other? Like between here and there in the mail?
Yeah. And they still do now, some. Like *quinceañeras*. For example, my sister's one in the United States was completely this big thing, and it was sent to all my family in Mexico. So when something happens, a wedding happens there, everybody gets a copy here.[22]

The experience of this FIOB staff member is not unique. As in other communities, for Oaxacan migrants, audiovisual skills often develop through the desire to document and share life experiences and popular cultural events such as weddings, *quinceañeras*, *guelaguetzas*, and funerals. Daily community media practices thus accumulate over time to shape new pathways through the changing media ecology. These practices might also be read as everyday forms of digital resistance against the erasure of translocal community citizenship.[23] In times of social crisis, these same media skills are used for transmedia organizing. It is the FIOB's regular use of digital video to circulate cultural practices, combined with the organization's long history of using video as a tool for struggle, that has proved decisive for their members' effective use of digital video during moments of translocal mobilization.

The Cultural and Political Logic of the *Tequio*

Some immigrant rights activists use the term *horizontalism*, adopted from Argentine social movements, to talk about organizing in ways that are directly democratic, nonhierarchical, rooted in consensus decision making, and consciously cultivate shared leadership.[24] Many movement groups use other terms to refer to similar directly democratic decisionmaking processes, such as popular assemblies. For example, the structure of the FIOB is based on the cultural and political logic of the *tequio,* an indigenous term for "community work for the benefit of all."[25] Formally, it could be said that the FIOB is a kind of representative democracy, with the membership electing officers to three-year terms. However, the overall decision making process is more directly democratic. The FIOB follows indigenous law (Uses and Customs), and makes decisions about goals, strategies, campaigns, and resource allocation after extensive discussion during a general assembly of the FIOB base, rather than by a simple ballot or through representatives. Leadership is also considered accountable to the base, and is responsible for reporting back on organizational activities, keeping members informed about the work of the FIOB, and bringing key decisions back to the assembly.[26]

For some of the FIOB organizers I talked to, the idea of separating media work from other aspects of organizing made little sense. They described media making as a supporting activity that ends up "just happening," based on community members and supporters stepping up when necessary:

I think one quality of the FIOB actually for being indigenous … is the fact that everybody does everything. As far as a strategy on how do we shoot, do outreach through the media, independent media, we don't have one. But everything happens because we have so many allies. [An ally] will probably write something about the mobilization and send it to us. Or somebody else will document the mobilization and send us pictures.[27]

The community the FIOB organizes does have members who are considered to be "specialists" in video production. One FIOB interviewee mentioned a man who receives regular payment to shoot and produce videos of community events. Thus, it would be inaccurate to assume that the FIOB has no dedicated movement videographers because their community "lacks capacity." Rather, as a migrant indigenous social movement organization, the FIOB draws on existing community norms to operate with a cultural structure of decision making that is more horizontal than seen in most of the incorporated nonprofit organizations in the immigrant rights movement. Hiring a videographer to document social movement activity seems unnecessary, because this work will be done by community members who have those skills, within the ethic of the *tequio*. Yet the FIOB also makes decisions to invest resources in higher-production-value media projects, and invites specific media-makers to work more closely with them, when it makes sense to do so.

APPO-LA

This section explores how the translocal media practices used by the FIOB and by Oaxacan migrant workers in Los Angeles, discussed in the previous section, enable transmedia organizing among indigenous migrant workers who otherwise have very limited access to digital media tools and skills. The example I focus on is a movement group called the Asociación Popular de los Pueblos de Oaxaca de Los Angeles (APPO-LA). This group was born out of political violence, electoral fraud, and indigenous resistance.

Ulises Ruiz Ortíz, governor of Oaxaca, took office in 2004 following a questionable electoral victory.[28] By June 2006, a mass mobilization by the Oaxacan Teachers' Union against job cuts had been joined by other unions, as well as by indigenous, women's, student, and other groups, in a general strike and occupation of the central plaza of Oaxaca City. The movement coalesced around the Popular Assembly of the Peoples of Oaxaca (APPO), and launched demands for, first, Ortíz's resignation, and second, that a constituent assembly be called to rewrite the state constitution.[29] In August 2006, at the end of a women's strike and a *cacerolazo* (a march accompanied by the beating of pots and pans) involving some 20,000 participants, Oaxacan women in the movement leadership entered and took control of the studios of Channel 9 at the Oaxacan Radio and Television Corporation. They also occupied several commercial radio stations. The state government responded by expelling activists from the stations, and so the movement generalized the media insurrection, seizing commercial TV and radio stations across the state.[30] Police attempts to invade and shut down broadcasts by "Radio APPO" were met with determined resistance from a blockade of several thousand people, who fought a pitched battle that lasted for days. The battle ended with the police in retreat and the radio station still in the hands of the movement. This series of events, now referred to as the *toma de los medios* (taking of the media), inspired social movements and media activists around the world, and increased the visibility of media infrastructure as a key space of contestation for Oaxacan activists both in Oaxaca and in Los Angeles. The *toma* is documented in the film *Un Poquito de Tanta Verdad* (A Little Bit of So Much Truth) and in *The Taking of the Media in Oaxaca,* two films that were screened widely around the world at events organized by activists from the global justice movement (see *La Toma de Los Medios en Oaxaca,* http://vimeo.com/6729709). Traditional forms of social movement media, such as feature-length documentary films, thus continue to serve as key vehicles for the global circulation of media strategies and tactics, beside newer trans-media organizing practices.

As the struggle in Oaxaca City intensified, the state government esca-lated its tactics and began to employ armed gunmen to attack the APPO. On October 27, 2006, New York City Indymedia video activist, Bradley Roland Will, was shot and killed in Oaxaca City, in the neighborhood of Santa Lucía del Camino, while filming an armed attack by undercover state police.[31] Will's death, although only one in a string of political murders that occurred during the 2006 struggles, resulted in greatly increased international attention to the mobilizations in Oaxaca. At least twenty-six Oaxacan activists were murdered (including José Alberto López Bernal, Emilio Alonso Fabián, Fidel Sánchez García, and Esteban López Zurita), with many more detained and disappeared during this mobiliza-tion wave.[32]

Figure 4.3
Bradley Roland Will.
Source: The Indypendent.

I had worked with Will in 2003 as part of an Indymedia video collective that produced *The Miami Model*, a participatory documentary about the Free Trade Area of the Americas (FTAA), the gentrification of Miami, and the brutal police repression of the 2003 anti-FTAA protests.[33] Since Brad Will was connected to the global Indymedia network, his murder brought the situation in Oaxaca into the consciousness of the global justice movement, and since he was a U.S. citizen, the story made international news.

In Los Angeles, the FIOB organized a series of protests and actions against the increasingly violent repression of the movement, first by the Oaxacan state government and later by the Mexican federal forces. APPO-LA imaginatively renewed the tradition of *Las Posadas*, a nine-day pre-Christmas celebration in Mexico in which groups of friends and family walk together to other community members' houses, playing music and singing carols and in return being offered hospitality in the form of food and drink. On December 16, 2006, the APPO-LA organized an *APPOsada* at the church of St. Cecilia in Santa Monica. The event was attended by around three hundred people, who gathered to celebrate resistance against the slayings in Oaxaca City. The event raised thousands of dollars, which went to support the movement in Oaxaca. At the height of APPO-LA mobilizations, the Koreatown Immigrant Workers Alliance (KIWA) lent its sound system and video projector to the FIOB. One of KIWA's staff was Oaxacan and had spent considerable time organizing the Oaxacan community in the Koreatown area. Video screenings of material from Oaxaca (much of it shot by the video collectives Mal de Ojo and Indymedia Oaxaca) became regular events during the winter of 2006 and the spring of 2007, with screenings held at KIWA offices in the evenings and in front of the Mexican Consulate in the northwest corner of MacArthur Park.

At one such gathering I attended, along with forty to fifty other people, several musical groups and a troupe of Aztec dancers performed. People bought tamales and *atole* (a hot, hearty drink) from FIOB members, who were selling them to raise funds to send to the movement assembly in Oaxaca City. I helped the event organizers hang signs and banners around the space, set up crosses on the ground to signify those killed in political violence, and set up KIWA's video projector and screen. One of the organizers placed a mobile phone call to an activist in Oaxaca and amplified the ensuing conversation through the sound system. The audience was then shown a video from the previous day's mass march of some 20,000 people in Oaxaca City. One FIOB interviewee, who was also a key organizer of the APPO-LA, described these media practices as follows:

We don't document everything because we do so many things, but that mobilization that I was talking to you about on November 11, we got video. I actually have the video how they leave, and show up to Oaxaca City. And the pictures, I could share with the members here.[34]

During this time, along with other allies from the global justice movement, I worked closely with activists from KIWA and the FIOB to support the APPO-LA's media work. We created a dedicated website for APPO-LA, built using the free/libre open-source content management system Wordpress, with graphics created by a designer from Oaxaca City. I recall coordinating in real time with Oaxacan activists via Internet relay chat (IRC) rooms on the irc.indymedia.org servers. Tech activists from around the world gathered there regularly, and worked especially hard to maintain servers that mirrored a live audio stream from the key APPO radio station. We also set up local phone numbers in several cities so that callers could listen to the radio stream on their (usually prepaid, non-Internet-enabled) phones. During one mobilization, we downloaded photographs of violent repression in Oaxaca from Indymedia Oaxaca and other sites (such as the blog *El Enemigo Común*), then printed the photographs and taped them to the gates of the Mexican embassy. Similar actions occurred outside Mexican embassies and consulates around the United States, especially in New York, Los Angeles, Houston, and Portland, and around the world.

The image in figure 4.4 was taken during a mobilization on the northern edge of MacArthur Park, across the street from the Mexican consulate in Los Angeles. The sign reads "Ulises, fascist, assassin of journalists." At the same mobilization, organizers used a projector to show videos produced by the FIOB and its allies (e.g., Sueños Binacionales), as well as raw footage from recent protests in Oaxaca City, often shot just hours or days before. Although the mobilizations did not directly force Governor Ulíses Ruiz Ortíz from power, on October 14, 2009, the Mexican Supreme Court found Ortíz "culpable for the human rights violations that occurred in Oaxaca as a result of teacher protests and political and social unrest in May 2006–January 2007 as well as July of 2008."[35]

Figure 4.4
APPO-LA protest at the Mexican consulate.
Source: Photo by pseudonymous poster Rogue Gringo, posted to L.A. Indymedia at
http://la.indymedia.org/news/2006/11/186082.php.

Translocal Media Practices: Conclusions

This chapter has explored how translocal media practices developed by
Oaxacan migrants were deployed during a translocal mobilization between
Oaxaca City and Los Angeles. Translocal media practices do not take place
exclusively online. Instead, community members and allied activists spread
media texts across platforms, as well as into offline ('real-world') spaces.
At the same time, while it is true that digital media literacy enables new
expressions of translocal citizenship, earlier media practices provide an

important foundation. Everyday forms of media use (such as VHS record-ing of cultural events) by transnational Oaxacan migrant indigenous com-munities serve as important precursors to, if not a precondition for, the effective use of new digital media tools during key moments in the mobi-lizations. This is especially important in the context of a community that has one of the lowest general levels of Internet access among all demo-graphic groups in the United States. The immigrant rights movement is best able to use digital media when the base of a particular movement group is already familiar with the tools and practices of network culture.[36] For indigenous migrant workers, this familiarity evolves out of the media practices of translocal community citizenship.

Within the APPO-LA, everyday video sharing by indigenous migrant workers laid the groundwork for transmedia organizing. For other move-ment organizations, media-making must be fostered in other ways. The next chapter explores approaches that worker centers are taking to develop a praxis of critical digital media literacy among low-wage immigrant workers in Los Angeles.

Figure 5.1
VozMob (Voces Móviles / Mobile Voices).
Source: Images from VozMob.net, collage by author.

5   Worker Centers, Popular Education, and Critical Digital Media Literacy

It is June 2010. We've been driving for fourteen hours, and our van is starting to feel a bit cramped. Our route from Los Angeles to Detroit has taken us an extra 150 miles out of the way to avoid passing through the northwest corner of Arizona, where we've heard there are immigration checkpoints on the I-15. The Popular Communication Team from the Instituto de Educación Popular del Sur de California (the Institute of Popular Education of Southern California, or IDEPSCA), comprised of day laborers, household workers, and high school students, supported by a community organizer, project coordinator, and volunteers from the Mobile Voices (VozMob) project,[1] is on a trip to the Allied Media Conference (AMC),[2] back to back with the United States Social Forum (USSF). The AMC is focused on media-makers and cultural workers, and will be attended by about 1,500 people. The USSF is a social movement megaconference; it will draw more than 30,000 activists, especially those from base-building organizations and those who work with low-income communities of color, from all across the country and around the world. When we get to Detroit, we'll be running a series of popular education workshops for more than one hundred grassroots activists. In our workshops, we'll share the story of the VozMob project, critically analyze mass media coverage of day laborers, and conduct hands-on small-group training sessions on how to blog from inexpensive mobile phones. Our workshops are one small part of a massive cross-movement convergence.

Our group is a bit overwhelmed by it all, but not too much so—after all, we've conducted similar workshops many times before over the past two years. The Popular Communication Team has provided VozMob workshops to day laborers at five Day Labor Centers around Los Angeles, for students and professors at the University of Southern California, and in an online webinar with remote participants from the Humanities, Arts, Sciences, and Technology Advanced Collaborative (HASTAC) Digital Media and Learning Network, underwritten by the MacArthur Foundation.[3]

We've rented a shared house for the two weeks we'll be in Detroit. As soon as we arrive, we scramble to set up a computer and video projector, connect to the neighbor's wifi, and start projecting a live stream of a World Cup game on the wall. Over the course of the AMC and the USSF conferences, our house becomes a welcome resting place from the elevated energy of the daily combination of workshops, meetings, street marches, presentations, and interviews. We share cooking and exchange recipes; Manuel Mancia's Salvadoran *chimol* salsa, purple and white, with radishes, cilantro, tomatoes, and onions, is a huge hit. After dinner one evening, Manuel demonstrates a streaming Internet radio station he and a friend have created using a hosted service, and Madelou shows us how she uses the free audio editing software Audacity to edit clips for *Enfoque Latino*, a radio show she now volunteers with on local Pacifica affiliate KPFK.

The AMC and USSF are important convenings. They both host deep strategy sessions that inform the evolution of some of the most powerful social movement networks, campaigns, and coalitions to emerge in the United States in decades. At these events, as at any conference or large gathering, much of the most valuable work takes place not during the big plenary sessions but in the margins. A mix of formal and informal learning, structured workshops, and peer-to-peer skill sharing takes place, including in the realm of transmedia organizing. Our VozMob group shares media skills through workshops but also informally, along with cooking recipes; this is true for many social movement participants. People build critical digital media literacy through both formal and informal processes: how to record and edit photo, video, and audio content, how to talk to the press, how to use social media, how to critically analyze mass media stories, how to remix commercials, how to effectively integrate new tools with tried-and-true organizing techniques, and so on.

Both formal and informal media skill-sharing efforts are important, because critical digital media literacy is a fundamental precondition for transmedia organizing. As we have seen, transmedia organizing takes advantage of changes in the media ecology to amplify social movement voices. Yet which voices get to speak? On the one hand, more people have access to media-making tools and skills now than ever before in human history. On the other, access remains deeply structured along intersecting lines of class, race, gender, age, and geography. Indeed, as transmedia organizing emerges as a crucial strategy for social movements, digital inequality is more troublesome than ever. Digital inequality may have a growing impact on the trajectory of social movements as transmedia organizing becomes increasingly important to the circulation of struggles, the formation of movement identity, and the transformation of public consciousness. The immigrant rights movement, especially, operates in a context of radically unequal access to digital media tools and skills. A detailed review of statistics on digital inequality is beyond the scope of this book; here it is enough to point out that multiple studies, conducted at neighborhood, city, state, and federal levels, find that foreign-born, Spanish-speaking, low-wage immigrant workers have less access to digital media tools, skills, and connectivity than any other group of people in the United States.[4] Yet at the same time, the immigrant rights movement uses digital media in innovative ways. Community organizers are taking steps to integrate critical digital media literacy into their daily work. This chapter begins by grounding our understanding of critical digital media literacy in Paolo Freire's ideas about popular education. I then trace the development of a praxis of critical digital media literacy within the immigrant rights movement in L.A.

Core Concepts: Praxis, Popular Education, and Critical Digital Media Literacy

To understand how immigrant rights activists use digital media, it is important to discuss the concept of *praxis*. IDEPSCA, the community-based organization (CBO) that is the home of the VozMob group (described in this chapter's introduction), uses the term to describe its approach to community organizing. For IDEPSCA, whose motto is "Reading reality to write history," praxis denotes an iterative process whereby liberatory theory is used to inform action, which changes reality. This, in turn, requires the modification of both theory and action to reflect and reshape the new reality.[5]

Praxis originates in the ancient Greek term meaning "practical knowledge for action." In the 1970s it was widely popularized by radical educator, organizer, and (post-dictatorship) Brazilian minister of education Paolo Freire. Freire is perhaps best known for his book *Pedagogy of the Oppressed*, in which he opposed what he called the "banking model" of education, or the one-way transmission of knowledge from educator to student, and posited instead a practice of critical pedagogy. He encouraged educators to pose problems, creating space for learners to build shared critical consciousness, plan for action, and develop agency. Freire defined praxis as "reflection and action upon the world in order to transform it."[6] Latin American popular educators, using the methods of critical pedagogy and praxis, taught hundreds of thousands of rural peasants and urban poor how to read and write while also working together to expose oppression and question unjust power relationships. For popular educators, literacy is a key tool that can enable oppressed individuals to become subjects who are able to act on the world and transform their conditions of oppression.[7]

Many popular educators linked to Latin American liberation movements fled U.S.-backed state and paramilitary repression in the 1970s and 1980s; some ended up in the United States, and many came to Los Angeles.[8] Popular education had already long played a role in U.S. social movements, from labor organizing to the civil rights movement and beyond. For example, the Highlander Research and Education Center, in New Market, Tennessee, had a history of using popular education to provide training in grassroots organizing and leadership.[9] Project South, based in Atlanta, Georgia, has used popular education since 1986 to organize young people in the struggle against poverty, violence, and racial injustice.[10] The tradition of popular education that emerged from the context of the U.S. civil rights movement, bolstered by a new wave of people, ideas, and practices from Latin America in the 1970s and 1980s, thus informs present-day social movements in Los Angeles.[11]

While these histories provide important grounding, at the same time, the changed media ecology requires new approaches to popular education. If print literacy was the primary tool of liberatory pedagogy during the era of popular struggle against the centralized power of authoritarian Latin American nation-states, critical digital media literacy assumes central importance as a tool of liberation against the networks of corporate and state power in the information society.[12] This may seem self-evident. Yet if we take the long view, the present moment is only the beginning of the growth of critical digital media literacy. The tools of audiovisual production and distribution are being spread, if unevenly, across an ever-growing proportion of the population. The history of print literacy offers clues to what this will mean for social movements. For example, in "The Growth of the Reading Public" and "The Growth of the Popular Press" in *The Long Revolution,* as in his work on television, Raymond Williams draws evidence from a wide range of sources to argue for the strong social impact of the spread of print literacy.[13] He also analyzes the class needs fulfilled by the expansion of print literacy. Initially, Williams writes, literacy was the province of the church and the aristocracy, or a small group of elites. The growth of commerce and of a middle class in the 1800s required an expansion of access to literacy to meet the demands of accurate accounting and to increase the exchange of trade knowledge. Higher literacy rates provided fertile ground for new forms of literature and for the growth of reading publics, which came to see themselves as political actors. Nick Dyer-Witheford takes a similar historical approach, but uses the lens of critical political economy of communication to analyze the rise of digital literacy. He argues that capital requires an ever-increasing number of knowledge and information workers, who must be trained and given access to advanced information and communication technologies (ICTs). In addition, the production of ICTs as mass commodities for profit impels their diffusion to the widest possible consumer base.[14] However, until very recently, the structure of the global economy limited advanced ICT tools and skills to the 1/3 world (residents of the wealthiest countries, plus local elites in the global south.[15] Earlier, powerful computers were available only to nation-states, multinational firms, and large institutions. Now they are pushed out for home use in ever-greater numbers. In the new millennium, Dyer-Witheford writes, the diffusion of ICTs took hold on a global scale. Even more than the personal computer, the arrival of mobile telephony further extended this logic. Networked ICTs are now, for the first time, in the hands of the majority of the planet's population.

As Dyer-Witheford suggests, the present moment is the beginning of a historic expansion of media-making skills. Everyday people are now making media, far beyond the small class of cultural producers who dominated the arts of audiovisual manipulation until the end of the twentieth century.[16] Indeed, a certain degree of digital media literacy is increasingly a basic requirement for participation in society. In many ways, the growing ubiquity of social media works in favor of social movements. The spread of print literacy laid the groundwork for the revolutions of the new middle class against the old aristocracies. The spread of critical digital media literacy—the ability to analyze, produce, remix, and circulate multimedia texts, not just consume them—may not determine a new wave of social transformation, but it is certainly a key enabling factor.

At the same time, however, the cultural industries continue to retain the lion's share of power over the creation and circulation of symbols and ideas. These industries, increasingly globalized, have also moved rapidly to monetize social media, transforming what Manuel Castells calls mass self-communication[17] into profitable platforms and services. The owners of social networking sites extract free labor from their users[18] and engage in both corporate data mining and state-backed surveillance of social movement activity.[19] Although social movements in communities of color have long been targeted by extensive state surveillance and systematic disruption, as in the infamous COINTELPRO program,[20] the widespread adoption of ICTs has spawned new and unprecedented surveillance threats. In 2013, the extent of the surveillance state become the subject of widespread debate when whistleblower Edward Snowden and journalist Glenn Greenwald released hitherto undisclosed information proving the extent of collaboration between the U.S. National Security Agency (NSA) and the largest web companies through PRISM and other massive data gathering programs.[21] For these and other reasons, it would be a mistake to assume that digital media literacy alone produces critical consciousness or supports the growth of liberatory social movements. On the contrary, participation in Internet culture all too frequently feeds patriarchy, heteronormativity, and racism. Without conscious intervention by organizers, educators, and critical thinkers, people use digital media literacy to reproduce all manner of historical and structural inequalities.[22]

Recently, the MacArthur Foundation's Digital Media and Learning initiative, and the associated conference series and network, have brought sustained scholarly attention to the importance of digital media literacy. A network of scholars engaged in ethnographic fieldwork and surveys of teenagers has developed a growing body of work to characterize the ways that digital literacies develop and circulate. For example, Henry Jenkins and co-authors have identified low barriers to participation, a supportive community, and informal mentorship as key characteristics of a participatory culture. They also note a persistent "participation gap," described as "unequal access to opportunities, experiences, skills, and knowledge."[23] Mizuko Ito and coauthors explore the ways that digital media literacy is acquired through peer networks and through social practices of "hanging out, messing around, and geeking out."[24] Samuel Craig Watkins found that young people increasingly access media "anytime, anywhere." He notes that they struggle to overcome "digital gates" that reinforce race and class inequality, and his work explores youth's use of social media to organize around the 2008 elections.[25]

These ideas also inform a new set of pedagogical interventions, as scholars working with the digital media and learning network develop approaches that are increasingly deployed both by existing institutions (such as schools, libraries, and museums) and in new digital learning spaces. This work is quite valuable and has an important role to play in pushing educators and institutions toward more flexibility. At the same time, most (although certainly not all) research conducted under the aegis of the MacArthur Foundation's Digital Media and Learning initiative focuses on a broad cross section of teenagers, with less attention to youth who are already involved in transformative social movements.[26] The model of learning and of civic engagement is primarily individualized, rather than focused on collective action. Broadly speaking, this framework emphasizes the individual acquisition of technical skills and social capital rather than the development of either a critical consciousness or a social movement identity. Unsurprisingly, within the formal educational system there is active resistance to the idea that it is important for young learners to develop a critical consciousness, much less participate in social movements. Existing community-based media literacy organizations, some of which have decades of experience, strong ties to community organizing, and active roles in social movement networks, are often marginalized within the digital media and learning initiative's discourse, funding, and project implementation.

Within social movements, the conversation is quite different. Rather than assume that the acquisition of digital media literacy will guide us unerringly toward a more just and sustainable world, savvy organizers understand the importance of a *praxis of critical digital media literacy*. This means that critical digital media literacy can be taught, learned, and shared in ways directly linked to both critical analysis and community organizing. Paolo Freire urged popular educators to teach print literacy using texts that simultaneously developed critical consciousness and an awareness of human rights. This was done through print literacy (reading and writing) workshops embedded in grassroots social movements. For example, the Brazilian Landless Workers' Movement (Movimento dos Trabalhadores Sem Terra) teaches peasants to read and write using the Brazilian constitution, which includes a section that guarantees land to those who productively use it. They do this in the context of a movement that has successfully acquired millions of acres of land previously unused by large landowners, now productively farmed by thousands of formerly landless families.[27] In similar fashion, some organizers in L.A. are developing a praxis of critical digital media literacy grounded in the experiences of the immigrant rights movement. Worker centers are key sites for this work.

Worker Centers and the Praxis of Critical Digital Media Literacy

In the introduction to this book, I described the rise of worker centers as part of the broader transformation of the labor movement. Vanessa Tait and Janice Fine have both written excellent accounts of the growth of the worker center model, in which community organizing is being rewired for intersectional liberation strategies.[28] Worker centers are geographically focused, tightly linked to their communities, and engage in cultural work, as well as in organizing, policy, and electoral strategies. Advocating for workers' rights remains at the core of what worker centers do, but organizing workers into unions has become only one part of a larger nexus of intersectional strategies that link together land use and gentrification battles, LGBTQ rights and gender justice, education and health, environmental justice, the prison system, and immigration rights.[29] Los Angeles is an important location in the history of the worker center model.[30] In the late 1990s and early 2000s, worker centers in L.A. won a series of important victories: the Garment Worker Center (GWC) won a major settlement against the clothing label Forever 21; the Koreatown Immigrant Workers Alliance (KIWA) helped win significant gains for sweatshop, restaurant, hotel, and supermarket workers;[31] and IDEPSCA made advances in education reform and day labor organizing. Worker centers have also struggled to increase affordable housing, gain regularization for undocumented people, maintain affirmative action, raise the minimum wage, and increase access to public transportation, as well as fight for LGBTQ rights. During the seven years I lived in Los Angeles, I spent time at each of these organizations. At IDEPSCA, GWC, and KIWA, I organized, conducted, or took part in digital media workshops with staff members, organizers, volunteers, workers, and community members. I also interviewed key staff and members at each center about the way they saw media work in relation to community organizing. This section draws on my experience and these interviews to explore the praxis of critical digital media literacy in L.A. worker centers.

The Institute of Popular Education of Southern California (IDEPSCA)

IDEPSCA uses popular education to educate and organize low-income immigrant families from Mexico and Central America. Established two decades ago during a struggle for better schools in Pasadena, by 2013 IDEPSCA had grown and expanded to a number of organizing projects across the city. IDEPSCA has a contract with the City of Los Angeles to operate six Day Labor Centers; runs a K–6 children's educational program called *Aprendamos* (We Learn); trains community health *promotoras* (promoters), who provide basic health care and education; created a Green Gardeners certification program and a household cleaning co-op called Magic Cleaners; provides ESL and Spanish literacy classes for adults in a program called *La Escuelita de La Comunidad*; and has a youth organizing component called Teens In Action, among other programs. IDEPSCA also acts as a key node in national networks. It is an anchor organization for the National Day Laborer Organizing Network (NDLON), the National Domestic Workers' Alliance (NDWA), and the Media Action Grassroots Network (MAG-Net).

From 2007 to 2010 I volunteered on a weekly basis for IDEPSCA's popular communication project. During that time I also interviewed a number of IDEPSCA staff, volunteers, and workers. Organizers from IDEPSCA described their long-term efforts to develop *comunicación populár* (popular communication) capacity among their base of low-wage immigrant workers. They had many years of experience working with day laborers and domestic workers to create and distribute their own media, including several radio and audio projects, video projects, and a newspaper called *Jornada XXII*. One IDEPSCA staff member had a long history of using popular communication in social movement struggles in Central America during the late 1970s and 1980s. He described popular communication as his main activity in those times, during which he worked with a team of three other organizers to create a nationwide network of social movement radio, as well as a newspaper that collected and distributed articles by students, workers, peasants, and women's organizations throughout Honduras.[32] He migrated to the United States as a refugee fleeing right-wing political violence. Once in L.A., he connected with IDEPSCA, and during the early days of the organization he helped create a newspaper, a radio program, and later a short video documenting the organization's activities. In the mid-2000s, IDEPSCA partnered with the Bay Area Video Coalition to produce a video titled *Neidi's Story*.[33]

IDEPSCA works to provide computers and Internet access to the community at sites around L.A. The organization's facilities include six computers located in the main office in Pico Union, four computers in the Hollywood Day Labor Center, and four computers in the Downtown Day Labor Center, among others. It also provides intermittent classes in basic computer literacy. Organizers at IDEPSCA are interested in developing the capacity of their base to critically analyze the mass media, and they run a number of workshops with this aim. For example, in 2006 they screened a series of documentaries about the anti-immigrant group the Minutemen, with screenings taking place at their main office, at Day Labor Centers, and at community sites. One organizer said that seeing the way the Minutemen and other anti-immigrant hate groups used the Internet to spread their message and circulate racist depictions of Latin@s filled her with rage, but also inspired her. She wanted to see IDEPSCA's base become digitally literate and gain access to ICTs so that they could "become subjects who speak, and authors of our own history."[34]

One of the organization's long-term goals is to organize L.A.'s 26,000 day laborers, using the network of Day Labor Centers and organizing corners spread throughout the city. They run a streaming radio station out of the Downtown Day Labor Center, and are exploring the possibility of setting up low-power FM stations to reach workers on the corners. However, mobile phones are the communication technology that day laborers have the most access to. By 2006, IDEPSCA organizers had become very interested in the possibilities of appropriating phones as tools for popular communication.

VozMob (Voces Móviles / Mobile Voices)

In 2006, as a doctoral student at the University of Southern California's Annenberg School for Communication & Journalism, I worked with Amanda Garcés, a community organizer from IDEPSCA, to develop a participatory research project focused on media, organizing, and immigrant rights. In 2007, this project grew to include day laborers, household workers, students, and volunteers from IDEPSCA, as well as additional graduate students and a faculty member from USC, François Bar. We chose to focus on researching the potential of mobile phones as a media production platform, and together we planned, then implemented, a survey of mobile phone use by day laborers at IDEPSCA's Day Labor Centers around the city. We found that nearly 80 percent of day laborers had mobile phones, although half had never used a computer and less than a quarter owned a computer.[35] In addition, we worked together to produce a successful application to the Social Science Research Council's 2008 Large Collaborative Grants program, followed by a successful application to the MacArthur Foundation–funded HASTAC Digital Media and Learning initiative. We created a community mobile blog at VozMob.net, where several thousand digital stories created by IDEPSCA's community can now be found.

VozMob (Voces Móviles / Mobile Voices) has several components, including critical media literacy training, popular education workshops, participatory research, and free/libre software development through participatory design. The team continues to produce *Jornada XXII*, a print newspaper that contains edited versions of stories initially seeded as posts from mobile phones to VozMob.net. The newspaper comes out several times a year and is printed in runs of 10,000 copies that are distributed throughout L.A. at Day Labor Centers, community spaces, on public transportation, and during mass mobilizations. VozMob participants also work with other CBOs. Workers and staff from IDEPSCA have led VozMob workshops for low-income downtown L.A. residents from the Los Angeles Community Action Network, for youth at the Southern California Library, and for organizers from across the city and around the country, to highlight just a few examples. VozMob members have also traveled widely to domestic and international conferences to conduct workshops, training sessions, and presentations. In 2011 the project won the United Nations World Summit Award for mobile content in the e-empowerment category.[36]

In 2013 the VozMob team continued to meet every week at IDEPSCA's main office and spend time together learning how to use mobile phones as tools for popular communication. For IDEPSCA, VozMob also provides a means to incorporate new technology into its existing popular communication practice. The VozMob project coordinator described these efforts:

I've always believed in pop ed [popular education].... These stories that happen here every day at the Centers are not told, and the media obviously doesn't have the workers' humanity in mind.... [We] use open-source tools to empower workers to tell their own stories.[37]

The project is designed to counter anti-immigrant voices, to enable immigrant workers to participate in the digital public sphere, and to serve as a space for the development of critical digital media literacy. Organizers from IDEPSCA have developed an intentional approach to digital media literacy that is tightly linked to struggles over community representation, base building, and the long history of popular communication as articulated through Latin American social movement struggles. At the same time, they are able to meaningfully engage the discourses of funders and academics, especially digital inclusion, digital storytelling, and technological empowerment, and this enhances their ability to gather resources for popular education and a praxis of critical digital media literacy.

Garment Worker Center (GWC)

While IDEPSCA organizes day laborers and household workers, the GWC organizes among L.A.'s approximately 60-80,000 workers who labor in the apparel industry, largely concentrated in the Fashion District just south of downtown's financial district. Garment workers suffer extensive abuses and violations, from unpaid wages to unsafe working conditions, sexual assault, and more.[38] GWC, created in 2001, is an independent worker center that has trained more than one hundred garment workers as organizers, successfully pushed for the implementation of antisweatshop laws, conducted a three-year boycott against the clothing label Forever 21, and won more than $3 million for workers in back wages and penalties. The organization's mission is "to empower garment workers in the Los Angeles area and to work in solidarity with other low wage immigrant workers and disenfranchised communities in the struggle for social, economic and environmental justice."[39]

In 2007, GWC had a computer lab with about five computers and a DSL connection. One of the computers was a G4 tower capable of running Final Cut Pro (professional grade video-editing software); this was donated by a film student from USC who occasionally helped with technical support and who started a video workshop with workers during the fall of 2006. GWC workers played key roles in, and participated extensively in the production of, the award-winning documentary *Made in L.A.* At the time, GWC also had two recording devices, one digital camera and one "old-school" camera (VHS or Hi8). They estimated that about 50 percent of garment workers had cell phones, mostly prepaid, and in their experience workers kept them turned off a lot because of the high cost of credit.

In general, at the time garment workers at GWC did not have access to the Internet, although some said they were connected. A few young adults came in to the GWC space on Saturdays to use the computer lab, mostly for email and video games. There were sporadic computer classes, but the organization did not have staff capacity to keep the machines maintained or to turn the lab into a real media production and distribution hub. GWC often tried to recruit volunteers to participate in projects or conduct training sessions but found it difficult to get people to commit time over the long term on a volunteer basis.[40]

Garment workers, volunteers, and staff produced a semiregular newsletter, but also said that they would like to see a lot more happen with multimedia production. Specifically, they dreamed of having a radio station, since radio remains the most popular form of media used by the majority of garment workers. GWC's long-term aim was for worker-produced audio to reach the 60,000 to 80,000 workers concentrated in the Fashion District. GWC workers said that they listened to the radio with headphones at work, especially when employers told them that they were not allowed to talk to each other.[41] One worker added that in some shops they were neither allowed to talk nor listen to music with headphones. Staff felt that audio content circulation would ideally be via FM radio, but might also be done initially via CDs.

Radio Tijera

Based on this reality, beginning in 2007 I worked with organizers Amanda Garcés and simmi gandi and garment workers Mariarosa, Cristian, Nayo, Edilberto, and Consuelo to create a critical digital media literacy workshop focused on audio production. From 2007 through 2009, the group of three to eight garment workers, one to two community organizers, and allies met regularly (every week, sometimes every other week) in a workshop initially called *El Proyecto de Radio* (The Radio Project), later *Radio Costurera* (Radio Garment Worker), and finally *Radio Tijera* (Radio Scissors). Between 2007 and 2009 we produced interviews, PSAs (public service announcements), know-your-rights clips, news, poems, calls to action, oral histories, and a range of other audio material. This material was distributed via CD audio magazines dubbed *Discos Volantes*.[42] We pressed hundreds of copies of CDs packed with worker-produced audio materials mixed with music, and garment worker organizers distributed these CDs inside downtown L.A.'s garment sweatshops (audio from these CDs is available online at http://garmentworkercenter.org/media/radiotijera). Workers also designed and completed an evaluation survey through which they documented the number of CDs distributed, the number of new contacts made during the distribution process, and the number of new workers who came in to the GWC based on the process of distributing the CD.

This distribution process offers a powerful example of how the principles of transmedia organizing can apply offline as well as online. GWC workers saw value not only in the recordings per se but also in the opportunity they provided for face-to-face contact between garment workers. *Radio Tijera* was therefore a useful space not only for building the media production skills of workshop participants but also as one component of a larger organizing process. The *Discos Volantes* provided a focal point for conversations about industry conditions, workers' rights, and GWC's organizing efforts.[43] During the summer of 2008, the group also built a low-power FM transmitter with the help of activists from the Prometheus Radio Project. This transmitter was later used for live microradio broadcasts from the 2008 Fast for Our Future hunger strike for immigrant rights in Placita Olvera.[44]

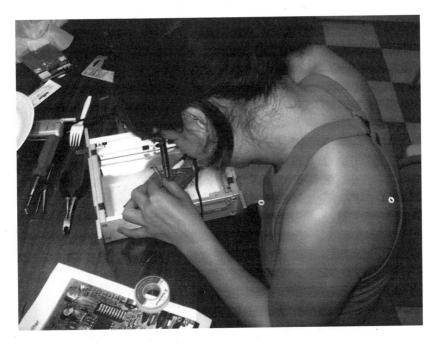

Figure 5.2
Building the transmitter for *Radio Tijera.*
Source: Photo by author, for the Garment Worker Center, Los Angeles.

In 2009, participants in the *Radio Tijera* workshop were invited to present some of their interviews and other material on Pacifica affiliate KPFK (90.7), which reaches the entire city.[45] In the week leading up to the KPFK appearance, GWC organizers took the broadcast as an opportunity to initiate face-to-face contact by distributing flyers on the streets and inside the factories, announcing the air date and time for garment worker–produced radio segments. In many ways, this project was a success: garment workers gained skills in digital audio recording, mixing, editing, and distribution, as well as increased computer literacy and live radio broadcast experience. Audio produced by garment workers was distributed inside sweatshops and over the air, spreading important messages about labor law, wages, health and safety, immigration policy, and organizing history. However, *Radio Tijera* was never able to become self-sufficient, with a process entirely run by garment workers themselves.

While low initial levels of digital literacy contributed to the challenges, the problems in building *Radio Tijera* into a self-sustaining project
were not primarily about access to resources or technological skills. It
was relatively easy for the project to raise the funds necessary to purchase digital audio recorders, microphones, a mixer, the parts for the
radio transmitter, and other equipment. Rather, the biggest challenges
were those faced by any organizing effort in an industry with long
hours, bad conditions, and low pay: limited time and energy. No garment
workers were able to step forward to consistently lead the project. For
larger labor organizations, this problem is to some degree mitigated
through the use of paid organizers—a solution that introduces its own
difficulties with respect to accountability and sustainability. However,
during 2006–2007 the GWC collective decided to move away from a
nonprofit model of paid staff or a union model of paid organizers. This
decision was based on the ideal that any sustained organizing effort
must be firmly rooted in the desires and organized efforts of garment
workers themselves, and eliminating paid organizer positions would
ensure the greatest possible degree of accountability to the base. At the
same time, this model is very difficult to sustain. Over the course of
three years, three different groups of garment workers came into the
project and produced audio material, before *Radio Tijera* was put on
hold. More recently, GWC has decided to switch back to a worker center
model with paid staff and organizers, and at the time of writing it is
gearing up for a major new participatory research study of industry
conditions and a new organizing drive.

Informal Learning and Key Sites

As we have seen, many CBOs involved in the immigrant rights movement
work to develop a praxis of critical digital media literacy with their community, largely through workshops, projects, and formal classes in computer labs. Yet research has shown that a great deal—perhaps the bulk—of
digital media literacy develops through peer-to-peer learning and informal
skill sharing.[46] This is also the case in the immigrant rights movement,
where digital media learning takes place constantly between friends and
within families. For example, many organizers whom I interviewed and
asked about where they learned media skills mentioned friends and

coworkers: "From my friends, I think that's the truth.... It's not like you learn base building, campaign strategizing, and media. It hasn't become that yet. I have been exposed to this because of friends, of people who have an interest in it."[47] Peer-to-peer learning also takes place between family members. Youth often spend time teaching parents or grandparents how to use computers, the Internet, and mobile phones:

Nowadays we get more parents coming and say, "Oh *mira*, I just got Internet but I don't know how to use it," or something like that. And so there's been a few times where we'll come into the home and set it up, or teach them how to do their email, set up their account. Even in my family I still get phone calls from my *tio* or my mom. I was trying to get my grandma to learn how to text, and that became a project on its own.[48]

Informal learning remains important even for organizations that do offer formal digital media literacy training. At IDEPSCA, where popular communication is a strategic goal, there are computer labs in the main office and in Day Labor Centers. In the previous section, we explored the VozMob project, itself largely a formal, weekly, face-to-face workshop organized according to the principles of popular education. Yet an organizer at IDEPSCA emphasized that informal learning is key: "For me it's really amazing actually to see some of the workers very interested in computers. Now the non-Mobile Voices workers ... a lot of people are coming to learn computers very informally."[49] Sometimes formal critical digital media literacy projects serve to gather resources and capacity that then become more readily accessible to the social base of the movement, even to those who do not "officially" participate.

Many immigrant rights activists also talked about developing their media skills in the context of ongoing media work within broader campaigns. An organizer with the UCLA Labor Center (the generally used public name for the UCLA Center for Labor Research and Education) described cutting her teeth on media organizing as a high school student. At that time, she worked on access to education with a youth organizing initiative called Inner City Struggle. She described intensive afterschool workshops with the group's media collective. They analyzed and deconstructed mass media messages, learned about media ownership, and, most important, according to her, learned how to create their own media in the context of campaigns, as well as how to control the message during interviews with reporters:

It was work around how do we get the Los Angeles Unified School District to invest more resources into low-income schools, when the message that goes out there is that Latino low-income children cannot learn, they can't go to college, they can't master these skills. For us, it was great turning that around and asking the questions, one, that we deserve to go to college, why aren't resources being placed in our communities? That was my first experience in really shifting the public discourse in terms of messaging, framing, and using media as a tool and as a resource.[50]

Youth organizers with Inner City Struggle thus learned to challenge mass media narratives about Latin@ youth. They took these skills with them into future movement activity, including in the immigrant rights movement. This experience is consistent with recent research observing that youth media projects succeed in producing longer-term outcomes when they are directly integrated with community organizing efforts rather than compartmentalized into "skills-focused" training programs.[51]

Both formal and informal digital media learning takes place in key learning sites, where people have access to equipment, connectivity, and mentorship. This is especially important in the context of the low levels of computer and broadband access in low-wage immigrant worker households. Many new immigrants build their digital media skills in computer labs at libraries, schools, universities, and community based organizations. These skills can later be applied to movement building. One organizer said that despite her lifelong involvement in the immigrant rights movement, she did not think seriously about how digital media could be used as an organizing tool until pushed to do so by the university environment:

I gotta be honest.... Technology is not my strength. But I realized that I had to. Little things, like being able to share documents, and things like that. I had to learn how to do it, and even though I had been organizing here in L.A. for so long, it was really in [UC] Santa Cruz that I learned that all these tools existed for me to be a better organizer.[52]

The same organizer talked about how students at UC Santa Cruz, as well as at nearby Cabrillo College, took advantage of their access to university cameras, editing equipment, and computer labs to produce video and audio testimonials that were useful organizing tools on campus and in the community. She also described a process of peer learning that developed into more structured approaches based in popular education. She later applied this experience to the development of IDEPSCA's *Aprendamos* (We Learn) educational program for kindergarten through sixth graders. In turn, workshops developed for children through *Aprendamos* proved useful in the context of adult education:

For example, a camera might have the button that says On and Off, which is a word in English, right? But if you're able to teach the "O" and the "N" and then at the same time be able to say, "The On is *Prender* and Off is *Apagar*," it's like you're doing three things at the same time for a person, and also learning how to use a camera. We have to do a lot of that because we realize that a lot of the workers that we were also organizing with, they didn't know how to read and write as well.[53]

Another interviewee, who had worked as a high school teacher, related her experience with working-class youth who had access to the Internet only at school or in public libraries: "I would have at least ten of my thirty students ask if they could use my computer during lunchtime because they just wanted to be on the Internet, you know? When I would take them to the library, they would just go straight to the Internet."[54] Her experience points to the continued importance of public computer labs. Another organizer discussed how computer labs at Day Labor Centers were often the only place where day laborers could connect to the Internet: "There's no access, really. Many people that I speak with at the centers don't have a computer at home. Only the ones that have kids that are born here, or that have kids in school, have computers."[55]

Other interviewees noted that many spaces for informal technology learning, including computer labs at libraries and schools, as well as DIY sites such as hackerspaces and makerspaces, are deeply gendered.[56] They are often dominated by straight white men and can be difficult to access for women, people of color, and queer and transgendered people. This dynamic stands in sharp contrast to many of the critical digital media literacy efforts taking place at worker centers in L.A. That is not to say that worker centers are ideal spaces, free of racism, sexism, and heteronormativity. However, many organizers promote an explicit intersectional understanding that includes race, class, gender, and sexual identity. Digital media workshops at worker centers often include developing this understanding as one of their goals. For example, when digital stories created by workshop participants reproduce oppressive assumptions about gender, facilitators at GWC or IDEPSCA often step away from the planned agenda in order to hold a conversation directly addressing the issue. Many organizers use digital media workshops to build a shared space where everyone in the room feels able to speak up and challenge the reproduction of oppressive images and narratives in mass media, popular communication, and everyday conversation. It is possible to develop this kind of space intentionally. In this way, critical digital media literacy can be integrated into a broader strategy of popular education, designed to develop critical consciousness and build movement capacity. Critical digital media literacy thus spreads through both formal and informal learning between friends, family, coworkers, and peers in the movement. Digital tools and skills are accessible, to some degree, to the base of the immigrant rights movement at key sites, including schools, universities, public libraries, and workplaces. Yet many barriers remain.

Barriers to the Praxis of Critical Digital Media Literacy

While worker centers in L.A. have begun to build critical digital media literacy into their organizing work, for the most part these efforts remain small in scale and sporadic, and reach only a limited part of the relevant communities. Lack of resources, inadequate training capacity, fear of technology, generational divides, and a lack of vision remain key barriers. The biggest obstacle, according to most of those I interviewed, is lack of resources, specifically money to hire dedicated staff. Money is also necessary to purchase computers, nicer digital cameras, and high-bandwidth Internet access, as well as to invest in other kinds of media production. For example, one FIOB (Frente Indígena de Organizaciones Binacionales) staff member hoped to make the organization's flagship communication platform, a print and online magazine called *El Tequio*, self-sufficient.[57] I asked her what she saw as the biggest obstacle to realizing that goal, and her answer was unequivocal:

Money. We don't have money. Money's a challenge. But you know, one of my wishes is for the ally organizations, the immigrant movement, to buy ads in this magazine that could make us self-sufficient.[58]

While this organizer, like many others, said that money was the biggest obstacle, most also mentioned the need for increased capacity to conduct training. This was the case for KIWA's attempts to increase digital media literacy among both staff and membership. One staff member described the biggest barriers as follows:

Our own capacity, I think. If we can hire someone to be just assigned to do something like that, it'll benefit the organization a lot.... Like we were talking about earlier, the computer class, if you have someone that could dedicate their time in terms of curriculum development and running it, it would be really helpful.[59]

Another interviewee emphasized that the inconsistent pedagogical quality and time commitment of volunteer teachers were major obstacles to successfully building digital media literacy capacity, and expressed hope that a new grant her organization had received to teach computer classes would allow it to hire a teacher and improve the quality of the program.[60] The chief barrier to an effective praxis of critical digital media literacy is lack of resources to hire dedicated, paid staff. Most interviewees believed that dedicated staff would be able to transform underutilized computer labs into hubs of training, formal and informal skill sharing, media-making, and transmedia organizing.

In a few cases, organizers said that fear of unfamiliar technology was the biggest barrier to access:

I know my mom went to school to get trained on computer lit.... They just have this fear, and I think the scary part is that technology and this tech equipment changes so much that they don't understand the fact that if they learned the skill, it could be applied to any machine. To my mom it's like, "Oh my God, it's a new machine, I can't touch it, I have no idea where to turn it on."[61]

The rapid pace of technological change and the endless marketing of new digital media technologies exacerbate this fear. It's also important to mention that the discourse of technophobia is highly gendered, as well as based on age. In other words, women and elders are assumed to be fearful of technology, which is portrayed as the domain of men and younger people.[62] Unsurprisingly, these broader societal assumptions are often replicated within movement spaces.

Even for those who are unafraid of digital media, have relatively high levels of access to ICTs and critical digital media literacy, and actively seek to incorporate digital media into their organizing, figuring out how to do so can be confusing, time-consuming, and unsettling. Organizers often feel pressure to stay up to date with emerging social media tools, practices, and norms. They frequently end up participating in new media spaces even when the value of doing so seems vague. The executive director of one organization described the experience of creating a blog, a Twitter persona, webinars, an online survey through Survey Monkey, and a Facebook presence:

We started this project, and we had an intern who created a blog for us. I mean we should check to see if anyone actually visits us, but we're pretty sure no one does. And I think that that's the thing, it was great because we had someone who could do it, but there's actually—you can't just create it, there's a maintenance level. There's a participation, there's a relationship that you have to build within it for it to work.[63]

In this organization, younger staff and volunteers were asked to create the entirety of the organization's social media presence, and resources were not available for maintaining that presence.

Younger staff members often act as de facto "online organizers," and end up working to adopt and integrate online tools into the life of movement organizations. Many enjoy this role. Others, however, point out that although students are often assumed to be so-called "digital natives,"[64] innately familiar with all digital media tools and skills, there is a wide range of digital media literacy among young people. At the same time, older staff who may have extensive experience with campaign communications, effective messaging, and movement strategy may not work together with younger staff or volunteers to figure out how to strategically use new tools for movement goals.[65] Younger organizers are often frustrated by the slow pace of organizational adoption:

I see more organizations using video and all these things to bring more awareness or put themselves out there. But still in the most immediate ways we could use it, it's sort of on the back burner.... It always is that one person that is into it that brings it up, but it hasn't become a basic tool.[66]

Put plainly, nonprofit leaders are only beginning to think of social media as key spaces for organizing, even as many younger activists feel that all organizers should now be trained in effective social media use, just as they are currently training in meeting facilitation, note taking, and door knocking.

Developing digital media literacy is also constrained by the moral panic induced by sensationalist broadcast media accounts of online spaces. Caught up in such panics (moments of intense, usually raced and gendered, fear that the social order will be disrupted, often used to justify repressive policies), adults often limit young people's access to social media, even as social media have become key platforms for political participation.[67] Parents and teachers sometimes restrict young people's access, especially if they are not comfortable with the technology or if their primary information source is the mass media, which tend to emphasize stories about scary, sensational, and negative uses of the net:

These were middle schoolers, these are what, eleven, twelve, thirteen, fourteen? Well, first there was a whole craze of not allowing kids to go on MySpace because, you know, crazy men go after girls. Or even—what was the one controversial case of a mom harassing a teenager and the teenager killed himself?... And it's just so TV perpetuating this craze about MySpace being a bad space.... I think a lot of my students hadn't seen that was just crap the media was putting in their parents' eyes. And then their parents weren't allowing them to do that.[68]

As this interview reflects, moral panics are also deeply gendered.[69] The introduction of new communication technologies is often accompanied by narratives of moral, physical, and sexual disorder, and especially by patriarchal fear of loss of control over female sexuality.[70] As a result of moral panics, parents, educators, and administrators impose different constraints on boys and girls.[71] Even when parents are not afraid of digital media, they may not recognize its educational value.[72] Parents sometimes push back against educators and organizers when they attempt to spend time developing children's digital media literacy. As one organizer noted, "Parents don't necessarily feel that teaching their kids how to use a camera to take pictures is as important to teaching them how to do math, you know? And it's not that we're replacing either/or, it's that they could do everything."[73] To try to persuade parents that digital media literacy is important, she would tell them, "Look, there's so many people out there that write about our lives, that document our lives, that come into our communities and then all of a sudden, write about it to try to create change. And it's in a good intention, but at the same time what makes us so different that we can't do it ourselves when we have these tools now much more accessible to us than before?"[74]

Finally, some immigrant rights organizers talked about vision as the most important obstacle. They felt that resources were available but that organizations failed to effectively grasp the strategic and tactical possibilities of digital media. One interviewee said that the biggest obstacle to reaching her goal of teaching digital storytelling skills to workers who came to the UCLA Labor Center was "getting people on board. Is this something the Labor Center would like to dedicate resources to?"[75] Without a strong vision of the possibilities, even the best-resourced movement organizations can remain far behind in developing a praxis of critical digital media literacy. Another activist described what he called a "disconnect" between the organizing approaches of a majority of movement groups and the possibilities enabled by broader access to digital media. He felt that this disconnect was increasingly based not on lack of access to technology but rather on a lack of understanding on the part of the organization's leadership.[76] He also noted that concrete transmedia organizing examples, such as the Basta Dobbs campaign (discussed in chapter 2), would go a long way toward generating buy-in from movement leaders.

A Praxis of Critical Digital Media Literacy: Conclusions

Digital inequality is a persistent and powerful force. Low-wage immigrant workers, who form the social base of the immigrant rights movement, on average have less access to media-making tools and skills than most people. Movement groups that work with them have not yet tightly integrated critical digital media literacy into their broader organizing efforts. However, organizers increasingly consider digital media literacy to be important, and have taken steps to try to advance these skills in their communities. Many CBOs now have computer labs and offer computer literacy classes. Indeed, the falling costs of equipment and connectivity have meant that even less well-resourced organizations are better able to acquire computers, media-making equipment, and broadband Internet access. However, higher-quality digital video cameras and other high-end equipment often remain out of reach due to cost. At the same time, mobile phones are approaching near ubiquity, even among the lowest income and least-connected populations of immigrant workers. The immigrant rights movement is learning to take advantage of mobile phones, with innovative media projects like VozMob providing inspiration across the field.[77] There is great potential for community organizers to fully integrate mobile media into their efforts. Some CBOs, among them IDEPSCA and GWC, have created popular education workshops around digital media. They are actively working to build a praxis of critical digital media literacy.

Besides formal digital media literacy trainings, tools and skills circulate through the immigrant rights movement through informal and peer-to-peer learning among friends, family, and coworkers. Critical digital media literacy develops at key sites, including universities, schools, libraries, and community computer labs. The major challenges include funding, training capacity, and lack of familiarity with new tools. Language issues, trust, and low-wage workers' lack of time and energy to participate also make developing facility with digital media a challenge. Fear of new technology and the moral panic induced by TV coverage of the Internet and digital culture create additional, gendered obstacles. There is also a generational divide. Younger people and students who volunteer with immigrant rights organizations, as well as younger staff, are often the ones who initiate online organizing strategies. Frequently, staff at CBOs feel pressure to adopt new digital media tools without a clear understanding of how they work, or how to evaluate whether they are effective.

In the past, digital media literacy was usually seen as peripheral not only to organizing but also to communication strategy. Until the late 2000s, online tools were still considered experiments by many senior staff and were not necessarily part of strategic communication plans. This began to change by the end of the decade, especially with the high visibility of digital tools and social media as fully integrated components of the 2008 and 2012 presidential campaigns. Still, besides low levels of access among the immigrant worker base, the greatest barriers to adoption and integration of transmedia organizing by the immigrant rights movement are insufficient resources to hire dedicated staff and the lack of a shared vision about the possibilities.

Overall, critical digital media literacy is crucial to effective transmedia organizing. Digital media literacy on the part of a movement's social base shapes and constrains that movement's ability to take advantage of the changing media ecology. In the long run, media-making tools and skills are becoming available to an ever-broader proportion of the population, but the distribution of skills and tools remains highly unequal. Some immigrant rights activists are developing a praxis of critical digital media literacy that has the potential to transform the lives of immigrant workers, students, and their allies and to reconfigure the movement.

While this chapter has focused on worker centers, it would be a mistake to impose an artificial separation between low-wage immigrant workers and student activists. The next chapter focuses on transmedia organizing by undocumented youth.

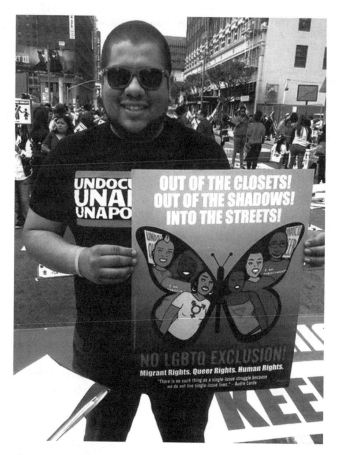

Figure 6.1
Undocuqueer artist Julio Salgado with his poster, "Out of the Closets! Out of the Shadows! Into the Streets!"
Source: Culturestrike.net, photo by Juan Castillo Alvarado.

6 Out of the Closets, Out of the Shadows, and Into the Streets: Pathways to Participation in DREAM Activist Networks

As the 2012 election built up steam, the Obama campaign focused increasing resources on Latin@ voters in key battleground states. Both Democrats and Republicans knew that these voters would be crucial. The Obama campaign was also aware that it would need strong Latin@ support, despite the administration's systematic increases in border militarization, detentions, and deportations, the controversial Secure Communities program, and the lack of progress on comprehensive immigration reform. While mainstream immigrant rights organizations and Beltway insiders concentrated their efforts on TV advertisements and get-out-the-vote campaigns, undocumented youth (widely known as DREAMers, after the proposed Development, Relief and Education for Alien Minors Act, first introduced in Congress in 2001 by Senators Dick Durbin and Orrin Hatch) decided to take bold, risky steps to force concessions from the administration. On June 5, 2012, Veronica Gomez and Javier Hernandez, undocumented youth leaders with the National Immigrant Youth Alliance, entered the Obama campaign offices in Denver to engage in nonviolent civil disobedience. A picket line of supporters circled outside the campaign office doors, chanting slogans in time to the staccato roll of snare drums. Veronica and Javier, wearing graduation caps as symbols of DREAMer demands for education, not deportation, sat calmly in the middle of the office, with friends and supporters taking pictures and starting a live video stream.[1] Over the next six days, these young undocumented activists conducted a sit-in and hunger strike that captured attention across social media, print, TV, and radio. Thousands watched their live stream, and thousands more signed petitions in support of their demands. Veronica and Javier, and overlapping networks of immigrant rights groups of which they were a part, demanded that President Obama take immediate administrative action to halt deportations of DREAM Act–eligible youth. They threatened that failure to do so would result in similar actions at campaign headquarters across the country, especially in key battleground states.[2]

This was not the first time that DREAMers had employed the sit-in as a tactic, nor was it the first time they live-streamed their own acts of non-violent civil disobedience. For example, in 2010, queer undocumented youth activists Mohammad Abdollahi, Yahaira Carrillo, and Tania Unzueta occupied the Arizona offices of Senator John McCain, and in 2011, Dream Team Los Angeles activists Adrian, Francisco Javier, Nancy Meza, Neidi Dominguez, and Tony Ortuño staged and live-streamed a sit-in at Immigration and Customs Enforcement (ICE) offices in Los Angeles.[3] By 2012 the movement had grown stronger and the networks of DREAM activists more robust; their media connections across platforms were much broader, and they had developed a degree of leverage over the Latin@ vote. On June 15, 2012, President Obama announced the Deferred Action for Childhood Arrivals (DACA) program, which provides a two-year, temporary permit that allows some DREAM Act–eligible youth to remain in the United States without fear of detention and deportation.[4] The DACA program is only a small step on the long path toward justice for immigrants, and some activists refer to the program as the smallest possible bone the Obama administration could have credibly thrown the immigrant rights movement in the run-up to the election.[5] However, it was a hard-won victory: undocumented youth battled for more than a decade to gain even this temporary administrative reform. It came through their dedication, creativity, and bravery.

As Prerna Lal, undocuqueer founder of DreamActivist.net, has so eloquently described, DREAM activism and the broad new wave of immigrant rights organizing have not only been led by undocumented youth, they have been disproportionately led by young, undocumented, queer people of color.[6] How did undocumented youth create such compelling, cutting-edge strategies and develop so many new leaders? How did DREAMers become one of the most powerful organizing forces in the United States, not only for immigrant rights but across social movements, from LGBTQ struggles to the resurgent labor movement and beyond? This chapter addresses these questions by focusing on transmedia organizing, pathways to participation, and public narrative in DREAM activist networks.

These terms bear explanation and review. In this book, I have proposed that *transmedia organizing* is the strategic practice of cross-platform, participatory media-making for social movement ends. DREAMers, like many grassroots activists, have organically developed effective transmedia organizing methods. *Pathways to participation* are the trajectories by which people come to identify with, and take part in, social movements over the course of their lives. Undocumented youth become DREAMers through friends, family, community-based organizations, and movement groups. Many also follow mediated pathways: for example, their entry point into social movement identity is through taking part in movement media production, circulating information during crises and mobilizations, and otherwise engaging in transmedia organizing. A *public narrative* is a story about a social movement that is intended for public consumption and has specific public goals: to build a shared identity among movement participants, draw in sympathizers, and generate new allies. DREAM activists have struggled to develop their own public narrative, reject discourse they feel harms them and harms the broader immigrant rights movement, and shape the ways they are framed across the media ecology. This chapter begins with a short discussion of DREAM activism and transmedia organizing, then moves on to explore the larger issues of pathways to participation and the development of public narratives. Along the way, I'll trace the links between social movement media and the rise of a new generation of committed organizers.

DREAM Activists Make Media and Make Trouble

According to data from the U.S. Census Bureau, in 2010 approximately 4.4 million immigrants under the age of thirty were undocumented.[7] Many were brought to the United States as children by their parents, either without documentation or on temporary visas that have since expired. In California, there are about 26,000 undocumented youth. Nationwide, each year about 65,000 undocumented youth graduate from U.S. high schools.[8] Yet without access to federal or state financial aid, many are unable to go on to university study, even if they are academically prepared to do so. In most states they are also denied driver's licenses and are not allowed to participate in the formal labor market. Over the last decade, undocumented youth, along with their families, communities, and supporters, have organized an increasingly visible campaign to gain access to higher education, become eligible for driver's licenses, achieve the right to work legally, and normalize their status as U.S. citizens.

In California, undocumented youth initially organized around key state legislative initiatives. The California Assembly Bill 540 (A.B. 540), which became law in 2001, did not provide access to financial aid but did allow undocumented youth to qualify for in-state tuition fees within the California university system (including community colleges, California state colleges, and the University of California). The California Senate Bill 65 (S.B. 65), or the California Dream Act, allows A.B. 540 students to access financial aid to attend any of the state's institutions of higher education. At the federal level, the DREAM Act would authorize temporary legal residence for young people who were brought to the country without documents before they were fifteen. The bill was introduced in the U.S. Congress multiple times between 2001 and 2011; in most versions, the bill would allow high school graduates to apply for up to six years of legal residence. Those who graduate from a two-year college, complete at least two years of a four-year degree, or serve in the military for at least two years during this six-year time period would become eligible for permanent residence.[9] Early versions of the bill also offered a community service option as an alternative to military service. After organizing for more than a decade, by December 2010, DREAM activists had managed to build bipartisan support for the DREAM Act in the U.S. Senate. However, support fell five votes short of the sixty needed to overcome a filibuster. More recently, in 2013, most provisions of the DREAM Act were incorporated into various federal legislative proposals for comprehensive immigration reform.

DREAM Act Debates

In addition to predictable resistance from the anti-immigrant right, DREAM Act organizing has been contentious within the broader immigrant rights movement. Some immigrant rights organizers, including many undocumented youth themselves, are concerned that proposals for a stand-alone DREAM Act play into a broader narrative that delinks undocumented youth from workers—often their own parents. One organizer I interviewed, a staff member at a worker center, noted that the most visible DREAMers are what she called the "cream of the crop:" the most successful immigrant youth who managed to make it to college. She worried that the outcome of organizing undocumented youth primarily around their own ability to advance in higher education and in high-skilled employment would be to separate them from the larger immigrant rights movement.[10] Others I interviewed, including some who themselves identified as DREAMers, voiced criticism of the military recruitment implications of provisions in the currently proposed DREAM Act legislation. The military provision offers a pathway to citizenship to students who enter military service. In the immigrant rights movement, this has mostly been framed as "the military option," in comparison to the much more visible pathway through higher education, despite the reality that actual passage of the legislation would result in far higher numbers of immigrant youth entering the armed forces (half a million or more would be eligible) than higher education.[11] Some interviewees thus questioned DREAM Act organizing, which they felt divided the movement by allowing a small group of students with higher education to become citizens while providing a larger number of immigrant youth a pathway to enter the military directly out of high school in order to achieve the same benefits.[12] The likely outcome—potentially hundreds of thousands of new Latin@ military recruits, in a time of war—prompted some critics to suggest that the DREAM Act was actually a military recruiter's dream in disguise.[13] A small but vocal contingent of undocumented youth has made this charge publicly, for example in the film *Yo Soy El Army*.[14] The group 67 Seuños, which organizes working-class immigrant youth in Oakland, also emerged in part out of frustration with a DREAM Act narrative that its members felt was dominated by college students.[15] In response to these criticisms, other DREAMers have defended the military option, pointing to the historical importance of military service as a pathway to immigrant integration and the U.S. middle class. Others, while themselves also critical of the U.S. military, have responded that military recruiters already target Latin@ youth and will continue to do so regardless of what takes place in the realm of immigration reform.[16]

DACA

In June 2012, President Obama announced the DACA program. DACA provides approximately 1.6 million DREAMers with a formal mechanism by which they can be recognized by the state, a promise that they won't be detained and deported for at least two years, and legal permission to work in the United States.[17] Most of those I talked to felt that this was an important victory. At the same time, some also saw it as a cynical electoral ploy by the Obama administration. A few worried that DACA might serve, along with both the Secure Communities program and the federal E-Verify employment verification system, to build a database of undocumented people that would be used to feed the steadily rising number of detentions and deportations. The growth of the detention and deportation industry over the past decade is not surprising, in light of the power of lobbyists from the for-profit prison industry to advocate for building new private prisons and detention facilities. These lobbyists coauthored the infamous Arizona S.B. 1070 and then, through the American Legislative Exchange Council, transformed it into "model legislation" that has spawned numerous copycat state bills.[18] Obama's victory in the 2012 election proved to be, unfortunately, no safeguard against this process. Indeed, the Obama administration has broken records for detentions and deportations year after year: from 369,221 removals in 2008 to 396,906 in 2011, according to figures released by ICE.[19] Under the Obama administration an average of 33,000 people are deported per month, compared to 21,000 per month under the George W. Bush administration and 9,000 per month under the Clinton administration.[20] By 2014, the Obama administration has overseen more than two million deportations. Among immigrant rights activists, this has earned Obama the nickname "Deporter-in-Chief."[21]

Still, despite disagreements about the overarching implications of the DACA program, most immigrant rights activists agree that it was a victory for the immigrant rights movement, won by a combination of tactics that included both lobbying and highly visible, heavily mediated direct actions. Meanwhile, the debates over the merits and problems of a stand-alone DREAM Act were (at least temporarily) suspended in April 2013, when most provisions of the proposed bill were rolled into the comprehensive immigration reform package introduced by the Senate's bipartisan "Gang of Eight."[22] Regardless of the outcome of the current round of legislative debates over comprehensive immigration reform, DREAM activists have clearly been among the most effective organizers within the broader field of the immigrant rights movement.

Undocuqueer Leadership

As noted earlier, the leadership of the immigrant youth movement disproportionately identifies as queer. Many DREAM activists are publicly out as
gay, lesbian, bisexual, queer, and/or *jot@*. DREAMer leadership also includes
many transgender people, as well as others who claim unconventional
gender identities or whose gender expression is non-normative. Prerna Lal
has summarized the role of queer undocumented people in a highly accessible article covering the last decade of the immigrant rights movement.[23]
Undocumented queer immigrant rights activists created the web portal
DreamActivist.net in 2007, helped organize Education Not Deportation
(END) campaigns beginning in 2009, and in 2010, led by Chicago's Immigrant Youth Justice League, launched the National Coming Out of the
Shadows Day.[24] In 2011 the National Immigrant Youth Alliance coined the
term "undocuqueer," which has emerged as a powerful shorthand for a
number of complex, intersectional, collective political identities with concrete political demands, such as the inclusion of same-sex couples in the
family reunification provisions of comprehensive immigration reform.
Also in 2011, United We Dream (the largest national DREAMer network)
launched the Queer Undocumented Immigrant Project (QUIP). Queer
undocumented youth led a nationwide escalation of nonviolent civil disobedience on the streets, in political offices, in campaign headquarters,
and even inside detention centers.[25]

Queer DREAMers face additional burdens and pressures. For example,
undocumented people who marry opposite-sex partners may gain legal
status more rapidly, whereas same-sex marriages, possible only in some
states, don't confer the same advantages. In this way, the nation-state
continues to regulate sexual identity and exclude queer folks from full
integration. As one activist stated,

[Immigrant youth] are often able to find, whether it's a friend or someone they
genuinely love, [a way] to get married to them and they're able to get status that
way. But there's a whole group of immigrant youth that don't get married because
they're identified as queer, and so disproportionately the leadership in immigrant
youth movement actually identifies as queer.[26]

At the same time, queer DREAMers often find themselves in the position
of challenging oppressive norms internalized by communities they otherwise feel a part of. Another interviewee described this struggle succinctly:

"If you're in a queer space, do you tell them you're undocumented, or if you're in an undocumented space, do you tell them you're queer?"[27] The artistic collective DREAMers Adrift addresses these challenges in part through illustrations, poster art, and videos that explore intersectional identity and the idea of a "movement within the movement." They challenge homophobia within immigrant communities more broadly and the immigrant rights movement specifically, and also challenge anti-immigrant narratives within the queer community. As Julio Salgado from DREAMers Adrift put it, "Guess what? You're part of an oppressed group; do not oppress other groups."[28]

Undocuqueer leadership has also played a key role in innovative media strategies, such as "coming out" as undocumented. Undocuqueer leaders organized a national day of action on which undocumented youth publicly declared their immigration status on Facebook:

> The DREAM Act has been around for more than ten years, and it had taken a whole decade for us to do something like this. And not even publicly, although in Chicago they had a public event where seven students went to the Federal Plaza and had a whole press conference, and one by one said "My name is blah blah blah, and I'm undocumented, and I support the DREAM Act." ... The conversations were tough. There's a lot of fear. Some people said it's the perfect way of just giving ourselves up.... So it's a risk, but I think for many of us it's just been too long.[29]

The same interviewee said that a DREAMer collective she was part of had extensively discussed and been inspired by LGBTQ coming-out videos on YouTube as a strategy to build queer visibility. Their Facebook campaign made intentional reference to the long history of the queer movement, and to the YouTube genre of the coming-out video.[30] Overall, undocuqueer youth mobilize their own fluency with digital media tools and skills in the service of visibility strategies that parallel (and are part of) those of the LGBTQ movement.

DREAM Activists and Transmedia Organizing

Transmedia organizing involves creating cross-platform media, inviting the movement base to participate in media production, and linking attention directly to action. DREAM activists employ all three strategies. First, while DREAMers have been highly visible in social media spaces, they by no means limit their media activism to the Internet. Rather, they use social media within a broader set of media practices, including print publishing, appearances on Spanish-language commercial radio and television shows, and, most crucially, face-to-face presentations in high schools, at community centers, and in other spaces across the country. Second, DREAMers' generally participatory approach to media-making is notable. Rather than attempt to produce a homogenous message and convince others to disseminate it, DREAM activists use social media to create spaces for conversation. They focus on featuring the stories of undocumented youth and on sharing information about the legislative process across their networks, and they use participatory media to build shared identity. Third, DREAMers make media designed to attract more undocumented youth to the movement.

DREAM activists are producing their own powerful stories, in a wide range of media; these accounts should be the first stop for those interested in learning from the movement.[31] The history of the last decade of organizing by undocumented youth can be seen in the gorgeous graphic art of Julio Salgado,[32] in compelling, humorous, and emotional videos,[33] in thoughtful blogs like *Undocumented and Unafraid* and DreamActivist.net; in poetry, theater, and films, such as *Mi Sueño, Papers*,[34] *Define American*, and *The Dream is Now*, and more. Indeed, media-making across platforms has been one of the key strengths of DREAM activism.[35]

Many (although by no means most) DREAMers are university students, and their cultural work also includes publication of both popular and scholarly texts about their movement. In Los Angeles, DREAM activists at the UCLA Labor Center's Dream Resource Center have produced two books that are must-read accounts of the organizing history of the undocumented youth movement. The first, *Underground Undergrads: UCLA Undocumented Students Speak Out*, was published in 2008. It provides personal stories from undocumented immigrant student leaders, has sold more than ten thousand copies, and has been used as an organizing tool at events across the country.[36] The second, *Undocumented and Unafraid: Tam Tran, Cinthya Felix, and the Immigrant Youth Movement*, published in 2012, highlights the lives of Tran and Felix, pioneering undocumented student organizers. It also narrates the decade-long transformation of a legislative campaign, focused on the first version of the DREAM Act, into a vibrant, multifaceted nationwide movement that brought together those working on immigrant rights, workers' rights, LGBTQ rights, educational justice, and more.[37]

Rogelio Alejandro López has developed a comparative analysis of the media practices of the present-day immigrant youth movement and the farm workers movement. He draws on interviews, findings from participant observation, content analysis, and movement archives to explore how media strategies are situated within organizing models; how strategies from the broadcast era persist, evolve, and change; and how social movement actors articulate their relationship to the media system. In analyzing media practices, repertoires, and tactics from both movements, he finds that both deploy transmedia mobilization, take great care to shift mass media frames, have participatory media cultures, ground their media practice in organizing needs, and are innovative under conditions of scarce resources.[38] López also finds that, in comparison with the farm workers movement, immigrant youth today have a more developed intersectional analysis of the dynamics of race, class, citizenship, gender, and sexuality in oppression and resistance, have less visible leaders, and use more horizontal organizing structures. Additionally, he proposes that media strategies need not be institutionally formalized or technically sophisticated to have a powerful impact, and that digital media should be seen as an important part of immigrant youth media practices, but not mistaken for the whole. He also notes that grassroots activists all agree on the preeminent importance of face-to-face organizing in movement building.[39]

Transmedia organizing by DREAM activists provides an interesting counterpoint to media literacy efforts in worker centers (as we saw in chapter 5), in part because DREAM Act organizers have grown up surrounded by digital media, social networking sites, and mobile phones. Immigrants to the United States, they are also so-called "digital natives."[40] I use the term cautiously both because it unthinkingly reproduces nativist discourse and because it's important to be wary of universalizing assumptions about young people's facility with computers and digital media. Nevertheless, many DREAM activists I worked with and interviewed did express the view that, in their experience, youth activists in the immigrant rights movement have been among the earliest adopters of digital tools and skills. For example, one student organizer described the importance of blogging to the growth of the Underground Undergrads campus organizing network. Underground Undergrads emerged out of student organizing at UCLA, with support from the UCLA Labor Center. The group later went on to produce a book about its organizing efforts, then launched the

Dream Resource Center. As early as 2006 it set up and maintained a blog about legislative progress, student organizing efforts across campuses, and immigration issues more broadly.[41] This organizer also described the origin of United We Dream, which as of 2013 was the largest, best-resourced, and most visible national organization advocating for DREAMers, though it started as an informal, nationwide blogger network:

That's a really interesting story. It actually was a small group of students that came together and realized the power of media, and felt like they could contribute to the DREAM Act and to issues of undocumented youth through a blog. So they feature a lot of stories of students, they have YouTube videos, they are updating people about the issue. It's also a place where they conduct polls, things like that. That started as something small but spread because this issue obviously affects a lot of students nationwide.[42]

Underground Undergrads was created when an intern decided to put together a blog; it began as a zero-budget, ad hoc project. In comparison with some larger, better-resourced immigrant rights organizations that invest a great deal of resources, time, and energy in top-down public relations strategies, the visibility, size, and impact of DREAM activist organizing have grown rapidly.

This growth can be attributed in large part not just to the technological skills of younger, digitally capable people but to DREAMers' active approach to a praxis of critical digital media literacy. DREAM Act organizers systematically share media-making and communication skills across their networks in formal and informal workshops as well as online skill-sharing events. Rather than attempt to produce a homogenous message and convince others to disseminate it, they use commercial blogging and video platforms to create spaces for conversation. These spaces are open to immigrant youth across the country who occupy similar positions, and who come to develop shared identities and political goals. DREAM Act organizers and activists focus on the stories of other undocumented youth, as well as on sharing information about the legislative process. They also use social media to build a conversation, create a shared identity, and develop participatory strategy. Perhaps most important, DREAM activism is not "online activism" alone. For example, Underground Undergrads developed a blog hand in hand with a printed book that was used to organize face-to-face presentations to high school students across the country. The blog was initially conceived as a way to maintain contact with high school students who attended presentations by DREAM activists. DREAM activists thus engage in their own forms of transmedia organizing. They provide multiple entry points to a larger narrative that extends across platforms, beginning with face-to-face presentations and maintaining contact online, while encouraging participatory media-making throughout.

Like any social movement, DREAM activism has its share of internal tensions. One organizer described a split between student groups at one of the University of California campuses, and provided insight into the way activists use social media to facilitate the development of ad hoc movement groups. Students frustrated with a vertical organizing model at UCLA formed a Facebook group, initially as a kind of backchannel where they could express discontent and critique. This group was soon perceived by others as a new organization: "They gave us an identity—because we formed a Facebook group, we were automatically a group."[43] This took place even though the initial creators of the group considered it a "loose network." The influx of students who were interested in developing a more participatory movement space brought additional energy, and soon the group expanded beyond UCLA to additional campuses, as well as to students from high schools and middle schools. Other people I interviewed also gave examples of how social media had facilitated the ad hoc formation of new movement groups. For instance, in the aftermath of Proposition 8, the organizer of a Facebook group called Queer Koreans individually contacted all those who had joined the group. Almost overnight, they agreed to launch a new organization, called KUE (pronounced "Q," for queer), Korean-Americans United for Equality.[44]

I suggest that DREAMers ground their media practices in concrete organizing needs and use every opportunity to invite deeper engagement with the movement. The work of the graphic artist Julio Salgado provides an additional window into this dynamic. Salgado creates artwork that, in its online forms, includes links to actions that viewers can take. For example, he produced a series of illustrations of undocumented, DREAM Act–eligible youth who were detained and facing deportation. These illustrations included links to online petitions organized by families and supporters of these youth, as well as to campaigns encouraging calls to elected officials and detention center administrators to urge their release. In an interview, Salgado also repeatedly emphasized that his artistic work is used by activists as they organize. For example, videos produced by DREAMers Adrift are played in community meetings:

In my case, I can draw, and Jesús is an amazing spoken word artist. He does these great things with editing. So using that talent definitely goes into the movement, because people use those videos when they're having a meeting, when they're facilitating a know-your-rights campaign, they've used these things that we've made.[45]

Movement media, whether social media, videos, books, spoken word, posters, or other forms, provide opportunities for organizers to engage people face to face. This leads us to the central question of this chapter: How did isolated, undocumented youth come together over the past decade to form new political identities, step into leadership roles in the immigrant rights movement, and win both cultural shifts and policy victories?

Pathways to Participation

Many social movement scholars argue for a biographical or "life-course" analysis of social movements. Put simply, this means exploring those aspects of social movement participation that unfold over the course of an individual's life, rather than focusing solely on the shorter-term, more easily quantifiable elements. For example, Doug McAdam explored the biographical consequences of participation in Freedom Summer by interviewing participants decades later.[46] Donatella Della Porta calls for social movement scholars to pay careful attention to the life histories of individual activists.[47] Silke Rothe, in a long-term study of the Coalition of Labor Union Women, takes a biographical approach to understanding women's social movement participation.[48] Manuel Castells dedicated the entire second volume of his *Information Age* trilogy to the power of social movement identity, including an extensive analysis of how individuals arrive at shared "resistance identities" and "project identities" through long-term social movement participation.[49] Verta Taylor and Nancy Whittier, in a case study of lesbian feminist collectives, explored how individual activists come to take part in collective identity formation over time,[50] while James Jasper emphasized the role of both cultural context and individual biography in the formation of strong social movements.[51] A biographical or life-course approach is also useful to understanding the contemporary immigrant rights movement.

Biographical social movement scholarship tells us that the most common pathways to movement participation are through family, friends, community, and direct lived experience. We also know from both surveys and biographical studies that many activists move from one group to another. An initial movement experience often shapes the subsequent life course of participants. Put plainly, people become engaged in one movement group, and that experience shapes the rest of their lives. They often become more deeply politicized, and go on to participate in additional social movement activity. This is the case for many DREAM activists. For example, one activist described her politicization as a high school student by the organization Inner City Struggle in the early 2000s: "I always go back to that organizing because I think that is where I learned all those skills I then put into use, to the immigrant rights organizing work."[52] Several years later, as an undergraduate at UCLA, she became involved with the student immigrant rights organizing group IDEAS. This is not an uncommon experience; many immigrant rights activists describe moving from group to group. Often, they cut their teeth on student organizing, then pass through multiple movement organizations, from informal groups and collectives to paid organizing positions:

I've been doing immigrant rights work for about, I guess it's six years now, maybe going on seven.... I locally organize here with the Student Immigrant Movement, so I consider myself a member of the Student Immigrant Movement. Nationally I work with the United We Dream Network, and I was also a part of DREAMActivists.org as that came together, which is another kind of national network. So that's where I kind of cut my teeth organizing, and now I became associated with presente.org.[53]

I heard many stories like this one, beginning with activists' participation in an initial ad hoc or informal movement group, followed by connection to national or transnational networks, and then occasionally moving into full-time organizing work.

Taking part in mass mobilizations and large-scale protest actions also profoundly shapes one's sense of social movement identity. Mass mobilizations have life-course impacts, as well as their more frequently studied if less often successful policy impacts. One interviewee who now works as a paid online organizer at a national immigrant rights organization described the massive 2006 marches against the Sensenbrenner bill (discussed in chapter 1) as a key inspiration for his own decision to apply his blogging and media-making skills to immigrant rights work.[54] Following that experience, he decided to use the media skills he had honed as editor of a college newspaper to create a blog tracing the steps of an immigrant coming to the United States on a long, dangerous route from Central America. He also noted that by creating media about their own experiences, undocumented youth become movement actors and take part in shaping history.

In addition to politicization along the path from group to group, or through participation in mass mobilizations, activists deepen their involvement by learning directly from other, more seasoned activists. For example, the DREAMers I interviewed often wove a complicated tapestry when describing where they learned how to use media as an organizing tool. Most teach themselves new tools and techniques; they consider social media to be something they understand "naturally" as part of everyday life. At the same time, many also attend formal training sessions, events, and conferences, where they learn media tools and strategies from other DREAMers, immigrant rights activists, or other progressives. Many mention conferences such as Netroots Nation, capacity-building organizations such as the New Organizing Institute, and progressive blogs as influences. In addition, they talk about past social movements, as well as key individual organizers and educators. For example, many United We Dream leaders learned about public narrative from Marshall Ganz, who worked with Saul Alinsky and Cesar Chavez as an organizer with the United Farm Workers.[55]

Learning from Other Movements

While some interviewees felt that certain kinds of student organizing had a tendency to split the interests of immigrant students away from those of workers, others noted a reverse dynamic. Students organizing against the University of California fee hikes specifically went to great lengths to link student and worker organizations. In addition, these partnerships occasionally challenge the assumption that youth organizers are always on the cutting edge of digital media use. In at least one case, interviewees pointed out that student organizers also learned digital media practices from migrant worker organizations. For example, when I asked where student activists got ideas about how to use digital media as an organizing tool, one interviewee had this to say:

They set up a television in the park while there was a basketball game, like this Oaxacan town was battling another Oaxacan town, and in the basketball court, around the side, the research center had a huge television with [Video conferencing platform] Oovoo running. So that way, they made a *convocación* [invitation to participate] out in the town, saying, "There's going to be a basketball game in Los Angeles in this hour, if you want to talk to your family, come to the plaza, and there'll be a television and you could see your family." First to teach them how to use a phone over Oovoo, but also so they could just say hi. So a lot of people would be, like, "Oh God, I haven't seen you in ten years!" and they would see each other over television and we would all get to watch them.[56]

As we saw in chapter 4, migrants use digital media tools to build translocal communities. Translocal media practices in the Oaxacan community inspired student organizers to use videoconferencing tools during their own movement events. New tools and skills flow across interconnected social movement networks, to be deployed when the moment arises.

Organizers also look to other social movement media practices (from beyond immigrant rights activism) for ideas. For example, one interviewee described a specific style of participatory video production used by the Occupy movement that she hoped to incorporate into the repertoire of DREAM activist media practices:

Something we talked about before is like with the Occupy movement, they have videos where they show people holding up this paper that say their story. So kind of incorporating that and trying to humanize the issue of being undocumented.[57]

Activists talk about looking to predecessors within their own organizations, as well as to other movement groups and networks, for inspirational uses of media as an organizing tool. Many choose to explore new tools after seeing an example of their effective deployment elsewhere, and do so in an ad-hoc, hands-on process of experimentation rather than through formal training. One described this as a "do and learn process."[58]

Mediated Pathways: Make Media, Make Trouble

As I participated in immigrant rights mobilizations, engaged in media workshops, and interviewed organizers, I noticed an interesting pattern. When I asked people how they initially became involved in the immigrant

rights movement, many (although certainly not all) described some combination of being inspired by a media text, connecting to others through
social media, or taking part in a media-making activity. Among other
pathways, many individuals become connected to social movements
through viewing, sharing, and making media. Most conversations about
social movements' use of ICTs emphasize their importance as tactical tools
for mobilization, fundraising, or information circulation. Some focus on
the ways in which social movements are able to reach new audiences on
the net. Few emphasize the importance of the media-making process itself.
Yet making media, especially making media together with others in the
heat of a campaign or mass mobilization, can be a powerful force for social
movement identity formation.[59]

As digital media literacy spreads, more people than ever before are creating social movement media, with largely unstudied implications. Many
immigrant rights activists expressed the idea that the media-making process
itself is a powerful movement-building force. Recent work by scholars at
the University of Southern California also supports this point. Arely Zimmerman conducted an extensive case study of how DREAM activists use
new media to foster what she and the Civic Paths working group describe
as *participatory politics*. Based on interviews, fieldwork, and content analysis, Zimmerman argues that the affordances of new media support youth
political engagement. She emphasizes that undocumented youth use blogs,
social media, and video to build shared identity, create community, and
form networks, and that these activities in turn increase their feelings of
self-worth and political efficacy. Zimmerman also finds that online communities initially focused on friendship and interest-driven activity can
become politicized spaces, feeding into formal political participation. She
maintains that DREAMers' use of new media strategies is grounded in
traditional community organizing approaches, and encourages scholars to
view new media strategies from a perspective that recognizes the continued
importance of face-to-face movement organizations and community
institutions.[60]

Made in L.A.

Active participation in documentary film production can also be important
to social movement identity formation. One organizer I met took part in

the creation of *Made in L.A.*, an award-winning documentary about garment worker organizing, and described this process as crucial to her own politicization. She emphasized that one of the most important outcomes of the film was the set of connections formed between people and organizations that worked with the filmmakers:

I became involved with the anti-sweatshop student movement at Cal State L.A. because I worked at a sweatshop, my mother worked at a sweatshop, my whole family, my uncles, they worked for, they had a little business. They were the *costureros* [clothesmakers] themselves, right?... I think the one project that I was the most proud of was helping Almudena Carracedo transcribe interviews with garment workers for her film, *Made in L.A.* She actually interviewed me, but gosh! That woman interviewed a bunch of people and it was a three-, four-year project that took her four years to finish. And it was great! And I liked the outcome, and especially the connections that she made. And the fact that that film got distributed all over the world.[61]

Following this experience, she became increasingly involved in social movement activity. Currently she works with the Amanecer Collective, an anarchist affinity group that she calls her "political home." The group meets regularly via phone conferences, and once a year face to face. They also have a radio collective, Echos de Libertad (Echoes of Liberty), that produces a two-hour radio show for the online radio station Killradio.org. At the time of the interview they were preparing to begin broadcasts on a new pirate FM station in East L.A.

Media production practices in the immigrant rights movement thus generate new movement participants. Digital media tools enable these practices, and the media that emerges is widely circulated via the Internet. However, the Internet is not always the primary point of connection for media-makers, and transmedia organizing practices do not necessarily require always-on Internet connectivity. Another interviewee, who works as a social media consultant for immigrant rights organizations, emphasized that he finds the process of participatory video production to have great value, even in situations of limited Internet access.[62] Of course, the videos produced in his media-making workshops are later circulated online, but he maintains that a significant part of the value for movement building is in the actual experience of face-to-face collaborative production.

Propagandists of all ideological stripes have long shared a dream: to make media so compelling that the reader or viewer feels moved to join the cause. Although this does occasionally take place, it may be the least common pathway to participation. However, it does happen: one activist described how an organization's online presence, specifically its Facebook page, served as a tool to recruit her as a DREAM activist. She strongly identified with a video produced by the Student Immigrant Movement that described the personal story of one of the organizers:

I was undocumented, my family was going back to Brazil and I really, really felt like these students from the stuff that they put on their Facebook. They had videos of the kids running after the bus, they had a video of Mario telling his story, and then when I saw those videos I was like, "I am one of those students." Right away I wanted to be a part of them, and that's what I did. I was living forty-five minutes south of Boston and I came all the way on the commuter rail, just to check 'em out. When I met the organizer I was like, "I want to be a part of you guys, tell me what to do."[63]

In this case, DIY video not only helped generate shared movement identity among the video producers, it also provided a touchpoint to bring a new person into the movement through face-to-face organizing.

Who Controls the Story? Public Narrative, Messaging, and Framing.

Public narrative is a key mechanism for the production of collective identity and for social movement formation. The messages and frames employed in that narrative have important implications for the kind of movement that emerges. In a certain sense, whoever controls the story controls—or at least shapes—the movement. Indeed, over the past decade, DREAM activists have struggled mightily over the public narrative that swirls around them. They have argued with mainstream immigrant rights groups over the issue of whether to push for stand-alone DREAM Act legislation in the absence of comprehensive immigration reform and debated internally over the 'good immigrant/bad immigrant' narrative they were placed into by political operatives from both parties. They have wrestled with the language of "we are not criminals" and "we are not terrorists," discourse that reinforces the master narratives of an out-of-control criminal justice system and the "war on terror." DREAMers have discussed, and decided to move away from, the argument "we were brought here through no fault of our own," a statement that pits "good"' DREAMers against their own "lawbreaking" parents. Most recently, as they have gained visibility, they have encountered the challenge of how to work with powerful, highly skilled media producers. These ostensible allies sometimes create high-production-value media that are compelling and beautiful, but delinked from accountability to existing social movement processes. (I return to this dynamic in chapter 7.) This section explores how DREAMers make collective decisions about the public narrative of their movement. DREAMers consciously shape public narratives, struggle to control the frame, and work to shift public opinion, while building their own movement base and coordinating with other elements of the immigrant rights movement and beyond. They do this through face-to-face organizing, developing and executing strategic media plans, making decisions about shared messaging, forming media teams, and through formal and informal learning focused on both traditional PR skills and new media tools.

Several recent scholarly works provide an in-depth analysis not only of DREAM activism but specifically of DREAM activists' attempts to shape public discourse. Claudia Anguiano's 2011 doctoral dissertation uses critical race theory to analyze shifts in the discursive strategies of undocumented youth over the period 2001–2010.[64] She draws on her own extensive participation in the movement as well as on interviews with activists, and finds three key phases in DREAMer discourse. From 2001 to 2007, Anguiano observes, DREAM activists focused on creating a shared group identity as "exceptional students" to counter the dehumanizing right-wing frame of the "illegal alien." From 2007 to 2009, she found, self-identification as "undocumented and unafraid" served to build national coalitions that were able to take the stage as political actors. After 2010, she describes a marked identity shift to "unapologetic DREAMers," who burst into national consciousness through high-risk civil disobedience tactics.[65] My own movement-based research, including media training, mobilization participation, and interviews, supports these arguments. Notably, each of these shifts was accomplished not through top-down "message discipline" but through discussions and intentional processes of shared storytelling among committed activists. Today, in 2014, storytelling strategy continues to be an important component of immigrant rights organizing. While it often emerges organically during the formative stages of social movements, later it is increasingly adopted by more formal organizations and institutions. For example, groups like Underground Undergrads and DreamActivist.org initially emerged in part as avenues for participatory storytelling by undocumented youth. Later, many of the most visible DREAM activist organizations and networks formalized this approach. In part, this happened through workshops and training sessions that integrated Marshall Ganz's "public narrative" approach to organizing. Ganz famously urged organizers to develop a "story of self, story of us, and story of now."[66] DREAM activist summer training sessions, workshops, gatherings, conference calls, webinars, and the United We Dream National Congress all prominently feature this approach.[67]

As the immigrant youth movement gained steam, DREAM activist organizations proliferated. Since 2000, DREAM activism has developed from ad hoc and informal, campus- and city-level groups and collectives to multiple overlapping multistate and national networks and coalitions. One interviewee described how her work with University of California DREAMers shifted to citywide work with Dream Team L.A. Next, she talked about the process of connecting to a statewide network called the California Dream Team Alliance, followed by participation in the national United We Dream network.[68] As these networks and organizations grow, the process of constructing shared movement identity involves ongoing discussions about messaging and framing, as well as attempts to ensure that members are able to project the shared message and talk to reporters. DREAM activists explicitly create plans to circulate key messages across all platforms, both online and via traditional media (print and broadcast).

One interviewee from Dream Team L.A. described a "traditional media strategy" designed to reach print media, broadcast news media, and magazines, as well as a "social media strategy" to stay connected to supporters and participants via Facebook and Twitter. She said, "For us, it's really important to merge the two." In addition, she mentioned systematic press training at the beginning of campaigns:

Right before we engage in any campaigns, before we engage in any interviews, any lead or source, we really focus a lot on developing our messaging, and really framing our messaging, and developing our members to be able to project that message, right, and be able to really know how to talk to reporters. How not to talk to reporters, how to bring things back to our main goals and objectives.[69]

She talked about how DREAM activists struggle to shape the framing of their movement, not only against anti-immigrant forces but also against larger, better-resourced, immigrant rights groups. DREAMers had to start forming their own media teams in part to redirect frames by ostensible policy allies that depicted them as "model immigrants" and criminalized their parents. In 2010, during the height of the federal DREAM Act campaign, many DREAMers felt uncomfortable with the messaging used by mainstream immigrant rights organizations. For example, one interviewee talked about how professional nonprofits developed PSAs (public service announcements) about undocumented youth that described them as "model immigrants" who came to the United States "through no fault of their own." She and other activists I interviewed felt that this message was developed without input from undocumented youth. They created alternative framing and used it to push back. As she said,

> We use to come back at it like: we were brought here by our courageous parents, who are responsible parents, and wanted their children to have a better life, right? Because we don't want to—we don't have to criminalize our parents.[70]

This activist brought sophisticated media skills she had developed as a high school educational justice organizer to her work on the federal DREAM Act. She discussed writing press releases, developing relationships with reporters, testing messaging and framing with focus groups, and developing clarity about the core values that underlay the frames. Yet rather than assign messaging tasks to single spokespersons or professional communications staff, many DREAMers work to make collective decisions about framing, sound bites, media strategy, and spokespeople.[71] As media and communications chair for an organizing collective, this activist now focuses on working with other DREAMers to help them develop more effective media strategies. Her goal is not only to ensure that DREAMers' voices are heard but also to lift up and humanize the entire immigrant community, which remains under heavy discursive attack. In addition, she emphasizes a media strategy that is led by, and run by, undocumented youth. Another DREAM Act organizer noted the important role of both specialist training and peer-to-peer learning in gaining key skills, such as how to cultivate press contacts, write press releases, and organize press conferences. At the UCLA Labor Center, interns working on A.B. 540 and access to education received media training from professional P.R. consultants. The training sessions focused on how to organize a press conference, establish contacts with professional journalists, and tell the story of undocumented youth without mistakenly placing people at risk.[72] In this case, undocumented student organizers used a "train the trainer" approach. The first training session was provided by a media consultant, and subsequent training sessions were conducted by trained students who also had hands-on campaign experience.

Pathways to Participation: Conclusions

Undocumented youth have been organizing for more than a decade to attain regularization of their immigration status, both as part of the broader immigrant rights movement and in the struggle for a stand-alone DREAM Act. The Obama administration's 2012 announcement of the DACA program, while only a small step forward, was a hard-won victory earned by undocumented youth through a combination of inside and outside tactics, including direct action and sit-ins in streets, offices, and campaign headquarters across the country. DREAMers use innovative transmedia organizing tactics to build visibility, circulate their messages, and strengthen movement identity through participatory media-making.

DREAMers travel diverse pathways into the immigrant rights movement. Some move from group to group, for example by getting involved in high school organizing around access to education, fair trade, or workers' rights, then connecting to the immigrant rights movement. Others are politicized through mass mobilizations: many specifically joined the movement after the mass marches and walkouts of 2006. Still others are mentored by seasoned activists who are respected members of their communities. In addition, there are a number of mediated pathways to movement participation. Media production, circulation, and reception all provide possible entry points to movement work. Making media, in particular, often provides a powerful experience that shapes social movement identity and, frequently, has longer-term impacts on people's lives. Among the immigrant rights activists whom I worked with and interviewed, some initially became involved through working on a media production project, such as a film. Others connected through media bridging work, by acting as curators or amplifiers of movement media made by others—for example, by helping to promote an action by circulating flyers, physically or through social media. A smaller number described media reception as their pathway to participation: they saw a video, contacted a local organization to attend a face-to-face meeting, and eventually became movement leaders themselves.

Participation in movement media-making thus provides an entry point to further politicization and deeper involvement. This dynamic is not limited to social media. For example, it also had an impact on those who took part in the production of the documentary film *Made in L.A,* and those involved in participatory video and audio production workshops. Media-making may have always provided pathways to participation in social movements, but the growth of digital media literacy has greatly expanded these paths. The spread of audiovisual production skills to a broader set of participants also influences the movement's public narrative. Undocumented youth are increasingly able to tell their own stories, and connect their own story to the larger story of the movement, through media that they themselves produce. At the same time, traditional press strategies, including skills such as organizing press conferences, developing talking points, staying on message, and deploying frames and messages that adhere to the movement's objectives, are all seen by organizers as fundamental components of movement media strategy. Transmedia organizers explicitly understand the need to develop participatory media strategies that play out in social media while simultaneously mobilizing resources to gain coverage in print and broadcast outlets.

The development of a powerful public narrative has been crucial to DREAM activism. During earlier stages of the movement, most undocumented youth kept their citizenship status hidden from public view. As more and more DREAMers abandoned secrecy, came out as undocumented, and became more visible across the media ecology, they found it increasingly easy to organize actions, gather supporters, and increase event turnout. One organizer spoke of 2010 as a year of "big victories" in terms of mobilization and public visibility. Although the federal DREAM Act failed to pass (by five votes), more than 250 undocumented students mobilized on Capitol Hill for weeks. The organizer described the shift as follows:

We just became fearless, and it just became a lot easier to organize people to our actions because we didn't have to keep it a secret. We could put it all over Facebook, we could tell the media. At one of our events, we did it at a church and we got over 400 people inside the church. We didn't even take, it was two weeks of organizing to get 400 people there. It wasn't an extensive amount of organizing that we did. So it was really powerful that a lot of people came, and we didn't expect that.[73]

Ultimately, transmedia organizers hope to build movement participation, shift public opinion, win policy victories, and win both symbolic and material gains. Although passage of the federal DREAM Act was initially the key policy outcome around which DREAM activists organized, it is no longer their main goal. One interviewee described the DREAM Act vote in 2010 as a huge victory, even though the bill failed to pass. He felt that organizing around the vote "changed the public opinion in this country of what undocumented workers are," citing polls at the time that showed between 60 percent and 70 percent of the American people supporting DREAMers.[74] He emphasized that this was an unprecedented level of support, and an indicator of a broader cultural shift. The same organizer also felt that some of the most important victories came from local organizing that led to state-level DREAM Acts, specifically in Maryland, Connecticut, Illinois, and California.[75]

Queer undocumented youth have led the DREAM activist movement, and the broader immigrant rights movement, into ever-greater visibility and power. They have developed innovative forms of transmedia organizing across social media, mass media, and community media spaces. DREAMers receive extensive print and broadcast coverage as they engage in nonviolent civil disobedience and direct action. They develop media-savvy protest tactics that leverage arrests, detentions, and deportations to build awareness of their struggle. Print and broadcast media now regularly cover these activities and help DREAMers reach a much broader audience, although many activists find message control in these platforms difficult. Faced with tactical escalation, nonviolent civil disobedience, sit-ins, and direct actions, increasingly sophisticated management of public narrative, and a broader cultural shift that includes public opinion tilting toward widespread support for regularization of undocumented youth, in 2013 the U.S. Congress had no choice but to put comprehensive immigration reform back on the table. Also by 2013, multiple professionally produced transmedia campaigns focused on the DREAMers and on immigration reform. The next chapter explores the opportunities and challenges these campaigns present for the immigrant rights movement.

Figure 7.1
Screenshot from FWD.us.
Source: FWD.us.

7 Define American, The Dream is Now, and FWD.us: Professionalization and Accountability in Transmedia Organizing

Real reform means strong border security, and we can build on the progress my administration has already made—putting more boots on the southern border than at any time in our history, and reducing illegal crossings to their lowest levels in 40 years. Real reform means establishing a responsible pathway to earned citizenship— a path that includes passing a background check, paying taxes and a meaningful penalty, learning English and going to the back of the line behind the folks trying to come here legally.... Our economy is stronger when we harness the talents and ingenuity of striving, hopeful immigrants. And right now, leaders from the business, labor, law enforcement, and faith communities all agree that the time has come to pass comprehensive immigration reform.

—President Barack Obama, State of the Union address, 2013

As President Barack Obama's second term unfolded, comprehensive immigration reform again took center stage. At the beginning of 2013, a group of U.S. senators known as the "Gang of Eight," including Republican senators McCain, Graham, Flake, and Rubio and Democrats Schumer, Durbin, Menendez, and Bennet, announced their intentions to develop a bipartisan comprehensive immigration reform bill. Soon after, the Obama administration leaked its own version of an immigration bill, and signaled that it would be introduced to both houses of Congress unless representatives and senators moved quickly to bring their own bills out of committee. Both the Senate framework and Obama's proposal contained the same set of provisions as the last several attempts at comprehensive immigration reform. Both began with an emphasis on heightened enforcement, continued border militarization, and a nationwide expansion of the federal E-Verify system to all employers. Both included a process to naturalize DREAMers, if they enrolled in college or the military and were "morally upstanding." Each proposal included an expanded guest worker program, designed to allow the agricultural industry to bring in migrant workers to harvest crops at low wages. Finally, both included a "pathway to citizenship" for undocumented immigrants who registered, paid a fine, paid back taxes, learned English, and "went to the back of the line."

The immigration bill that passed the Senate in 2013 was nearly identical to the proposed 2007 bill, but the political context had shifted. Mitt Romney's defeat in the 2012 elections drove home a reality that the Republican Party was no longer able to ignore: the Latin@ electorate is huge, overwhelmingly in favor of immigration reform, and voted for Obama by a margin of 44 percentage points nationwide.[1] Latin@s now make up 17 percent of the U.S. population, and their numbers are growing, including in many states that have traditionally been Republican Party strongholds.[2] To put it bluntly, the Republican leadership knows that the party must shift on immigration if it hopes to attract Latin@ voters. What's more, the fact has hit home that the party must broaden its base beyond Anglo conservatives if it wants to remain viable in the twenty-first century.

Transmedia Organizing: The New Normal?

One of the most striking aspects of the current stage of mobilization around immigration reform is the rise of transmedia organizing as a mainstream strategy. Organizing efforts that center storytelling by undocumented people, that operate across platforms, and that provide multiple opportunities for people to contribute their own voice have begun to proliferate rapidly. This approach is moving quickly from the margins to the center. Most of the transmedia organizing practices described throughout this book arose organically from grassroots networks, in part out of necessity. The transmedia organizing we have explored so far was often cobbled together, in a context of lack of access to the resources needed to run traditional, top-down messaging campaigns. However, by 2012–2013 larger, better-resourced groups and institutions had begun to adopt transmedia organizing. There are many examples, but it is worth describing the three best-resourced efforts to date in more detail: Define American, The Dream is Now, and FWD.us.

Define American

On June 22, 2011, Pulitzer Prize–winning journalist Jose Antonio Vargas came out as undocumented in an essay in the *New York Times Magazine* titled "My Life as an Undocumented Immigrant."[3] He was inspired to do so by four undocumented students who walked from Miami to Washington to raise awareness of the federal DREAM Act, in an action known as the Trail of Dreams.[4] In the essay, Vargas tells his story. He reveals how, as a young undocumented student born in the Philippines and sent to live with his grandparents in Mountain View, California, he negotiated one hurdle after the next. He had help from family, friends, and allies: the grandfather who doctored his Social Security card at Kinko's so that he could find employment; the high school choir teacher who changed a planned class trip from Japan to Hawaii so that Vargas could participate; the school principal who helped him find a college scholarship that was agnostic about his immigration status. In one moving section, he describes coming out as gay in his high school history class after watching a documentary about Harvey Milk, then writes, "Tough as it was, coming out about being gay seemed less daunting than coming out about my legal status."[5] Vargas describes the delicate dance he performed as a staff reporter at the *Washington Post*, working hard and climbing the ladder, but always living in fear that his status would be discovered.

After his essay appeared in the *New York Times Magazine*, Vargas became a visible and vocal activist for immigrant rights. In June 2012 he wrote a cover story for *Time* magazine that described the long struggle of undocumented immigrants for public visibility and the battle for comprehensive immigration reform.[6] He was accompanied on *Time*'s cover by the faces of more than a dozen undocumented youth, themselves DREAMers and leaders in the immigrant rights movement, several of whom I interviewed for this book. Vargas, who is queer and undocumented, has continued to use his visibility and credibility in both mainstream and movement circles to launch a transmedia campaign called Define American (http://defineamerican.org). Define American encourages people to produce and upload videos discussing what it means to be American; material from these videos has been woven into Vargas's feature-length documentary film, *Documented*, that at the time of this writing is appearing in major film festivals and is scheduled for broadcast on CNN. Define American was explicitly conceived, implemented, and promoted as a transmedia organizing campaign.

I talked with one of the project staff, who has worked in the past with the Harry Potter Alliance to foster fan activism and connect people to civic action through transmedia strategies and "cultural acupuncture."[7] He described working with the project team to leverage the theatrical release of the film *Man of Steel* to generate attention to immigration reform through the meme "Superman is an Immigrant" (see http://wearetheamericanway.tumblr.com).[8] Several activists who were interviewed for this book specifically mentioned Vargas's coming out and the Define American campaign as catalysts for their own decision to publicly reveal their own undocumented status, as well as for inspiring their own journey to deeper social movement participation.[9] The campaign has thus successfully linked a powerful narrative frame, participatory media-making, and a media strategy that crosses platforms. Vargas has sustained this narrative from the *New York Times* to the *Colbert Report*, from *Time* magazine to YouTube videos, and from social media platforms to a feature-length documentary. Define American has also linked storytelling directly to legislative action, as well as to community organizing efforts; Vargas frequently includes DREAM Act organizing and the broader immigrant rights movement when discussing his own history and immigration status.

Define American is a transmedia organizing campaign that is largely led and staffed by undocumented people, immigrant rights activists, and close allies. The campaign often highlights the stories of immigrant rights activists. It frames these stories in ways that are consistent with the public narrative the broader movement decides to project. For example, Define American avoids the problematic "we are not criminals" framing. This frame has been extensively promoted by Spanish-language mass media (as we saw in chapter 1) but has the unintended consequence of dividing immigrants into "good" and "bad," while reinforcing a master narrative about criminality that provides support for the continued growth of the already bloated prison industry. From its inception, the Define American campaign also intentionally moved away from a '"DREAMers-first" narrative to include voices across a wide range of age groups, countries of national origin, class backgrounds, educational levels, and so on. While it lacks a formal accountability mechanism, the leadership and staff of Define American, many of them activists with deep ties to the immigrant rights movement, have kept the project's goals, messaging, and actions linked to the needs of the movement's social base.

The Dream is Now

In 2012, Laurene Powell Jobs, widow of Apple cofounder Steve Jobs, launched a transmedia campaign called The Dream is Now (http://www .thedreamisnow.org). This campaign initially focused on building support for the passage of stand-alone DREAM Act legislation. Jobs funded the campaign through the Emerson Collective, her philanthropic organization, and teamed up with Academy Award–winning filmmaker Davis Guggenheim, director of *An Inconvenient Truth* and *Waiting for Superman*, to produce the project. The Dream is Now was conceived as a public communications campaign designed to educate a broad spectrum of people about the human stories that lie behind the highly politicized debates over immigration policy. Visitors to TheDreamisNow.org are encouraged to watch videos of DREAMers telling their stories, and, as on the Define American site, to record and upload their own videos. Those who do so are encouraged to think about the act of sharing their personal story as "joining the movement," and storytelling is framed as a radical new form of political organizing. In addition, visitors are asked to sign a petition supporting passage of the DREAM Act (or at least, this was the case during the first several months of the site's launch).

As The Dream is Now built momentum in the spring of 2013, I had the opportunity to participate in several meetings and calls with the project team. The producers had many conversations with immigrant rights activists, some of whom repeatedly asked how they planned to use the attention their campaign was sure to generate to help support the existing organizations and campaigns that DREAMERs themselves had built over the years. In general, The Dream is Now team seemed to feel that informal conversations with activists would be enough to guide their efforts. In addition, they soon put out a call for paid community organizers, whose mission would be to travel to college campuses across the country, organize screenings, and capture more stories in HD video. Many activists questioned how The Dream is Now organizers would relate to existing movement networks like United We Dream (UWD), DreamActivist.net, the National Immigrant Youth Alliance, and so on. For example, UWD had been running a Share Your Story project for some time.[10] Videos submitted through UWD's Share Your Story project were nowhere near as nicely produced as those uploaded to The Dream is Now, yet the process of gathering the stories was more closely linked to UWD's nationwide ground game. UWD's Share Your Story project was designed to directly connect DREAMers to an existing network of organizers, training, actions, and events built up over a decade of community organizing. Participatory media-making was, for UWD, linked to a complex strategy involving movement identity building, public narrative and public opinion shifts, and state- and federal-level policy demands.

Most critically, The Dream is Now project was initially developed with an exclusive focus on passage of a stand-alone DREAM Act. However, as comprehensive immigration reform came back on the table in early 2013, most DREAM activists switched from an emphasis on stand-alone DREAM Act legislation to efforts to move a comprehensive bill, one that would include the best possible provisions for undocumented youth alongside regularization of all eleven million undocumented people. This shift was carefully discussed at face-to-face convenings of DREAM activists across the country, including at the nationwide UWD summit in Kansas City in December 2012. There, more than six hundred "Dream Warriors" from across the United States came to consensus to switch from a focus on a stand-alone DREAM Act and a public narrative that primarily emphasized the stories of DREAMers to a focus on comprehensive immigration reform and a narrative of "all 11 million." This meant a different demand: immigration policy reform that would benefit every undocumented person living in the United States.[11] In light of the broad consensus among DREAMers themselves about how to frame their stories in 2013, multiple activists asked The Dream is Now team to consider shifting its overall message, including the language of the petition drive, to reflect the new context. The team declined to make the change, and when the project launched, it included a petition calling for passage of a stand-alone DREAM Act.

Eventually, The Dream is Now did change its petition language to fit the context of the actual comprehensive immigration reform bill. More important, it began to shift its frame to call for immigration reform that would provide a pathway to citizenship not only for undocumented youth but also for their families. Yet initially, by launching its own petition over the express objections and criticism of movement activists, using an outdated framing, and failing to link to existing campaigns and organizations, The Dream is Now team's efforts were delinked from the organizing priorities of the immigrant rights movement. At each step of the way, this team of experienced media-makers fumbled attempts to connect with the movement on the ground. Charitably explained, this may well have been from a lack of experience, as they also seemed ignorant of movement history. For example, the original version of the DREAM Act had three pathways to citizenship: through a college degree, military service, or community service. Most DREAMers I talked to preferred that the community service option be included, since most can't afford a college degree and many oppose the military on moral grounds. Yet The Dream is Now petition mentioned only college and the military, ignoring the community service option, and the short film produced by the team prominently highlights the potential importance of DREAMers to the future viability of the U.S. military.

The site also had weak "do no harm" protections. Along with other activists from the UndocuTech project, I advised The Dream is Now team that, as people uploaded their stories, it would be crucial to warn them prior to upload that they not share any story that could potentially put them at greater risk, trigger deportation, negatively impact their chances to apply for DACA or for other regularized status once the bill went through, and so on. However, the site designers implemented only a boilerplate privacy warning.

As mentioned, the organization also hired a team of community organizers who focused on visiting college campuses, where they met with student groups that already supported immigration reform. These organizers were tasked with shooting and uploading high-quality video stories from supportive students. This took place at the same time as movement groups such as UWD received large grants to hire additional community organizers in the push for comprehensive immigration reform, thus placing The Dream is Now and UWD in direct competition to hire media-savvy immigrant rights activists. Some organizers floated an alternative proposal: The Dream is Now could work closely with community organizers from existing DREAM activist networks and provide movement activists with media production trainings and higher-quality cameras in exchange for good-quality videos of DREAMer stories. This proposal was ignored. Although The Dream is Now producers eventually agreed to change some of their language to reflect the broader movement's goals, at each step of the way, grassroots organizers as well as D.C. insiders struggled to communicate with the media production team about the evolving social movement strategy.

Overall, the project created a beautiful, nicely produced video, and managed to attract a good deal of mass media attention. It amplified the voices of undocumented youth, including Erika Andiola, one of the leaders of the Arizona DREAM Coalition, and contributed to the movement's broader efforts to use public narrative, shift public opinion, and advance concrete policy goals. The Dream is Now has evolved, learned from past mistakes, and made significant strides toward becoming an amplifier of stories from within the immigrant rights movement. My point here is thus not at all to denigrate the efforts of The Dream is Now project. It is a powerful, high-production-value, transmedia campaign that has served an important purpose, not least in helping to shape the public conversation during the 2013 debates in Congress. However, at least in the initial stages, the project repeatedly stumbled because it lacked accountability. It did not build a strong connection to the immigrant rights movement. It included undocumented youth as camera subjects and as powerful voices, but it failed to meaningfully include them in framing, decision making, and strategic process. By failing to implement a concrete accountability mechanism, The Dream is Now suffered both ethical and practical problems. Ethically, the project sacrificed accountability and democratic process for speed and efficiency. Practically, this resulted in demands that were out of sync with the movement and overall reduced impact: a transmedia campaign delinked from the social movement base is far less able to leverage attention for meaningful action.

FWD.us

The first transmedia campaign this chapter explored came more or less organically from the immigrant rights movement: as described above, Define American is a transmedia organizing campaign led by queer undocumented author and activist Jose Antonio Vargas, and staffed by many DREAMers themselves. The second transmedia campaign discussed here, The Dream is Now, was initiated by a professional filmmaking team. It told DREAMer stories through a very high-production-value, professional documentary aesthetic. However, it had a slightly rocky relationship with movement networks on the ground, wrestled with framing decisions that should have been clear, and tended to move ahead with a centralized approach to action alerts that weren't necessarily linked to grounded movement strategy. The third transmedia campaign for immigrant rights, FWD.us, was created by Silicon Valley.

FWD.us is the most recent entrant into the growing set of transmedia organizing campaigns around immigration reform, and it is another animal entirely. The project was launched in the spring of 2013 by a group of technologists and businesspeople, including Facebook founder and CEO Mark Zuckerberg, LinkedIn cofounder Reid Hoffman, various executives from Dropbox, several Silicon Valley venture capitalists, and Bill Gates. Some of the founders identify as immigrants, and the main narrative they advance is that of the immigrant entrepreneur. In addition, the organization hired experienced political operatives such as Clinton administration official Joe Lockhart and Republican Senate adviser Rob Jesmer to guide their policy strategy.[12]

FWD.us employs many of the same techniques as Define American or The Dream is Now. Like these campaigns, FWD.us calls on the public to share their immigration stories. It models this request by providing short, nicely shot videos of immigrant tech entrepreneurs talking about their life experiences, their desire to become citizens, and the difficulty of doing so under the current system. The website calls on viewers to sign up for a campaign via their Facebook, Twitter, or email account; asks for a signature for an online petition; and asks people to upload their own immigration stories to contribute to the growth of "the movement." The campaign has also hired "community organizers," whose responsibilities focus on organizing the tech community to support comprehensive immigration reform. By the summer of 2013, FWD.us had also begun to organize face-to-face meetups in multiple cities.

On a technical level, FWD.us is cutting edge. The campaign is powered by Nation Builder, a for-profit platform for constituent relationship management built by techies with backgrounds at Facebook and in the Obama campaign. Nation Builder provides sophisticated tools for campaign managers, such as the ability to integrate, manage, and visualize contacts across platforms, including email, Facebook, Twitter, and mobile phones. It has powerful analytics that reveal the views, open rates, and conversion rates to an asked-for action (such as liking, sharing, calling a congressperson, or donating money).

While it launched as a sophisticated transmedia organizing campaign around immigration reform that used the latest digital tools, FWD.us (at least initially) had very little connection to the existing immigrant rights movement (although this relationship has changed over time). At launch, the campaign rhetoric advanced demands based on the narrow needs of high-skill knowledge industry employers while ignoring the reality, agency, and movement history of the more than 12 million undocumented people who have fought for decades to make immigration reform a political possibility. FWD.us supports border militarization proposals that run counter to the spirit of the immigrant rights movement and that would cause increased deaths on the border. The organization also supports expansion of the E-Verify employment verification system. E-Verify will make the lives of millions of working-class undocumented people significantly more difficult; in addition, according to U.S. Citizenship and Iimmigration Services' own evaluation, the system suffers a 50 percent failure rate.[13] In a tangential but telling development, shortly after launch, FWD.us generated a wave of criticism from across the immigrant rights movement and the environmental movement when it paid for a series of political ads supporting the controversial Keystone XL pipeline, designed to carry oil from the Canadian tar sands to the United States.[14] The leadership of FWD.us responded to these criticisms by arguing that these are simply the political compromises necessary to attain their objectives.

FWD.us thus represents a new level of corporate-led transmedia organizing. It is cross-platform, combining a sophisticated social media strategy with the ability to place stories in mass media outlets. It is participatory, calling on people to produce and upload their own stories as well as to "like" and "share" nicely produced videos on social networking sites. It links attention to action by asking supporters to sign an online petition and call their elected representatives in Congress. However, it lacks both formal and informal accountability mechanisms to the social base of the immigrant rights movement. Instead, the campaign's strategy, narrative, and calls to action are guided from the top down by paid staff, ultimately accountable primarily to the interests of the Silicon Valley firms that are the financial backers of the "movement." While it may be logical for these firms to support policy positions that primarily advance their own interests, in the name of "building a movement" for immigration reform, FWD.us takes stances, such as support for border militarization and E-Verify, that are directly harmful to the vast majority of undocumented people. What's more, the organization actively positions itself as "the immigrant rights movement," erasing the history of decades of grassroots organizing led by young people of color, many of them queer and undocumented themselves.

In summary, Define American is a transmedia campaign led by undocumented activists, with organic ties to the broader movement that produce a strong if informal accountability mechanism. The Dream is Now is a transmedia campaign led by well-meaning funders and professional media-makers; it produces high-quality video stories and generates mass media attention but struggles to link its framing, calls to action, and strategy to those of the broader immigrant rights movement. FWD.us is a tech-industry backed transmedia campaign that (at least initially) consciously positioned itself at a distance from the broader immigrant rights movement. It has a clear main goal: to increase the number of visas available for high-skill information workers. Many immigrant rights activists dismiss FWD.us as "astroturf:" a campaign that attempts to leverage the credibility of grassroots organizing to advance a policy goal but is backed directly by powerful private corporations that stand to directly benefit. More recently, this analysis has become more complicated, as FWD.us has partnered with Define American and Mark Zuckerberg has helped Jose Antonio Vargas promote his film, *Documented*. Yet speaking broadly, we can say that each transmedia campaign has more resources, produces higher-production-value media, and is more professionalized than the last, but each is less accountable to the immigrant rights movement.

Professionalization and Accountability in Transmedia Organizing: The Revolution Will Not Be Funded

The trend toward the professionalization of transmedia organizing, and the questions about accountability that it raises, must be seen as part of a broader process. Social movement professionalization is not unique to the immigrant rights movement, and it is not new. In the wake of the civil rights, anti-Vietnam War, gay liberation, and feminist movements during the 1960s and 1970s, social movements in the United States underwent a period of increasing professionalization. Social movement scholars such as John McCarthy, Meyer Zald, Suzanne Staggenborg, and others have documented how, over time, private foundations stepped in to fund, mediate, and increasingly shape social movement activity in the United States.[15]

Social movement groups outside the academy have also developed a critique of foundations and incorporated nonprofits over the last two decades. In 2004, INCITE! Women of Color Against Violence organized the conference, "The Revolution Will Not Be Funded." INCITE! members and other conference attendees unpacked the ways that many feminist organizations, initially committed to ending all forms of violence against women and to dismantling patriarchy, ended up spending all their time as professional service providers for battered women. Service provision is important, they argue, but if it is decoupled from movement building, the root causes of violence will never be addressed and violence against women will never end. The conference invited organizers from multiple social movements to reflect on the dynamics of private foundation support and the rise of professional nonprofits.

The conference proceedings were published as the book *The Revolution Will Not Be Funded: Beyond the Non-profit Industrial Complex*.[16] The main arguments of the authors are as follows: all foundation money is in a sense "stolen" money. It is initially stolen from the workers who produce value for corporate owners, and it is "stolen" again when wealthy donors avoid taxes by creating private foundations. These funds would otherwise become available to the state, and would thereby be subject to formal democratic accountability. Instead, they are used to establish privately governed organizations with mandates to spend funds according to directives written at the will of their individual (white, male, ruling-class) founders. The book's authors go on to argue that the creation of professionalized nonprofits has in many ways served to weaken social movements in the United States and, increasingly, internationally. Case studies of the civil rights movement, the women's movement, and the environmental movement demonstrate how what the authors term the nonprofit industrial complex (NPIC) has systematically drawn movement leadership away from radical or even broad-based progressive social movement building and into issue-specific, organization-centric, professional careerism.[17] People who otherwise might be building value-driven social movement networks, able to mobilize large-scale societal shifts, instead end up isolated into issue silos. There they compete with one another for limited foundation funds. They spend much of their time writing proposals and project reports instead of organizing and movement building.[18] Additionally, organizations registered as nonprofits under section

501(c)3 of the U.S. tax code are prohibited by law from engaging in many forms of political activity, including lobbying and supporting political parties or candidates. Nonprofits are thus quite literally instruments of depoliticization.[19]

Elements of this critique are widely shared in social movement circles. In the immigrant rights movement, almost all the activists I worked with and interviewed, whether they had jobs in nonprofits or not, were critical of foundations and of the nonprofit system. As the financial crisis triggered by the collapse of the housing market struck the endowments of private foundations, ambivalence about the nonprofit sector became especially salient. Many nonprofit organizations and movement groups found themselves defunded in the midst of a climate of economic austerity.[20] Some immigrant rights activists used their experience within the NPIC to develop new movement structures with strong internal policies that govern who they will accept funds from, and under what conditions. A few decided not to accept any funds from either the state, or the corporate sector, or private foundations. In some cases this was based on their critique of the NPIC; in others, it was simply because they desired to maintain autonomy from foundations and avoid the professionalization of social movement activity. For example, when I asked an FIOB organizer about foundation support, she had this to say:

No, we're pretty much autonomous. We don't want any foundation money, we're not a nonprofit. We want to maintain our autonomy, not committing with anyone on what stand we're going to have on any issue, don't want to owe anybody a favor.[21]

However, this is the exception that proves the rule. Overall, it would be fair to say that the immigrant rights movement has undergone a long-term process of professionalization. Today, incorporated nonprofit organizations with paid staff often present themselves, and are presented by the mass media, as "the immigrant rights movement." Yet almost all immigrant rights activists, including most nonprofit staff, recognize that the movement is much broader than the incorporated nonprofit organizations that operate within it.[22]

Many organizers discussed their own personal experience of the ongoing shift to movement professionalization and centralization. They talked about how the past ten to fifteen years especially have seen a transition from social movement groups fully governed by those most directly affected to incorporated nonprofit organizations controlled by boards of directors, executive directors, and paid staff.[23] One interviewee described the transformation of day laborer organizing in Los Angeles, from a day laborers' union that was governed directly by general assembly to the current formal network governed by a committee of executive directors of immigrant rights organizations.[24] He stressed that the intentions of the directors remain good, the services offered by the organizations are important, and many of the directors came from the base they now represent. However, he also felt that the consolidation of organizing within formally incorporated nonprofits led, in the long run, to the progressive removal of decision-making power from the hands of day laborers themselves. For this organizer, the implications for movement media strategies were clear:

> Classically what tends to happen is that there's a centralization. Within that centralization, even within the messages, even if the base is asking for another message, once that request gets filtered through their communications department, through their EDs, and through their board, it's changed completely. It's become maybe a little bit more acceptable, or more responsible of a message, or not as extreme a message.[25]

Like many activists, he felt that the professionalization of immigrant rights organizations tends, over the long run, to distance the social base of the movement from decision making. This is a dynamic that social movement theorists have long observed.[26]

As the movement professionalizes, many smaller and mid-size organizations struggle to keep up with larger, better-resourced nonprofits. This plays out in specific ways when it comes to communication strategy more broadly, and in transmedia organizing specifically. For example, most smaller immigrant rights organizations do not employ full-time communication staff, but are under increasing pressure to develop an online presence. Organizers who work for less-resourced nonprofit organizations describe experiencing tension between their own desire to include their social base in meaningful decision making, framing, and media-making and the need to "just get it done." They often want to share communication and technology skills more broadly with their communities but feel pressure from funders and organizational leadership to complete communication projects quickly. In addition, without resources to hire full- or even part-time staff with media production skills, many told me that they move from volunteer to volunteer, with an occasional small contractor, in efforts to release more professional-looking multimedia materials, without the time to establish full accountability to their base.[27]

As movement organizations grow into nonprofits, at a certain point many do hire full-time communication staff and develop an explicit social media strategy. This process is supported by funders and advanced by communication consultants within the nonprofit field. However, increased capacity does not necessarily lead organizations to develop a praxis of critical digital media literacy, as discussed in chapter 5. In other words, the voices of the movement base do not always become the center of professional nonprofit communication strategy. Instead, better-resourced nonprofit organizations often approach social media strategy from the perspective of building a brand, fundraising, and constituent relationship management. Often, they hope to appropriate some of the functionality—and excitement—of "Web 2.0" while retaining top-down control over messaging and framing.[28] The desire to adopt social media is in part driven by the apparent success of other professionalized nonprofit organizations, which also happen to be competitors for a limited pool of philanthropic funds. Social media adoption among nonprofits also accelerated after the display of the power of online organizing by the Obama campaign machinery.[29] However, even as the idea of social media is valorized by nonprofit leadership, social media labor is frequently devalued. Thus, even in better-resourced nonprofits, social media work often ends up relegated to the realm of underpaid labor, assigned to volunteers or to the lowest-paid staff.[30] This makes it quite difficult to develop transmedia organizing strategies that are tightly linked to organizing, policy, and broader communications efforts.

At the same time, an industry of 'new media consultants' has sprung up around the nonprofit sector. In interviews with some of these consultants, I found that many are deeply interested in pushing top-down immigrant rights organizations toward more horizontal, or conversational, media practices and strategies. However, they expressed that this often ends in failure and frustration.[31] In some cases, social media consultants told me that they were able to move new media initiatives forward with much more success as outside 'experts' than as organizational staff. For example, one described how he ultimately left full-time nonprofit employment in order to work more independently with different organizations and networks on a contract basis:

I just found, within organizations there's a strange dynamic that when you're in an organization it's really hard to move through new initiatives and new approaches, yet when you're on the outside, and they have to pay for it, they're more interested.[32]

Thus, in some cases, participatory media strategies can make headway in top-down organizations, if pushed by someone operating from outside that organization's structural constraints.

One of the main barriers to effective transmedia organizing comes from what several interviewees described as "old-school" cultures of organizing. According to some interviewees, "old-school" organizers fail to engage in the social practices of sharing that characterize newer movement groups and networks. One activist described his experience with organizations refusing to share contact information, and the lack of trust between similar nonprofits, as the main block to successful online organizing during a national campaign against Maricopa County sheriff Joe Arpaio.[33] In this case, organizers within a movement network were unable to move a social media strategy forward because the leadership of vertically structured member organizations were wary of sharing contacts with each other. Sharing of resources, contacts, content, and platforms, so crucial to the cultural logic of networked activism,[34] is not well developed among professional immigrant rights organizations:

Part of the challenge with a lot of the larger organizations, the immigrant rights organizations that receive a lot of funding—they're kind of these institutions, they're very wary of sharing. They're very wary of, well, then who gets the credit for this, you know? And unfortunately it leaks back to kind of the funding issue, 'cause whoever gets the credit is the one that's going to get the funding. The funders aren't just going to fund this undefined movement, you know? This uncentralized movement, they'll just move on to the next topic on their funding list.[35]

In other words, funders currently play an important role in pushing movement organizations away from horizontalist organizational logics and away from the norms of network culture. In part this may be because funders themselves do not understand the new cultural logic of networking; in part it may be because they have a different model of social change; in part it may be because individual program officers do not want to (or in some cases are legally not allowed to) fund a diffuse "network." Funders want to build organizations and institutions, and want to be able to quantify deliverables such as service provision or key policy changes.[36] In this context, interviewees described how professional nonprofit organizations within the immigrant rights movement often compete for funding and project ownership rather than work toward network coordination and resource sharing.[37]

Many organizers are also deeply frustrated by what they find to be pervasive attempts by nonprofits to use social media as a new kind of broadcast channel. Interviewees described various organizations that have this problem and said that it was a constant struggle to get "old-school organizers" to realize the possibilities of creating a conversation with their online audience. This is especially a problem for national organizations:

Some of these national groups are using social media, but they kind of use it as a broadcast medium.... It's really hard for organizations to understand about opening it up and allowing people to add content to what they have to say, you know? And it's kind of scary to them, and they're very wary of it.[38]

This social media consultant mentioned two national organizations based in D.C. as examples, and said that many movement organizations in L.A. suffer from the same problem. When I asked for a specific example of top-down social media use in L.A., he began by describing how one well-known immigrant rights organization tried to use Twitter:

They cut and paste different things from the [conference] program, like "We're gonna have a workshop on social media," and they put that in the Twitter feed and just sent it. And there was no kind of—they didn't follow anybody, they didn't ask any questions, it was "This is what we're doing, and maybe somebody out there will be intrigued enough by the title of this workshop that they'll want to come to our conference."[39]

In another instance, the same organization hired a consulting firm to manage its Facebook page, but then got upset when the firm changed the profile picture without authorization.[40] The logic of social media, which requires constant attention to human connections, conversation, and regular foregrounding of "new and fresh" content, conflicts deeply with the practices of branded identity that nonprofits have inherited from the private sector.[41] In the social media space, nonprofits often struggle to implement the advice they have received from corporate communications consultants who counsel them to maintain strong brand identity. This manifests in the micropolitics of daily communication practices. Nonprofit staff especially push back against the more fluid social media practices of youth.[42]

As we have seen, the danger that a movement's base will be exposed as more radical than the leadership is one reason why nonprofit leaders remain wary of opening up to social media. The fear of too much transparency comes into play not only in terms of political positioning but also in the potential for social media to expose the behavior of organizational staff as 'unprofessional.' Another interviewee talked about a situation in which the executive director of a nonprofit angrily called in the younger staff to berate them for posting pictures of people drinking and dancing at an organizational fundraiser on Facebook.[43] In this case, social media again generated tension: on the one hand, the executive director worried that revealing staff and members drinking, dancing, and having fun would appear unprofessional and reduce the chances of securing foundation funds in the future; on the other hand, staff members felt that showing this side of the organization on social media would make it easier to attract interest from new potential members and volunteers.

Finally, younger organizers talked about how organizational leaders simply do not understand social media as a space for the production and circulation of digital culture. For example, one articulated a concern that more hierarchical movement organizations are unable to effectively bring arts and music into their culture of organizing, in contrast to the dynamic use of social networking sites by youth activists.[44] When asked how art, creativity, and music within social movement groups relate to communication technology, she responded, "I feel like these are different organizing strategies.... Alternative media strategies or tools are in line with art and culture and music. So I feel it's about us thinking and using these as ways to organize and to develop."[45] She also expressed concern about the professionalization of social movement activity, and said, "I think that organizing sometimes is very businessy. I think about unions, or nonprofits that are very hierarchical." She felt that hierarchical organizations approach communication technology from a "hard" utility perspective. They assume that information and communication technologies are worth investing in only if they can be applied directly to nuts-and-bolts organizing, with outcomes that can be measured in clear quantitative terms, such as increased membership, greater donations, or more efficient use of staff time. In her analysis, this perspective fails to grasp the key value of networked communication, so evident from the transmedia organizing experience of high school and college student activists that we saw in chapter 2: direct participation in the production and circulation of movement narratives.

Media-makers who understand that social media are about creating a conversation but who work within movement groups that are afraid to abandon a "broadcast" model sometimes find that the only way to move forward is to "ask forgiveness rather than permission." When consulting on social media for a national immigrant rights network, one activist was given relatively free rein:

So I started this MySpace page and tried to reach out to a lot of these kids, 'cause a lot of what those kids were saying was stuff about enforcement issues.... I think this is part of the problem that we're finding now with the whole immigration reform debate. There's this very superficial statement about the need for reform, but nothing about necessarily what that means. So a lot of the groups very focused on enforcement feel shut out a lot, because we're seen as kind of too radical. We want to release all the criminals or something like this. But a lot of these kids, they were saying things like "Don't criminalize my family" and "Don't take my parents away from me."[46]

This interview also highlights the fact that conversations on social media, as framed by those most directly affected by immigration enforcement policies, are often more radical than the "safe" messages put forward by national or Washington, D.C.-based immigrant rights organizations. Others described how national messaging in 2006 often promoted a "we are not criminals" frame that emphasized "hardworking, Christian immigrant families who pay taxes and just want a shot at the American Dream," while conversations by young people on MySpace at the time often included critiques of racism, colonialism, genocide, and cultural imperialism.[47]

Organizers who hope to engage their base in social media spaces must be prepared to have difficult conversations, and cannot assume that the frames they have chosen will be the same ones generated through truly participatory communication processes. Effective transmedia organizing thus requires a significant cultural shift for movement organizations that are used to a top-down strategy of message control. In other words, one of the key goals of transmedia organizing is to create a space within which people can contribute to defining the larger movement narrative:

It goes back to looking at it as a tool for organizing. It's not about going into a community and being like, "Okay everybody, you all have to get together now, and you have to think this way and do it this way because we're right," even though a lot of people follow that model in organizing. And it's ridiculous because that shit falls apart anyways. The whole thing about organizing is, I think, and at least the people I've worked with that I really respect, it's about the creation of a space in conjunction with the people that you're working for.[48]

The accountable transmedia organizer sets up a space and then facilitates conversation, but does not impose one model or idea from the top down. In theory, transmedia organizing thus integrates the praxis of critical digital media literacy with more traditional strategies for outreach to mass media, since member-created media texts can serve as key "hooks" to generate interest from professional journalists.[49] In practice, even without engaging the deeper critiques of the NPIC, we can say that many professionalized nonprofits have failed to grasp the new media ecology. They continue to develop social media strategies that replicate top-down communication processes, don't take advantage of the possibilities of transmedia organizing, and in many cases lack community accountability.

The Reproduction of Structural Inequality through Volunteerism

Most immigrant rights organizers have quite complex feelings about movement professionalization. On the one hand, as we have seen, it can easily lead to distance from the movement's social base. Professional transmedia producers sometimes create narratives that are not grounded in community voices and desires, and calls to action that are delinked from the actual needs of the movement. Of course, transmedia strategy was initially developed by the cultural industries in order to capture attention and sell more branded commodities. It should, therefore, come as no surprise that professional nonprofits are beginning to employ transmedia strategy primarily to build brand visibility, increase the size of their mailing lists, and raise funds. In the worst cases, top-down organizations that lack accountability are using transmedia approaches to advance goals, narratives, and actions that are directly harmful to the immigrant community. At the same time, the professionalization of social movement organizations brings increased resources, staying power, and access to decision makers. In terms of transmedia organizing, professionalization can mean the ability to create higher-production-value media, reach a broader audience, and ultimately increase a movement's power to shape public consciousness.

INCITE!'s critique of the NPIC has been challenged by some theorists and activists. Pushback has come from those who work within more professionalized movement organizations, as well as from some who work in small, grassroots collectives and groups that are staffed largely by volunteers. One scholar and activist who has written extensively about the struggles of integrating digital media into community organizing put it this way: "As a member of a small grassroots welfare rights and economic justice organization with an extraordinarily horizontal structure, I have to say that we'd kill for a half-time staff member."[50] Many immigrant rights activists I worked with and interviewed, including those who volunteered for informal or ad hoc movement groups, expressed similar sentiments. Indeed, the most frequently mentioned barrier to effective transmedia organizing is lack of access to resources. Specifically, immigrant rights organizers frequently say that lack of paid staff is the greatest obstacle to successful implementation of communication strategies. In the absence of paid staff, those with the most free time typically end up running movement groups, and free time is shaped by class, age, and gender. In other words, failure to professionalize can make it difficult to set up structures that allow more people from the movement's base to fully participate, thereby strengthening accountability. While professionalization may distance movement organizations from their base, *not* professionalizing may reproduce structural inequality along lines of race, class, gender, sexuality, age, immigration status, and geography.

Ultimately, most activists thus have a complicated relationship with the nonprofit system. While many are critical of the demobilizing effects of 501(c)3s, few argue for the actual deprofessionalization of social movements. The harsh critique of "service providers" that some radicals employ often rings false when set against the daily realities of organizing among low-wage immigrant workers, who are often focused first and foremost on the struggle for survival. Many organizers with radical, intersectional analyses have jobs with nonprofits that provide direct services, meet people's material needs, and work to develop critical consciousness while organizing toward broader political goals. Although it is beyond the scope of this book, it is important to develop a nuanced discussion of the tensions between volunteer and paid labor in the social movement sector. There are many potential problems with, as well as synergies between, both ad hoc and professionalized movement groups. This discussion will have crucial implications for the future of transmedia organizing.

Professionalization and Accountability in Transmedia Organizing: Conclusions

The normalization of transmedia organizing is a powerful shift. We are turning an important corner: transmedia organizing is increasingly well-resourced. Advocacy campaigns have come to regularly include participatory media-making components, and media campaigns are hiring community organizers as core team members. This shift offers incredible opportunities. At the same time, it also reveals troubling dynamics. The professionalization of transmedia organizing has in some cases led to decreased accountability to the movement base. This is not only unfortunate in a normative sense, it also leads to numerous tactical problems, such as poor frame selection, or calls to action that miss the mark based on the current political opportunities. Unaccountable transmedia organizing projects are less likely to deploy frames that reflect the desires of the supposed subjects of the story. Sometimes this can mean strategic failure, missed opportunities, or irrelevance; in other cases it can actually be harmful to the movement's goals. Another pitfall is the failure to transform attention into meaningful action. In some cases these problems may be due to a simple lack of experience. For example, filmmakers who may know the craft of filmmaking quite well and desire to use their skills for good may be unaware of, and unconnected to, existing social movements that have a great deal of knowledge, experience, and strategic insight concerning how to move social change processes forward. In other cases, transmedia organizing strategy is used by "astroturf" organizations to advance the policy agendas of powerful industries, under cover of "popular" cross-platform mobilization.

The professionalization of transmedia organizing is only one small component of the long term professionalization of social movements. The segmentation of grassroots movements into issue-based nonprofits, dependence on foundation funding, and the adoption of top-down governance structures all militate against accountability to the movement base. Professionalized movement organizations that receive funding from private foundations, while they have greater access to resources than grassroots groups, organic networks, or ad hoc collectives, are almost always organized with top-down decision making structures. These organizations may come from and maintain strong ties to their base, but they also often centralize decision making. What's more, they are placed in the position of competing against each other for a relatively small pool of resources. Accountable transmedia organizing may be incompatible with the model of social change increasingly favored by private philanthropy, where change is driven by efficient, professionalized nonprofits engaged in single-issue, policy-centric advocacy rather than by broad-based, directly democratic, media-literate social movements.

Few grassroots movement groups think systematically about how to use online media to drive broadcast media coverage, or vice versa. In part, this may be a function of the fact that in smaller, understaffed movement organizations, there is a division of labor between "new" and "old" media: younger staff or volunteers spend time building the movement's online presence, while older and more experienced organizers focus on generating mass media coverage through press conferences and relationships with print and broadcast journalists. By dividing communications work in this way, movement organizations miss opportunities to effectively amplify interesting social media texts produced by their communities through mass media coverage. By the same token, they may miss opportunities to use mass media coverage to drive greater attention to online movement spaces. In addition, younger staff within professional nonprofits are often frustrated when their efforts to use social media for movement ends are blocked by organizational leaders. This often happens when nonprofit leaders fail to understand that social media are spaces for conversation, or when they fear losing control of the message. Overall, professional nonprofit culture does not usually mix well with transmedia organizing.

Organizers experience a catch 22: transmedia organizing strategies that reflect community voices emerge most organically from decentralized, open social movement networks. Yet these networks are difficult to sustain. They also often reproduce structural inequality along lines of race, class, gender, sexuality, and education, since those with the most access to time and resources may be able to participate more heavily in all-volunteer organizing. At the same time, professionalized nonprofits are increasingly

adopting transmedia organizing strategies but struggle to remain accountable to the movement's base rather than to their own institutional impera-
tives or to the demands of funders. The development of accountable,
well-resourced, transmedia organizing campaigns remains for the most
part a tantalizing possibility. Immigrant rights activists are working hard
to realize this possibility, and to engage in transmedia organizing that
remains accountable to the movement base, recognizes and lifts up grassroots movement history, and connects people to meaningful action guided
by the movement's needs.

Conclusions

This book began with an account of the unprecedented mobilizations for immigrant rights that swept the country in the spring of 2006. As I write these conclusions, in the fall of 2013, the movement has launched a new series of actions reminiscent of the moment that the "sleeping giant" awoke. While making final edits to the manuscript, I can't resist regularly switching tabs to look at my Twitter feed, where I find a steady stream of updates from the October 5 National Day for Dignity and Respect.[1] Immigrant rights supporters, including movement organizations, religious groups, businesses, radio hosts and journalists, musicians and celebrities, and thousands upon thousands of individuals across the country, are taking part in marches, rallies, vigils, and concerts this weekend. A new generation of queer undocumented activists is stepping up the level of both analysis and action, speaking out about the importance of intersectional organizing while committing acts of nonviolent civil disobedience. With bold moves that shook up both the Democratic Party and many Washington, D.C.-based immigrant rights nonprofit organizations, the Dream 9 and the Dream 30 immigration activists recently organized direct actions at the U.S.-Mexico border. These DREAMers, who at some point in the past had been deported to Mexico, publicly recrossed the border without papers and now face detention, endure solitary confinement, and engage in hunger strikes to pressure the Obama administration to take executive action and halt deportations.[2] These actions will be followed in the coming weeks by a new wave of nonviolent civil disobedience, mass marches, protest, and lobbying. All this activity takes place alongside rapid growth in the visibility and sophistication of transmedia organizing efforts by the immigrant rights movement.

The past few years have also seen policy gains, including the Deferred Action for Childhood Arrivals (DACA) program. Although criticized by some as a stopgap measure, or as a political ploy aimed at bolstering the Latin@ vote in the 2012 presidential election, the DACA program has provided temporary legal status for hundreds of thousands of previously undocumented youth. For many, this has meant increased access to jobs, credit, and driver's licenses.[3] While DACA is nationwide, most immigrant rights policy gains have occurred at the state level. For example, a federal judge recently ordered that unapologetically anti-immigrant Sheriff Joe Arpaio, of Phoenix, Arizona's Maricopa County, must have a court-appointed monitor for at least the next three years. California governor Jerry Brown signed A.B. 60, allowing more than 1.4 million Californian immigrants to register for driver's licenses starting in 2015, after more than ten states passed similar bills.[4] On October 5, 2013, Brown also signed the Trust Act, limiting California's cooperation with the federal Secure Communities (SCOMM) program.

However, despite pushback from some states, the Obama administration has expanded SCOMM across the entire country, linking local law enforcement with Department of Homeland Security databases in a network of algorithmic immigration enforcement designed to autodetect the citizenship status of every person detained by police.[5] In part because of the expansion of SCOMM, the Obama administration has now passed the historic milestone of two million deportations.[6] Meanwhile, comprehensive immigration reform, seemingly so close in 2010 and again in 2013, has come to a near standstill; the odds of both houses of Congress adopting a federal bill that includes a path to citizenship for all 11 million undocumented people living in the United States seem more remote each day. If a bill becomes law, it will most likely include more than $46 billion for increased border militarization, mandatory expansion of the federal E-Verify biometric employment database, and a winding, expensive path to citizenship that some analysts estimate would exclude more than half of all undocumented immigrants.[7]

If we step back from the immediate round of immigration policy battles in the United States, it is possible to see the broader context of a global political economy that has eliminated barriers to cross-border capital flows, while human beings face militarized borders, harsh migration policies, and ever more sophisticated systems of algorithmic surveillance and control.

Still, on the scale of human history, tight controls on migration are quite new. There is nothing natural or inevitable about closed borders. Migration policy is shaped in part by social movements—nativists on one side, immigrants and their allies on the other—that battle over attention, framing, and credibility. This battle is expressed and fought through a communication system that is increasingly globalized and is converging across platforms. The shifting media ecology also includes the ever-expanding, participatory, and frequently unruly space of social media, which coexist beside long-established immigrant media channels such as minority language print, radio, and television broadcasters. This book represents an attempt to make sense of how social movements negotiate such a rapidly changing media ecology, and how they leverage the opportunities it provides to build movement identity, mobilize people for action, shift cultural narratives, and advance policy goals.

My attempt to understand these dynamics is based on insights gained from participating in nearly one hundred media workshops, actions, events, and day-to-day media practices as a movement ally. This experiential knowledge was augmented by analysis of media texts produced by the immigrant rights movement over the past decade, and by the views that emerged from forty semistructured interviews I conducted with movement participants. Together with a wide network of organizers, students, media activists, community-based organizations, ad hoc collectives, and immigrant workers, I worked to develop research, theory, and practice around what I call transmedia organizing. Along the way, I took part in a social movement that is learning how to take advantage of transformations in the media ecology. Immigrant rights activists are adopting transmedia organizing strategies: they tell stories across multiple platforms, invite their base into participatory media practices, and connect attention directly to action by leveraging the affordances of new information and communication technologies. Some have shifted their role, from speaking for the movement (as "the voice of the voiceless") to aggregation, curation, and amplification of voices from the movement's social base. Many work toward a praxis of critical digital media literacy: they combine hands-on digital media workshops with popular education methods. This approach fosters critical consciousness and develops movement leadership among low-wage workers, while simultaneously strengthening their ability to participate in the digital public sphere. Over time, I also observed that media-making frequently provides a powerful pathway to deep, ongoing social movement participation. At the same time, I also found that transmedia organizing has become increasingly professionalized. Professionalization brings a new level of resources, high production values, and great potential power, but for both normative and pragmatic reasons, it requires accountability mechanisms. Otherwise, the public narrative can quickly become separated from the voices of the movement's social base. These closing pages summarize the key arguments I have made in each chapter, then end with a note about the implications for scholars and for social movement participants. I hope that my arguments here have been interesting, if not persuasive, and that they will be useful to scholars and community organizers alike.

Summary of Findings

We live in a culture that romanticizes the liberatory potential of new media technology. Too often, scholars and journalists credit social media with playing a lead role in mass mobilizations. Many funders, perhaps hoping for quick, relatively cheap fixes to structurally persistent problems, have begun to move away from long-term investment in community organizing and toward "seed grants" for tech-centric approaches. These projects, while exciting, are too often delinked from real-world movement needs. Even activists are sometimes seduced by the same logic. Although I am a media scholar, activist, and to some degree a technologist, I urge readers to reject mediacentric approaches to thinking about social movements. I believe it is possible to pay close attention to social movement media practices without insisting that they are the most important aspect of social movements.

In this book, I have described many cases in which social media use was indeed key to movement processes. For example, during the walkouts in protest of the Sensenbrenner bill (described in chapters 1 and 2), high school students used MySpace in innovative ways. During the struggle for the DACA program, DREAM activists live-streamed sit-ins in DHS buildings, congressional offices, and Obama campaign headquarters (chapter 6). In the aftermath of the MacArthur Park "melee," horizontalist organizers were able to leverage social media platforms to challenge the top-down narrative of the police, the mass media, and professional nonprofit organizations (chapter 3). Yet social media, new technologies, and horizontal organizing processes are not necessarily the most important variables in social movement success, if it is even useful to analyze social movements in such mechanistic terms. Other factors are frequently more crucial: access to resources, elite allies, splits between different factions among formerly unified opponents, support and solidarity from the broader public beyond the movement's base, tactical innovation, highly publicized acts of police repression, or a compelling narrative, to name a few. All of these, and many more, have long been identified by social movement scholars, as well as by organic intellectuals, as key to social movement success. I believe that transmedia organizing is important because it is a crucial part of movement building, not because it is the most important factor in social movement outcomes. Through media-making, social movement participants build collective identity. When movements open their narratives to participation from their social base, and when they apply directly democratic decision making to the stories they tell about themselves, they prefigure a more just and democratic world. I hope that it is possible to recognize this dynamic without placing media at the center of our stories about movements. Movements are ultimately about the power of organized people, not the power of any particular platform or technology—even a platform as revolutionary as the Internet.

A Changing Media Ecology

In chapter 1, I proposed that the immigrant rights movement, like all social movements, operates within a rapidly changing media ecology. On the one hand, most immigrant rights organizers still lack consistent access to English-language print or broadcast media. These channels continue to play the most important role in framing and agenda setting for the dominant political class, both locally and nationally. On the other hand, most of the organizers I interviewed agreed that they enjoy a steadily growing ability to generate coverage in the Spanish-language press (and in other minority language media), including print, radio, and television stations that have increasing reach and power. At the same time, commercial Spanish-language radio is the single platform with the most power to galvanize the social base of the immigrant rights movement to action, as we saw in the 2006 marches against the Sensenbrenner bill. When Spanish-language *locutores* (radio hosts) decided to call for mass mobilization, they were able to bring literally millions of immigrant workers into the streets. Minority language media, especially Spanish-language commercial radio, television, and newspapers, thus provide important new possibilities for the immigrant rights movement.

At the same time, the media ecology has been transformed from the bottom up by the widespread use of the Internet, social media, and mobile phones. The rapid adoption of social media by the children of new immigrants, and mobile phone access rates soaring above 90 percent even among the most marginalized groups of low-wage immigrant workers, enable new participatory practices of movement media-making. As we saw in chapter 2, this was evident as early as 2006, with the widepread use of the social networking site MySpace by middle school, high school, and college students during the walkouts. New tools and skills help everyday participants in the immigrant rights movement coordinate, document, and circulate their own actions in near real time, and generate space for bottom-up agenda setting, framing, tactical media, and self-representation. The power of social media extends beyond the obvious ability to distribute movement messages rapidly through extended friendship networks, as important as that may be. Media produced by activists and initially circulated through social networks also frequently passes into broadcast distribution, as print, TV, and radio journalists seek news tips and content that has "bubbled up" from social media and blogs. Movement actors who recognize these new openings in the media ecology and take steps to occupy them are more successful than those who continue to address all of their communications efforts directly to English-language broadcast outlets.

Transmedia Organizing

The most successful movement media practices can best be theorized in terms of what I call transmedia organizing. *Transmedia organizing* denotes cross-platform, participatory media making that is linked to action and, ideally, accountable to the movement's social base. During the 2006 walkouts, and in the aftermath of the 2007 police attack in MacArthur Park, transmedia organizers engaged both skilled media-makers and the movement's social base in the production and circulation of movement narratives across multiple media platforms (see chapters 2 and 3). Transmedia organizing provides opportunities for participation to people with varying skill levels. For example, transmedia organizers often invite movement participants to contribute simple media elements such as photographs, texts, or short video clips, which they later aggregate, remix, combine, and circulate more broadly. Some movement groups consciously employ social media solidarity tactics that encourage allies and supporters to identify more closely with the movement by personalizing larger shared texts, as we saw in chapters 6 and 7. Transmedia organizing is not limited by genre; it may also incorporate elements of commercial films, television programs, comic books, songs, and so on, which are then referenced, sampled, remixed, and recirculated in the movement context. These practices provide multiple entry points that strengthen movement identity across networked publics (chapters 1, 2, and 6).

Transmedia organizers strengthen movement identity formation by providing clear opportunities for supporters to produce and circulate their own movement media. For example, immigrant rights "artivists" such as Julio Salgado and Favianna Rodriguez lead face-to-face workshops to teach media-making techniques, such as how to create stenciled posters and cardboard protest signs. They also provide downloadable stencil templates, make instructional videos, and post them to YouTube and Vimeo, where they are circulated via social media platforms like Facebook and Twitter.[8] Transmedia organizers thus value the act of media-making as in and of itself a movement-building process (chapters 3, 5, 6, and 7). At the same time, transmedia organizing can result in broader movement visibility to nonparticipants, through cross-platform distribution. In addition, immigrant rights advocates are taking advantage of new tools for "constituent relationship management," such as ActionNetwork.org. These services help organizers translate attention to action by building and maintaining contact lists of supporters that span email, mobile phones, Facebook, and Twitter, replacing the previous generation of clunky list management and action alert services. Movement groups that become hubs of transmedia organizing are able to take advantage of the changed media ecology, build stronger movement identity among participants, link attention to action, and gain greater visibility for the movement, its goals, its actions, and its frames.

Changing Roles: From Spokespeople to Amplifiers

Many immigrant rights organizers are caught between the desire to act as spokespeople for the movement—a strategy that retains tight control over messaging and framing—and the need to become transmedia organizers. The latter approach requires learning new skills and can feel risky to those steeped in previous public relations paradigms. It marks a move from a focus on content production toward aggregation, remix, curation, and amplification. As we saw in chapter 3, in the example of the People's Network in Defense of Human Rights, transmedia organizers amplify messages and frames generated by the movement's social base. Some characterize this shift as a conscious decentralization of the movement voice. Top-down communicators inside social movements find it increasingly difficult to retain control over messaging, as "approved" frames are challenged by media produced by a social base with ever-growing digital media literacy. In some cases, as we saw in the aftermath of the MacArthur Park "melee" (chapter 3), bottom-up transmedia organizing forces movement leaders to modify their messages in order to regain credibility and the trust of the broader movement base. However, the tools and skills of transmedia organizing are only beginning to become an established part of daily communication practices within movements. Press conferences and actions staged specifically to draw mass media coverage continue to be the go-to forms of social movement media strategy. Over time, the many small tasks required to effectively organize a press conference have become tacit organizational knowledge. By contrast, effective use of social media tools, let alone an integrated transmedia organizing strategy, requires a new and different skill set. These skills often mystify the older generation of organizers. Many older organizers are used to dealing with broadcast media events but do not yet truly understand the new media ecology—the shifting terrain of communication power.[9] Even those who do pay close attention to changes in the media ecology and who have intellectually committed to adapt digital media to movement needs continue to struggle to transform their daily practices. This is slowly changing, as we saw in chapter 5. Many organizers feel that over time, the new tools and skills will fade into the background, and the ability to effectively deploy and integrate them within overall movement strategy will grow.

Translocal Media Practices

Translocal media practices also modify the broader media ecology. In chapter 4, we discussed this dynamic in the context of the Frente Indígena de Organizaciones Binacionales and the Associación Popular de los Pueblos de Oaxaca–Los Angeles (APPO-LA). Although access to information and communication technologies (ICTs) and to digital media literacy remains deeply unequal, immigrants often appropriate ICTs to strengthen practices of translocal community citizenship. In some cases, immigrant workers are early adopters of new digital media tools that allow them to remain closely linked with family and friends in their places of origin. In chapter 4, we saw that the Oaxacan community in Los Angeles has long engaged in translocal media practices. For decades, Oaxacan migrants have used home video technology to send VHS tapes of weddings, *quinceañeras*, and cultural festivals back and forth to friends and family in their hometowns. In the past, these practices also played an important role in social movement activity, as in the mobilization against the Alto Basas dam. As video sharing migrated online, primarily to YouTube, Oaxacan migrants followed, despite relatively low levels of ICT access. More recently, indigenous migrant Oaxacans have also appropriated real-time communication technologies such as push-to-talk, Skype, and Oovoo to support collective decision making and community governance by hometown associations and assemblies (*asambleas*). During mass mobilizations in Oaxaca against Governor Ulises Ruíz Ortíz, migrant Oaxacans in Los Angeles used these and other digital media tools and skills to share movement media with networks of supporters and media outlets in their communities of origin and around the world. They also generated transnational support by circulating footage from Oaxaca to the Spanish-language press in the United States. As we also saw in chapter 4, transmedia organizers who led the APPO-LA protests at the Mexican consulate in Los Angeles were able to establish real-time communication with protest leaders in Oaxaca City, rapidly download and project video from major mobilizations taking place thousands of miles away, and attract the attention of Spanish-language commercial media outlets.

Praxis of Critical Digital Media Literacy

Transmedia organizing has great potential. It can be used to help strengthen participatory democracy within social movements, and as a strategy to leverage changes in the media ecology. However, widespread disparities in access to ICTs and in digital media literacy pose significant challenges. In the worst-case scenario, activists may transfer most of their time and energy to "organizing in the cloud." This may lead some to become removed from their social base, and draw resources and attention to online activity that appears significant but lacks accountability to any real-world community. While some see this as a problem, few in the immigrant rights movement argue that the solution is to move away from online organizing. Instead, as we saw in chapter 5, community organizers are building on the history of popular education to develop a praxis of critical digital media literacy that links ICT training directly to movement building.

Overall, many community-based organizations (CBOs) know that critical digital media literacy is important for their communities. Often, they maintain computer labs, which they make available to community members. However, most struggle to sustain digital media literacy training along with their many other responsibilities as overworked, underresourced nonprofit organizations with few staff and constant crises. Many community computer labs are staffed by occasional volunteers, and the type of training that takes place often focuses primarily on job skills such as learning how to use Microsoft Office, creating résumés, and conducting job searches. Media production is not typically taught, and social media use is often prohibited or even blocked by filtering software.[10] Partly as a result, community computer labs are often underutilized. In other words, there is a great deal of untapped potential for CBOs to foster critical digital media literacy among their social base.

There are some CBOs that prove the exception to the rule; they develop innovative media-making projects, hold critical media literacy workshops on how to analyze and remix mass media messages, and systematically cultivate transmedia organizing skills among their base. For example, most immigrant workers now have access to mobile phones. As discussed in chapter 5, the Instituto de Educación Popular del Sur de California (IDEPSCA) and the VozMob project are taking advantage of this fact to develop a popular education approach that begins with the mobile phone as a point of entry to broader critical digital media literacy. Hundreds of day laborers and other workers have now been through VozMob workshops, and the group's Popular Communication Team has produced thousands of stories for the web (see VozMob.net). They also remix mobile stories for *Jornada XXII*, a print newspaper they distribute across Los Angeles, and incorporate audio from voice posts into a radio show on Pacifica affiliate station KPFK. Additionally, the project has repeatedly attracted mass media coverage from Spanish-language newspapers and TV networks, as well as from the *Los Angeles Times*.[11] Media-making workshops thus build the digital media literacy of immigrant workers while emphasizing both critical analysis of mass media frames and the integration of media-making skills into movement building and leadership development processes.

As we saw in chapters 5 and 6, there is also a great deal of informal learning that takes place within the immigrant rights movement. Critical digital media literacy may flow back and forth across generations and between social movement networks in largely informal processes of peer-to-peer learning. Workshops, community computer labs, courses, and convenings, as well as informal and peer-to-peer learning, are all important vehicles for the circulation of media skills. The key to an effective praxis of critical digital media literacy is to connect tools and skills-based training to concrete organizing practices, and to avoid siloed, technology centric trainings.

Pathways to Participation

More than 4.5 million immigrants under the age of thirty are undocumented, according to data from the U.S. Census Bureau.[12] Over the past decade, undocumented youth have created a shared movement identity as "undocumented, unafraid, and unapologetic." Through highly visible public narrative campaigns, including everything from coming-out videos on YouTube to nonviolent civil disobedience in congressional offices, DHS facilities, Obama campaign headquarters, and at border checkpoints, they have become visible as DREAMers. The name came initially from federal legislation that would regularize their status but has been transformed to signify a shared movement identity. DREAMers, often led by queer, undocumented youth of color, have been at the forefront of the new wave of immigrant rights activism. In chapter 6, we explored diverse pathways to participation: trajectories by which people, over the course of their lives, come to identify with and join social movements.

DREAM activists have worked hard to shape their own public narrative, even as their enemies, and sometimes ostensible allies, often reproduce discourse that they feel is harmful to them. Public narrative is the creation of a story about a social movement, one that can build a shared identity among movement participants, draw in sympathizers, and generate new allies. For example, DREAMers are actively challenging the frame that they were brought to the United States "through no fault of their own," since this supposedly supportive message works to criminalize their own parents and divide the broader immigrant rights movement. Instead, many prefer a frame that emphasizes the courage of their parents, who suffered great hardships to bring them to the United States as young children, in search of a better life.

In general, DREAMers leverage youth familiarity with digital media practices and network culture to strengthen their organizing efforts. The steady growth of digital media literacy among those under thirty does make it easier to create ad hoc groups and route around top-down organizations. For example, in chapters 2 and 6 we saw how back-channel conversations via social media were able to rapidly coalesce into new, ad hoc movement groups with horizontalist decision-making practices. At the same time, it would be a mistake to assume that critical digital media literacy is simply "natural" for immigrant youth (or for any young people). While immigrant youth do generally enjoy greater digital media literacy than older low-wage immigrant workers, this facility is unequally distributed across socioeconomic backgrounds. Instead of assuming an equal playing field, DREAM activists make conscious efforts to share media and organizing skills both informally and via workshops. As described in chapters 5 and 6, they also learn from and adapt media practices from other social movements, such as the translocal video practices of immigrant indigenous communities (which we first saw in chapter 4), or the genre of LGBTQ coming-out videos on YouTube.

Undocumented youth become DREAMers through a wide range of pathways, including friends, family, CBOs, and movement groups. Many also find their way into movement participation through mediated pathways: by helping to produce a media project, by circulating information during mobilizations, or by taking part in an existing transmedia organizing campaign. Making media and making trouble are thus often tightly interlinked.

The Professionalization of Transmedia Organizing

Finally, in chapter 7 we explored the dynamics of professionalization and accountability in transmedia organizing. In recent years, transmedia organizing has begun to shift from a process that emerged organically from movements to a domain of experts and professional producers. Professional transmedia projects such as Define American, The Dream is Now, and FWD.us urge people to submit their own immigration stories, then remix these DIY videos into short- and long-form documentaries for broader distribution. Along the way, they invite people to take specific actions, such as share a link, contact an elected official, or take part in a mobilization. Sometimes professional transmedia organizing projects link participants to networks of grassroots organizers and to a broader social movement; in other cases the producers themselves claim to be "the movement." However, the lack of accountability to the social movement base produces both normative and pragmatic problems for transmedia organizing—normative, because values of self-representation, self-determination, horizontalism, and direct democracy require that the actual participants in a social movement have control over the movement's public narrative, messaging, and framing, as well as over the actions and proposals it advances; pragmatic, because even well-meaning transmedia producers, if they are out of touch with the movement base, may use frames that no longer resonate or support policy proposals that no longer make sense given the political opportunity structure. For example, in chapter 7 we saw that The Dream is Now campaign site initially launched with a petition in support of a stand-alone DREAM Act, although a bill for comprehensive immigration reform had already been introduced in the U.S. Senate and the immigrant rights movement had shifted away from a piecemeal legislative approach.

In the same chapter, I suggested that the professionalization of transmedia organizing is best understood within a broader historical context that includes the long-term professionalization of social movements, the incorporation of movement groups as 501(c)3 organizations, and the rise of competition with other organizations for scarce resources. Private foundations often push organic movement networks toward issue-based policy advocacy, professionalization, and clear brand identity, all of which require top-down communication strategies and tight control over messaging and framing. For these and other reasons, nonprofit organizations often lean toward tighter message control. Nonprofit staff are under pressure to take credit for mobilization successes and increase their organization's visibility, to reframe broader social struggles in terms of issue-based campaigns, and to advance winnable policy proposals over deep structural transformation. Funders, program officers, and media specialists are also often experienced with communication strategies that have not caught up with recent transformations in the media ecology, the possibilities of transmedia organizing, or the growth of critical digital media literacy. In capacity-building workshops and professional training sessions, they therefore often replicate a discourse about the importance of top-down message control based on communication strategies geared toward the production of "news hits" in English-language broadcast media.

These realities should not necessarily be read as an argument for a simple solution, such as the deprofessionalization of social movements. Indeed, without funding, movement groups often end up dominated by those who are able to volunteer the most time. Reliance on volunteerism can easily become another way of replicating class, race, or gender privilege in movement leadership. The point is rather that any given group, organization, or network faces contradictory pressures in response to the new media ecology. Besides implicit and explicit pressure from funders, many feel that older organizers, who occupy leadership positions inside vertically structured nonprofit organizations, ignore, dismiss, or deprioritize the possibilities of transmedia organizing. In some cases, leaders actively push back against social media use because they fear loss of control in networked, participatory spaces. As discussed in chapters 1, 3, and 6, others worry that by hosting conversations rather than promoting talking points they will appear unprofessional or too radical to secure funding. Some are willing to take risks, open movement communication practices to their base, and incorporate the praxis of critical digital media literacy into their work. They are shifting from speaking *for* the movement to speaking *with* the movement. In the long run, as noted in chapters 2, 3, 5, and 6, these risk-takers are the most likely to reap the rewards of transmedia organizing.

By engaging in cross-platform, participatory, action-linked campaigns that are accountable to the social base of the immigrant rights movement, they are able to leverage the new media ecology, strengthen movement identity, win political and economic victories, and transform consciousness.

Key Gaps

There are, of course, many gaps in the arguments I've made here. First, and perhaps most critically, it will be important in the future to more fully elaborate and understand the very real dangers of transmedia organizing. I have touched on this only briefly, but in a post-Snowden world, it bears emphasis that transmedia organizing enables heightened surveillance, data mining, and social network analysis by state, corporate, and countermovement actors. As a social movement's activity comes online, its enemies are able to take advantage of a new set of tools to surveil, map, understand, and potentially disrupt that movement. Transmedia organizing makes social movements more visible to friends and enemies alike, and movement participants often create and circulate content online without regard to the potential implications for privacy and for future repression. The long-term persistence of online data generates unforeseen effects, as movement participants who leave traces of their daily practices in social media spaces may retroactively be held accountable for their activity far into the future. This is especially problematic in environments of extreme state repression, but it is potentially harmful to movement participants' life chances even in the most (supposedly) open environments. In the wake of revelations about the extent and lack of accountability of NSA surveillance under PRISM and related programs, this dynamic deserves much more sustained attention. Overall, transmedia organizing potentially enables heightened surveillance by adversaries. For immigrant rights activists in the United States, a country that now performs approximately half a million deportations per year, this is a daily reality rather than a potential dark sci-fi future.

Second is the matter of censorship. While social media platforms are great enablers of peer-to-peer movement communication, at the same time, overreliance on commercial platforms leaves social movements vulnerable to multiple forms of both intentional and algorithmic censorship. Censorship of movement media takes place for a variety of reasons:

content that contains music or video clips from commercial sources may be deleted by algorithms designed to eliminate copyright violations; images of police, military, or vigilante brutality are removed for violating terms of service that disallow the graphic display of violence; group accounts and pages are deleted for advocating positions seen by site moderators as too extreme. Terms of service tend to leave activists high and dry when web service providers hide or delete their content or accounts. In some countries, the state requires service providers to implement extensive content filtering, and in most countries, almost all commercial sites cooperate extensively with law enforcement and intelligence agencies. Transmedia organizing also opens the door to new forms of social control, such as user-generated censorship,[13] as well as to the incorporation of movement communication practices as free labor for the profitability of corporate media platforms.[14]

A third issue is the inadvertent contribution to the hegemonic power and legitimacy of for-profit, private, corporate media systems. Most of the self-documentation of struggles that takes place in the immigrant rights movement is circulated through commercial sites like YouTube, Facebook, Twitter, and Tumblr. While movement media may find broader audiences in these spaces, at the same time, activists are contributing to the profitability of transnational communication firms, some of which (especially Rupert Murdoch's Fox News) are active mouthpieces for anti-immigrant sentiment. Many activists and organizers I talked to were quite aware of, and critical of, their own use of corporate tools to do movement work. They use these spaces strategically in order to reach wide audiences. However, if viable autonomous alternatives were available, many would use them. On the margins, some media activists are working to construct stronger autonomous communication infrastructure, built using free/libre and open-source software. However, these tools are little known and are often difficult to use. Since corporate social media sites already have massive audiences, autonomous tools have much less chance of uptake even if they are functionally equivalent or superior. However, this situation can change rapidly during moments of great crisis, ruptures in the glossy facade of friendly corporate culture, or at other moments based on the fickle feelings of the multitude. Additional research into and concrete initiatives concerning free/libre infrastructure for transmedia organizing are much needed.

Implications

In the past, few social movement scholars focused sustained attention on the movement-media relationship. Press attention as measured by print and broadcast coverage was taken as a dependent variable, or outcome, of successful movement activity. While some scholars wrote about media produced by movements themselves, media-making was rarely considered a core aspect of social movement activity. The spread of digital media literacy and the increased visibility of participatory media in the broader cultural landscape require that we retheorize this relationship. The political economy of the communication system itself is being reconfigured around the social production and circulation of digital media. Social movements are becoming transmedia hubs, where new visions of society are encoded into digital texts by movement participants, then shared, aggregated, remixed, and circulated ever more widely across platforms. Despite persistent digital inequality, the praxis of critical digital media literacy can produce subjects able to fully participate in transmedia organizing. Transmedia organizers take advantage of the changed media ecology to mobilize networked social movements. Participatory media-making can help strengthen movement identity, win political and economic victories, and transform consciousness.

Within the immigrant rights movement, as in other social movements, this process is increasingly visible. However, activists and social movement organizations are continually pushed in contradictory directions vis-à-vis participatory media practices. Private foundations steer movements toward professionalization and vertical structures, and toward tight message discipline. Old-school organizers, often in leadership positions within nonprofits, often misunderstand, distrust, or fear the loss of message control. To build stronger social movements, transmedia organizers work to diversify resource streams and reduce dependency on private foundations. At the same time, they struggle to build trust relationships with old-school organizers, who have a wealth of knowledge about community mobilization but who learned a different model of communications work. Transmedia organizers are pushing nonprofit organizations and other social movement groups to share the elaboration of public narratives with their own movement base. In this context, social movement scholars must retheorize movements and the media as interlocking systems.[15] It would also be fruitful to further examine the role that media production plays in movement identity formation.

Recommendations for Organizers and Activists

One of my main aims as an engaged scholar is to develop new knowledge alongside the communities I work with, in order to advance both theory and real-world practice.[16] In accordance with that aim, I end this book with a brief set of recommendations for organizers and activists, based on key research findings. In addition, at the end of each interview I asked interviewees to reflect on what they felt the most important goals of the immigrant rights movement should be, with respect to media strategy. I also asked interviewees to imagine and describe the media system they would like to see in five years' time. This section therefore draws from organizers' responses to an invitation to imagine the future of social movement media.

Analyze the Media Ecology

Very few organizers systematically analyze the media ecology for new opportunities and threats. This book demonstrates that it is worthwhile to do so, since rapid changes in the media ecology have implications for how social movements might best approach media strategy. In plain language, this means that effective organizers think about who they are trying to reach, research which media platforms will be most effective at reaching that group of people, and shape their communication strategies accordingly. In addition, they integrate participatory media-making into their plans from the beginning. This form of analysis needs to be iterative and built into overall movement strategy, since the media ecology involves rapidly changing platforms, tools, and services. The process involves learning about the audiences and reach of various print, TV, and radio channels, as well as blogs, social media, and mobile media services and platforms. Movements can also take advantage of the changing media ecology by developing relationships with and allies among journalists, bloggers, and media-makers across various platforms.

Develop a Transmedia Organizing Strategy

We have also seen that effective organizers have learned to involve their social base in making media about the movement. Media created by the movement base can be aggregated, remixed, and amplified across plat-forms. Transmedia organizing also means systematically linking move-ment media in any one channel to the broader public narrative of the movement, a narrative that takes place across multiple platforms. For example, interviews with broadcast media should always mention a website or an SMS number where the viewer or listener can find out more. If a movement participant creates an interesting video about an action, a link to the video can be included in tweets or press releases that organizers send to journalists and bloggers. A high-quality version can be made available for download by TV and web video outlets. Online news sites and local bloggers can be contacted to embed the video in their stories, and so on. Transmedia organizing also requires reconceiving the communicator's role, from content creator to curator or from spokesperson to amplifier. Part of the responsibility of effective transmedia organizers is to constantly pay attention to media created by the movement base. When they find some-thing powerful, transmedia organizers repost it on their sites, send it to their social networks, and leverage press contacts to get it picked up by media outlets with greater reach. These practices privilege participation by the social base of the movement in messaging, framing, and the construc-tion of larger movement narratives, and help build movement identity among those who participate. It is also possible to conduct workshops where people from the movement's base are invited to develop messaging and framing. Those social movement organizations that are willing to relax top-down control over messaging and framing will benefit from stronger movement identity, greater participation, and ultimately more power.

Actively Foster Critical Digital Media Literacy

Movements whose social base is largely excluded from the digital public sphere are also developing a praxis of critical digital media literacy. Transmedia organizers in the immigrant rights movement link media production training directly to movement building. We have seen that the praxis of critical digital media literacy is most effective when techni-cal training is combined with organizing efforts, rather than when they are placed in separate silos. A praxis of critical digital media literacy involves more than volunteers teaching basic computer skills. Activists and organizers can strengthen the praxis of critical digital media literacy by sharing tools and skills in both formal and informal settings across movement networks. Regular hands-on skill-sharing workshops, open to all, can greatly strengthen a movement's capacity for transmedia organizing. The more people in the movement's social base that learn to make, remix, and circulate media across platforms, the more powerful the movement becomes.

Transmedia organizers are also challenging the tendency to assume that media production is too complex or too expensive. Effective media production is increasingly fast, cheap, and DIY. Movements with few resources can use free tools to make quick, inexpensive, multimedia that tells their story effectively. Expert advice or fears about poor production values should never be allowed to hamper the creative use of media for movement ends. Videos with high production values can be important tools if the resources are available, but movement groups do not need big budgets to have big impacts. Those who make a practice of regularly producing and circulating their own media improve their skills and abilities over time.

Community computer labs can become vibrant spaces for the development of critical digital media literacy and are key assets for transmedia organizers. It is possible to transform existing computer labs, which often sit empty and are used only for basic computer literacy trainings, into hubs of transmedia organizing. Social movement organizations have for the most part not thought creatively about how to find staff or volunteers to help make this happen. Partnering with community colleges, universities, and other institutions that have students skilled in media production is one possibility. Movement organizations might also explore pooling resources with others to help make dynamic media labs a reality.

In the long run, many activists and organizers I interviewed also felt that social movements should consider the possibilities of community-controlled communications infrastructure. For example, although cable access TV stations are rapidly disappearing, many of them still have resources to teach video production; the long struggle by microradio activists has finally begun to bear fruit in the form of new low-power FM licenses; organizers in L.A., Detroit, and Brooklyn created community-owned wireless networks, and so on.[17] Community control of media and communications infrastructure, combined with the development of critical digital media literacy, has the potential to be a decisive factor in building strong social movements in the United States.

Create Strong Accountability Mechanisms for Transmedia Organizing Campaigns

The structure of social movement groups shapes, but does not determine, the ways in which they use media as an organizing tool. Social movement groups in the U.S. context have become increasingly professionalized and vertically structured, in part because of the influence of private foundations and the rise of the issue-based nonprofit sector. Within the immigrant rights movement, some professionalized nonprofits and vertical organizations have been able to take advantage of the new media ecology and engage in transmedia organizing, when their leadership is open to shifting their communication strategy away from a top-down model. However, junior staff within nonprofit organizations are often frustrated by senior staff's refusal to abandon top-down communication practices. In contrast, horizontally structured movement groups are more easily able to deploy transmedia organizing approaches.

Regardless of the decision-making structure of the movement group, I have argued in this book that for those who want to take advantage of the possibilities of the new media ecology, it is essential to follow principles of democratic decision making. Social media provide a platform for a conversation, not a broadcast. Movement leaders who try to control the message across social media platforms will fail, since no one wants to participate if they are not allowed to speak. It is also crucial to let people innovate, play, and take risks. Those who try to overplan social media strategy will never get off the ground, while those who allow interested movement participants to set up accounts and play with new online services and networks, then incorporate them into overall communication strategy if they seem to be working well, will have more success. Movement groups must also avoid technological "lock-in": tools that do not seem to be working should be dropped in favor of others that seem more intuitive or effective. Perhaps most crucially, accountable transmedia organizing means opening the story of the movement to the voices of those who make up its social base. If movement participants want to push messages other than those preferred by the leadership, then the leadership needs to either do a better job of articulating the importance of the frame or a better job of actively listening to what the social base demands. The solution, in a social movement organization that actually wants to build shared power, can never be to silence or marginalize the voices of the community.

Effective movement leadership respects and values community knowledge and information. An effective praxis of critical digital media literacy and a strong transmedia organizing strategy should thus also serve to constantly strengthen movement accountability.

Finally, those I worked with and interviewed for this book repeatedly emphasized the importance of both sustainability and autonomy. A diversified stream of resources is important not so much to avoid explicit control by funders (although that does occasionally present a problem) but to escape the long-term process of social movement professionalization that tends to shift movements away from value-driven base building and toward issue-driven, top-down models of social change. This is not to say that social justice–oriented foundations cannot play a positive role in encouraging transmedia organizing among social movement organizations. However, so far most have not. Exceptions during the period of this research included the Funding Exchange's Media Justice Fund, now closed, and certain program officers within the Ford Foundation, the Open Society Foundations, and a handful of others. These programs supported a great deal of important community-based media work while also urging CBOs to get involved in media and communications policy battles. The California Emerging Technology Fund, Zero Divide, and the Instructional Telecommunications Foundation (now Voqal.org) have also all been important sources of funding for media-making capacity within the immigrant rights movement in California. Some foundations fund CBOs to train community members in basic computing skills, but usually in a "job readiness" framework that delinks digital media literacy from critical analysis or social movement participation. Others urge their grantees to develop professionalized public relations strategies, and too often see social media as a broadcast or branding tool. Yet we have seen that movements are most effectively able to incorporate networked communication tools and skills when their base is digitally literate, when they use digital media tools and practices in everyday resistance, and when they are willing to shift from top-down communication strategies to approaches that involve the base as much as possible in shaping the movement's public narrative. A long-term vision for community control of media thus requires a diversified funding model that does not remain wholly dependent on foundations for the bulk of resources.

The immigrant rights movement has already pioneered transmedia organizing, in organic forms built on top of existing media practices. The steady growth of critical digital media literacy makes broader adoption of transmedia organizing approaches possible. By beginning from the actually existing practices of social movement groups and tracing the ways that they create and circulate media across various platforms, we gain a deeper understanding of social movements in the twenty-first century. By listening to the experiences of those involved in day-to-day organizing within the immigrant rights movement and by learning from those experiences, it is possible to build stronger, more democratic social movements in the information age.

Appendixes

Appendix A: Research Methodology

In appendix A, I summarize my research methodology. I briefly discuss participatory research and collaborative design, communication for social change, and popular education. I also describe the media workshops, semistructured interviews, field recordings, and movement media archives that together provide the bulk of material I analyze and synthesize in this book. The appendix ends with a brief note about intersectionality, and thoughts on the limitations of my research approach.

Participatory Research and Design

I conduct most of my work within the broad frameworks of participatory research, popular education, and participatory design. Participatory research is not a unified methodology; rather, it denotes an orientation to research that emphasizes the development of communities of shared inquiry and action.[1] I consider the groups and individuals I work with to be coresearchers rather than simply subjects of my research. Along the same lines, for me, participatory or collaborative design takes place with community members as codesigners rather than simply "test users."[2]

I value participatory research and collaborative design on both normative and practical grounds. Ethically, I believe in democratic decision making, including decision making in research and design processes. I also believe in shared ownership of the outcomes of research and design. Practically, I believe that participatory methods involving people at all stages of a research or design process are most likely to produce innovative knowledge and tools that respond to people's goals, strengths, and needs in everyday life. A commitment to these approaches has connected me to strong communities of participatory research and codesign and helped me produce a range of work, including scholarly and popular publications; video, audio, web-based, and interactive media; free/libre and open-source software; and other texts.

That said, the incentive structures of the academy militate against participatory research. Single-authored publication is the gold standard in many fields, including media studies, and this is largely incompatible with shared community ownership of research. Thus, while this book does reflect insights gained from years of participatory research, media, and design projects that I have taken part in within the immigrant rights movement, it is not itself a participatory research project. The research questions, study design, and authorship are mine, along with responsibility for errors, omissions, and any misrepresentation. Between 2006 and 2012, I participated in more than one hundred popular education workshops, played a key role in multiyear, ongoing collaborative design processes, and took part in immigrant rights movement actions and events. I also employed traditional research methods, primarily semistructured interviews, field recordings, and textual analysis of movement media archives. At the same time, many of the projects that I describe in these pages fit within the umbrella of communication for social change.

Communication for Social Change

In participatory research, typically a community-based organization collaborates with a researcher or research team to generate a study that documents, deepens, and validates community knowledge.[3] This approach can help provide legitimacy and increased visibility for community demands while advancing broader scholarship by circulating community-based knowledge. This kind of work is also often used to generate attention from mass media and policymakers, often with the end goal of a specific campaign victory. For example, in Los Angeles Andrea Hricko's work with community-based environmental justice organizations,[4] Gary Blasi and Jacqueline Leavitt's work with the Los Angeles Taxi Workers' Alliance,[5] and Victor Narro's engagement with worker centers[6] all follow this model.

My own work with the immigrant rights movement has focused on building long-term communication capacity rather than on winning a specific campaign. All of the movement groups I became involved with already had histories of popular communication practice. They also hoped to build critical digital media literacy among their base. My role, over a period of about seven years, was to help plan, fundraise for, and support the implementation of various participatory media projects based in popular education approaches. I attempted as much as possible to do this not by imposing my ideas about what kind of project might be most fruitful but by employing communication for social change methods to explore the possibilities and develop plans together with community partners.

Communication for social change (CFSC) is both theory and method. It is an approach strongly influenced by the work of Paolo Freire. CFSC draws especially on the Freirian focus on conscientization and political education through literacy.[7] In this theoretical and practical tradition, literacy is seen as a process through which people acquire more than simply technical skills, such as reading and writing. Rather, literacy is seen as a process that builds our awareness of ourselves as actors who have the ability to shape and transform the world, as well as of the structural (systemic) forces that stand in our way.[8] CFSC emerged as a subfield of development communication that emphasizes dialogic communication rather than a one-to-many "knowledge injection" or "banking method" approach to education.[9]

CFSC overlaps with participatory research approaches and has been elaborated over time by several generations of communication scholars and activists. Contemporary proponents of CFSC include Alfonso Gumucio Dagron,[10] John Downing,[11] Cees Hamelink,[12] and Clemencia Rodriguez,[13] among many others. CFSC emphasizes principles of community ownership, horizontality (as opposed to verticality), communities as their own change agents, dialog and negotiation (instead of persuasion and transmission), and outcomes measured by changes in social norms, policies, and social structure rather than solely by individual behavioral change.[14] CFSC practitioners are also attempting to rethink critical literacy for the digital age. Practitioners work with community partners to develop a shared analysis and vision, create strategy, construct curriculum, work on media production and circulation, and evaluate project impacts.[15] Ideally, the community actively participates in each aspect of the communicative process, as far as possible. The outside researcher acts as a catalyst for a shared process with the community rather than as an observer of the community. Community participants are thus coproducers of knowledge and practice rather than objects of study.

I began to engage in this methodology, in partnership with immigrant rights organizations in Los Angeles, beginning in May 2006. In January 2007, Amanda Garcés from the Institute of Popular Education of Southern California, simmi gandi from the Garment Worker Center, and I received a Small Collaborative Grant in Media and Communications from the Social Science Research Council (SSRC). This grant provided a small amount of funding to work together to map the communication ecology of immigrant rights organizations in L.A. The project planted the seed that eventually grew into this book. Along the way, it catalyzed the creation of the Garment Worker Center radio project that would later become *Radio Tijera* (Radio Scissors).[16] It also laid the foundation for a larger university-community partnership. The following year, I worked with leadership, staff, and members of the Institute of Popular Education of Southern California (IDEPSCA), as well as with faculty and students at the University of Southern California's Annenberg School for Communication & Journalism, to secure a follow-up Large Collaborative Grant from the SSRC for the Mobile Voices project (VozMob).[17]

As described in more detail in chapter 5, VozMob was built by members of IDEPSCA's Popular Communication Team, including Madelou Gonzales, Manuel Mancía, Adolfo Cisneros, Crispín Jimenez, Marcos and Diana Mendez, Alma Luz, and Ranferi, as well as organizers Amanda Garces, Natalie Arellano, Brenda Aguilera, Luis Valentín, Pedro Joel Espinosa, and Executive Director Raul Añorve (later Marlom Portillo). At USC, research partners included Annenberg School faculty member François Bar and PhD students Carmen Gonzales, Melissa Brough, and Cara Wallis, later joined by Benjamin Stokes and Veronica Parades. Software developers Mark Burdett, Gaba Rodriguez, and Squiggy Rubio played key roles, as did graphic designer Poonam Whabi from Design Action Collective. This project later received a MacArthur/HASTAC Digital Learning grant to explore the use of mobile phones for digital storytelling by day laborers and household workers. Over time, VozMob has created thousands of stories, conducted workshops with hundreds of day laborers, household workers, and students, and won international recognition. The project continues today (see http://vozmob.net), and more can be read about it in the co-authored chapter "Mobile Voices: Projecting the voices of immigrant workers by appropriating mobile phones for popular communication," by VozMob, in P. M. Napoli and M. Aslama, editors, *Communications*

Research in Action: Scholar-Activist Collaborations for a Democratic Public Sphere (New York: Fordham University Press, 2010).

Although projects such as *Radio Tijera* and VozMob are not at the center of this book, I met many activists, friends, and colleagues through working with them. Several of my interviewees are participants in these projects. In addition, taking part in these projects through weekly face-to-face workshops over a period of several years provided me with a great deal of contextual knowledge. I was given the opportunity to develop key insights together with an extended and supportive community. That experience, more than any other, grounds this research in an understanding of day-to-day media practices in the immigrant rights movement.

Workshops

During the years 2006–2012 I took part in more than one hundred skill-sharing sessions and workshops in the immigrant rights movement. These workshops spanned a wide range of areas, from critical media analysis to audio and video recording and editing, from "social media 101" to how to work with developers and designers through agile development, user stories, and issue trackers. The workshops include a three-year ongoing audio production workshop at the Garment Worker Center and a weekly workshop in mobile digital storytelling (VozMob) that began in June 2008 at IDEPSCA and continues today. For an example of workshop facilitation guides I helped develop during this time period, see "Dialed in: A cell phone literacy toolkit," produced by the Center for Urban Pedagogy, with a section by VozMob (available at http://welcometocup.org/Store?product _id=42). There is also quite extensive process documentation available on the VozMob wiki at https://dev.vozmob.net/projects/vozmob/wiki.

Interviews

I conducted forty semistructured interviews with people who considered themselves part of the immigrant rights movement. Interviews were conducted both with individuals and in small groups, although the majority were one-on-one interviews lasting one to two hours. I conducted nearly all interviews face-to-face, but in a few cases they took place via phone, videochat, or IRC (chat). I recorded interviews using a small digital audio recorder, with the explicit permission of interviewees. These audio recordings were fully transcribed, some by the author and the majority by a professional transcriber.[18] The full questionnaire that guided the semistructured interviews is available in appendix C. The confidentiality of interviews and Institutional Review Board requirements preclude inclusion of a full list identifying individual interviewees, unedited transcripts, or audio recordings. Anonymized transcripts are available on request. For more on semistructured interviewing, see Sharan B. Merriam's excellent book on the design and implementation of qualitative research.[19]

I conducted interviews with individuals active in immigrant rights organizations, independent worker centers, service-sector labor unions, indigenous organizations, immigrant student networks, and day laborer, household worker, and garment worker associations and unions. Many individual activists and organizers in the immigrant rights movement are not single-issue organizers; they also fight for workers' rights, indigenous rights, the rights of youth, gender justice, environmental justice, access to health care, access to education, the right to the city, lesbian, gay, bisexual, transgender, queer (LGBTQ), and Two-Spirit rights, sex workers' rights, lower remittance tariffs, and against ICE raids and police brutality. In seeking interviewees in Los Angeles, I began with activists from key worker centers that focus primarily on organizing immigrant workers, then snowballed outward from there to include individuals from groups and networks that my initial interviewees considered important to the movement. After arriving at MIT, I worked closely with Comparative Media Studies graduate student Rogelio Alejandro López. Together, in 2011–12 we conducted a round of interviews that I transcribed, analyzed, and now reference in this book. This round of interviews also informed Rogelio's thesis, titled "From huelga! to undocumented and unafraid! A comparative study of media strategies in the farm worker movement of the 1960s and the immigrant youth movement of the 2000s" (available online at http://cmsw.mit.edu/rogelio-lopez-from-huelga-to-undocumented-and-unafraid).

Recordings and Notes

I took photographs, recorded video and audio material, and took extensive written notes during many immigrant rights mobilizations, meetings, and events. I used these recordings and notes both as primary source material for analysis and to incorporate into multimedia presentations of the research findings and/or design iterations. At no point did I make recordings of nonpublic meetings or events without seeking explicit permission from those present. For the purposes of writing this book, I organized recordings and notes using the software package Scrivener for Linux (available at http://www.literatureandlatte.com/forum/viewforum.php?f=33).

Movement Media

During the course of research for this book, I compiled an extensive archive of movement-produced media. As with the interviews, recordings, and notes, I frequently incorporate clips, stills, and short excerpts of movement-produced media into digital presentations of findings. Multimedia texts include photographs, audio and video recording, and texts posted to movement websites, as well as to popular social networking sites and video-sharing sites. I also gathered screen captures and transcriptions of SMS messages, and a large number of physical flyers, posters, and newspapers. I assembled a small library of physical CDs and DVDs produced by media-makers linked to the immigrant rights movement. This archive provided extensive primary source material for textual analysis.

Intersectionality

Throughout this book I deploy race, class, gender, sexuality, and other categories from a nonessentialist position and from the perspective of intersectional analysis. *Intersectionality* denotes the position, developed by Kimberlé Crenshaw and other feminist theorists in the late 1980s and early 1990s, that class, race, gender, sexuality, and other axes of identity, power, and resistance never operate independently from one another.[20] All subjectivity is located at their intersection. For example, there is no categorical subject position of "woman" who experiences gender oppression independent of her race and class position. A white middle-class woman will experience different forms of raced, classed, or gendered oppression than a working-class Latina. At the same time, as articulated by Judith Butler, identity categories are themselves constructed and performative.[21] Sandra Harding describes how social scientists have come to understand race, class, and gender as interlocking axes that form a matrix rather than as parallel but basically separate systems.[22] According to Patricia Hill Collins, each axis operates on three levels: the individual, the structural, and the symbolic; and every person is located (raced, gendered, classed) by society at a particular position within this matrix. These categories are mutually interlocking and reproduce each other, in addition to dividing subaltern subjects from seeking solidarity and constructing a unified project for social justice.[23]

Intersectional and anti-essentialist analysis may appear to be in conflict with institutional data categories and standard research methods. Yet data gathered by state agencies, corporations, and mainstream researchers according to essentialist identity categories often provide the best available indicator of the impacts of structural inequality. This is true even as uncritical reproduction of fixed identity categories by researchers also tends to normalize a reductive view of subjectivity. Wherever I use such data to support my arguments, I invite the reader to retain the critical perspective of intersectional analysis.

Limitations of the Research Approach

My own subject position as a white, male-bodied, queer, U.S. citizen, university-affiliated scholar with extensive training in multimedia production shapes both my theoretical and methodological approach. In addition, it shapes my regular interactions with activists, organizers, and community members in the immigrant rights movement. The limitations and advantages introduced by my own standpoint are further complicated as I gain increasing visibility and credibility based on institutional affiliation with a well-known university. My own participation in movement spaces, both off- and online, is additionally complicated by my multiple roles as ally, activist, and researcher.

Language also limits my research. My language fluency is limited to English and Spanish, with some limited ability to communicate in Portuguese (Portuñol, really). This means that all of my formal interviews were conducted in English and Spanish, and the movement media materials I examined were also almost all in these two languages. Given the immense diversity of immigrants to the United States, this fact undermines the generalizability of my study. That said, I did work with and interview activists from immigrant rights organizations, collectives, and networks that organize Korean, Chinese, South Asian, and Southeast Asian immigrant workers, and their perspectives also inform this work.

Finally, this study does not employ a comparative design. This fact limits any strong claim that my findings in the immigrant rights movement necessarily hold for other social movements, or even across geographic locations. It may be that the analysis in this book is unique to the movement actors I worked with and studied, at this particular historical moment. In the future, I plan to develop a comparative analysis of the transmedia organizing framework by exploring its applicability to other movements. I invite other scholars to do the same.

Appendix B: Interviewees

This appendix provides brief descriptions of interviewees, to provide more context for the reader. The interviewees participated in formal, recorded, semistructured interviews that were transcribed and analyzed for this book. To preserve the anonymity of the interviewees, the descriptions are of a very general character. The initials of all interviewees have been changed and do not reflect their real names.

Brief Descriptions of Interviewees

BC, radio producer, interviewed July 2008

BD, day laborer, interviewed October 2009

BE1, college student, DREAM Act organizer, interviewed spring 2011

BE2, college student, DREAM Act organizer, interviewed spring 2011

BH, staff member of a community-based organization, interviewed February 2010

CP, funder, interviewed March 2008

CS, volunteer with a news website, interviewed January 2009

DM, volunteer with various media projects, interviewed July 2008

DN, online organizer with a national immigrant rights organization, interviewed April 2013

EN, high school student, interviewed August 2009

EQ, director of a small nonprofit organization, interviewed May 2009

GN, video producer, interviewed December 2007

HH, taxi worker, interviewed November 2009

IQ, funder, interviewed September 2008

KB, volunteer for multiple collectives, interviewed July 2009

KD, staff member of a community-based organization, interviewed July 2009

KE, executive director of an activists' and artists' nonprofit organization, interviewed spring 2011

KL, tech activist, interviewed September 2008

KT, member of an undocuqueer activist and artist group, interviewed fall 2011

LC, online organizer with a national immigrant rights organization, interviewed fall 2011

LN, IT staff member of a large nonprofit organization, interviewed February 2010

NB, community organizer and media-maker, interviewed April 2009

ND, immigrant rights lawyer, interviewed April 2010

NH, household worker, interviewed August 2009

NI, student, interviewed May 2008

NN, day laborer, interviewed October 2009

NQ, community organizer, interviewed February 2010

OE, staff member of a medium-sized nonprofit organization, interviewed January 2010

ON, core member of a DREAM activist collective, interviewed fall 2011

PS, organizer with an indigenous organization, interviewed May 2009

QH, labor organizer, interviewed October 2008

QX, director of a community-based organization, interviewed April 2008

RF, student and media-maker, interviewed November 2009

SM, student, member of an undocumented student organizing group, interviewed spring 2011

TD, staff member of a community-based organization, interviewed July 2008

TH, member of various horizontalist collectives, interviewed February 2010

TX, employee of a small nonprofit organization, interviewed March 2010

WO, public interest lawyer, interviewed April 2009

XD, social media consultant, interviewed February 2010

ZP, radio host, interviewed February 2009

Appendix C: Interview Guide

The following guide was used to conduct all semistructured interviews. Not every question was asked of every interviewee, but each interview touched on the following main themes: an overview of the work the interviewee did in the immigrant rights movement; media practices in the movement; access; appropriation and learning; professionalization; organizational structure; and long-term vision.

Overview

• Organization: Briefly describe the organization or network you work with, its main areas of work, how you frame your work, and what social movements you consider yourself part of. What's the best source for more overview information?

• Personal engagement: How and why did you get involved?

• Daily communication practices: Please describe the day-to-day communication practices: within the organization, between the staff and the leadership of the movement network, with the base, with alternative and popular media, with the ethnic media, with the "public" media, with the mass (Anglo) media.

• Media use by those you are trying to organize: What media does the community you are trying to organize use most? What are the community's three most popular communication channels (specific radio stations, TV channels, newspapers, etc.)?

• Are the most popular channels the same for men and women? For younger and older people?

• How do you know?

- Networks: Are you, your organization, or movement part of a network or networks? What are they?
- Are any of them transnational? How has it helped or made things more difficult to be part of a network?
- Describe how communication flows through the network.

Mobilization

- Victory: Describe something you consider to be a major victory of your organization or of the movement.
- Crisis: How about something that was a major setback or crisis?
- Communication: Describe your own communication practice during these key moments.

Access

- Relationships to the media: Please describe the movement's relationship to: the mass (Anglo) media, the ethnic media, public media, independent and popular media, the print press, radio, TV, blogs, social networking sites, mobile phones, other forms of media.
- Relationship to the Internet: Describe how your organization and the movement use the Internet. In what ways has the Internet helped you, and in what ways does it present challenges or dangers?
- Barriers: What do you think are the key barriers for your organization in gaining access to the media?
- What are the barriers to learning and using new communication tools and skills?
- Do you think these same barriers are faced by other groups or networks in the movement?
- What do you think the key barriers are for your base or members?

Appropriation and Learning

- Popular communication strategy/practice: Is there or has there ever been any? If so, describe it. What worked or failed, and how do you know?

• Describe an example of how the immigrant rights movement has effectively used the mass media, and an example of how the movement has effectively used new media.

• Where do you get ideas for how to use new media as an organizing tool?

• Are there specific people, organizations, trainings, or examples you look to?

Specialists and Professionalization

• Specialists: Describe your following relationships:

• With tech activists in the movement.

• With movement media-makers.

• Do you have a dedicated communications person on staff?

• Do you work with outside communications consultants or strategists?

• Do you have an IT person you work with, or a software programmer?

• Do you have an online organizer?

• Do you use any corporate application service providers (for example, Democracy In Action)? Talk about that experience: what has been good and bad?

Structure

• Accountability: Describe whom your organization is accountable to, and the mechanisms for accountability.

• Structure: What is the decision-making structure in your organization or network?

• Technology: Do you think communication technology has any impact on accountability in the movement? If so, what is it?

• Traits: Please describe the gender, sexual identity, race/ethnicity, class, and age of the staff and leadership, the membership, and the communication activists. How do these features have an impact on communication practice in the movement?

• Funders: What role do funders play in developing movement communication tools, skills, and practices?

Long-Term Vision

• History: Has your use of media and communication technology changed over time? How?

• Desired capabilities: Are there communication projects or goals that you have as an organization or as a movement? What would you like to see in five years' time?

• Barriers and blocks: What is in the way of realizing your best-case scenario?

Thank you so much for your time!

Appendix D: Online Resources for Organizers

Additional resources for community organizers can be found online at http://transformativemedia.cc.

Notes

Acknowledgments

1. "Without a boss and without borders."

Introduction

1. Jesse Díaz, "Organizing the brown tide: *La gran epoca primavera* 2006, an insiders' story," PhD diss., University of California, 2010, http://www.escholarship.org/uc/item/3m92x4nb (retrieved August 1, 2013).

2. Leo Ralph Chavez, *The Latino Threat* (Stanford, CA: Stanford University Press, 2008); Priscilla Huang, "Anchor babies, over-breeders, and the population bomb: The reemergence of nativism and population control in anti-immigration policies," *Harvard Law and Policy Review* 2 (2008): 385.

3. W. Lance Bennett, Christian Breunig, and Terri Givens, "Communication and political mobilization: Digital media and the organization of anti-Iraq war demonstrations in the U.S.," *Political Communication* 25, no. 3 (2008): 269–289.

4. Todd Gitlin, *The Whole World Is Watching: Mass Media in the Making & Unmaking of the New Left: With a New Preface* (Berkeley: University of California Press, 1980).

5. Robert W. McChesney, *Rich Media, Poor Democracy: Communication Politics in Dubious Times* (Urbana: University of Illinois Press, 1999).

6. Alan B. Albarran, "Mergers and acquisitions in Spanish language media," in *The State of Spanish Language Media: 2007 Annual Report*, 38. Center for Spanish Language Media, University of North Texas, Denton, 2008.

7. Arlene Dávila, *Latinos, Inc.: The Marketing and Making of a People* (Berkeley: University of California Press, 2012).

8. Adrián Félix, Carmen González, and Ricardo Ramírez, "Political protest, ethnic media, and Latino naturalization," *American Behavioral Scientist* 52, no. 4 (2008): 618–634.

9. Clay Shirky, *Here Comes Everybody: The Power of Organizing without Organizations* (New York: Penguin, 2008); Nick Dyer-Witheford, *Cyber-Marx: Cycles and Circuits of Struggle in High-Technology Capitalism* (Urbana: University of Illinois Press, 1999).

10. Dan Gillmor, *We the Media: Grassroots Journalism by the People, for the People* (Sebastopol, CA: O'Reilly Media, 2008); Manuel Castells, *Networks of Outrage and Hope* (New York: Polity Press, 2012).

11. Orlando Fals-Borda and Muhammad Anisur Rahman. *Action and Knowledge: Breaking the Monopoly with Participatory Action-Research* (New York: Apex Press, 1991).

12. John Downing, *Radical Media: Rebellious Communication and Social Movements* (Thousand Oaks, CA: Sage, 2001); William A. Gamson and Gadi Wolfsfeld, "Movements and media as interacting systems," *Annals of the American Academy of Political and Social Science* 528 (1993): 114–125; Manuel Castells, *The Power of Identity, Vol. 2 of The Information Age: Economy, Society and Culture* (Oxford: Blackwell, 1997); idem, "Communication, power and counter-power in the network society," *International Journal of Communication* 1, no. 1 (2007): 238–266.

13. Sidney Tarrow, *Power in Movement: Social Movements and Contentious Politics* (Cambridge: Cambridge University Press, 1994).

14. R. Kelly Garrett, "Protest in an information society: A review of literature on social movements and new ICTs," *Information Communication and Society* 9, no. 2 (2006): 202.

15. Paolo Gerbaudo, *Tweets and the Streets: Social Media and Contemporary Activism* (London: Pluto Press, 2012).

16. Virginia Eubanks, *Digital Dead End: Fighting for Social Justice in the Information Age* (Cambridge, MA: MIT Press, 2011).

17. Douglas Kellner and Jeff Share, "Toward critical media literacy: Core concepts, debates, organizations, and policy," *Discourse: Studies in the Cultural Politics of Education* 26, no. 3 (2005): 369–386; Shelley Goldman, Angela Booker, and Meghan McDermott, "Mixing the digital, social, and cultural: Learning, identity, and agency in youth participation," in *Youth, Identity, and Digital Media*, ed. David Buckingham, 185–206 (Cambridge, MA: MIT Press, 2008).

18. Malcolm Gladwell, "Small change," *New Yorker*, October 4, 2010, 42–49.

19. Marina Sitrin, *Horizontalism: Voices of Popular Power in Argentina* (Oakland, CA: AK Press, 2006).

20. Jeffrey S. Juris, *Networking Futures: The Movements against Corporate Globalization* (Durham, NC: Duke University Press, 2008).

21. Dorothy Kidd, "Indymedia.org: A new communications commons," in *Cyberactivism: Online Activism in Theory and Practice*, ed. Martha McCaughey and Michael

D. Ayers, 47–69 (New York: Routledge, 2003); Victor W. Pickard, "Assessing the radical democracy of Indymedia: Discursive, technical, and institutional constructions," *Critical Studies in Media Communication* 23, no. 1 (2006): 19–38.

22. Tad Hirsch, "TXTMob and Twitter: A reply to Nick Bilton," http://publicpractice .org/wp/?p=779 (retrieved October 18, 2013).

23. Castells, *Networks of Outrage and Hope.*

24. David Graeber, "The new anarchists," *New Left Review* 13, no. 6 (2002): 61–73; Marina Sitrin, "Prefigurative politics: Weaving imagination and creation: The future in the present," in *Globalize Liberation: How to Uproot the System and Build a Better World,* ed. David Solnit, 263–277 (San Francisco: City Lights Press, 2004).

25. Zeynep Tufecki, "New media and the people-powered uprisings," *MIT Technology Review,* August 30, 2011.

26. Gerbaudo, *Tweets and the Streets.*

27. Andrew Sullivan, "The revolution will be Twittered," *The Daily Dish, The Atlantic,* June 13, 2009.

28. Philip Howard, Aiden Duffy, Deen Freelon, Muzammil Hussain, Will Mari, and Marwa Mazaid, "Opening closed regimes: What was the role of social media during the Arab Spring?," Project on Information Technology and Political Islam, University of Washington, Seattle, September 2011, http://pitpi.org/index.php/2011/09/11/ opening-closed-regimes-what-was-the-role-of-social-media-during-the-arab-spring/ (retrieved May 22, 2012).

29. Sasha Costanza-Chock, "Mic check! Media cultures and the Occupy movement," *Social Movement Studies* 11, nos. 3–4 (2012): 375–385.

30. Personal communication, ON, July 2013.

31. S. Vaidhyanathan, *The Googlization of Everything* (Berkeley: University of California Press, 2010).

32. Evgeny Morozov, *The Net Delusion: The Dark Side of Internet Freedom* (New York: PublicAffairs, 2012).

33. Stefaan Walgrave, Lance Bennett, Jeroen Van Laer, and Christian Breunig, "Multiple engagements and network bridging in contentious politics: Digital media use of protest participants," *Mobilization* 16, no. 3 (2011): 325–349.

34. Lance Bennett and Alexandra Segerberg, "Digital media and the personalization of collective action: Social technology and the organization of protests against the global economic crisis," *Information, Communication & Society* 14 (2011): 770–799.

35. Leah Lievrouw, *Alternative and Activist New Media* (Malden, MA: Polity Press, 2011), provides a welcome exception. Lievrouw first locates contemporary activist

media practices within a larger historical context, then traces five basic genres: culture jamming, alternative computing, participatory journalism, mediated mobilization, and commons knowledge production.

36. Annabelle Sreberny and Ali Mohammadi, *Small Media, Big Revolution: Communication, Culture, and the Iranian Revolution* (Minneapolis: University of Minnesota Press, 1994).

37. Laura Pulido, *Black, Brown, Yellow, and Left: Radical Activism in Los Angeles* (Berkeley: University of California Press, 2005).

38. Jack Kyser, "Manufacturing in Southern California," Los Angeles County Economic Development Corporation, Los Angeles, 2007.

39. Rick Fantasia and Kim Voos, *Hard Work: Remaking the American Labor Movement* (Berkeley: University of California Press, 2004).

40. David Harvey, *A Brief History of Neoliberalism* (Oxford: Oxford University Press, 2005).

41. Vanessa Tait, *Poor Workers' Unions: Rebuilding Labor from Below* (Cambridge, MA: South End Press, 2005).

42. Jonathan Walters, "Justice for janitors: 'Your hands make them rich,'" with Kamilo Rivera, Rafael Ventura, Dolores Martinez, and Marisela Salinas, Research Center for Leadership in Action, New York University/Wagner, September 2003, http://wagner.nyu.edu/leadership/reports/files/8.pdf.

43. Personal communication, KL, PG.

44. Edna Bonacich and Fernando Gapasin, "Organizing the unorganizable: Challenges of globalized manufacturing for the California labor movement," in *The State of California Labor,* ed. Paul Ong and James Lincoln, 345–368 (Berkeley/Los Angeles: UCLA and UC Berkeley Institute of Industrial Relations, 2001).

45. Hector Delgado, "The Los Angeles Manufacturing Action Project: An opportunity squandered?," in *Organizing Immigrants: The Challenge for Unions in Contemporary California,* ed. Ruth Milkman, 225–238 (Ithaca, NY: Cornell University Press, 2000).

46. Abel Valenzuela, Jr., Nik Theodore, Edwin Melendez, and Ana Luz Gonzalez. *On the Corner: Day Labor in the United States,* Los Angeles: UCLA Center for the Study of Urban Poverty, 2006, http://www.sscnet.ucla.edu/issr/csup/uploaded_files/Natl _DayLabor-On_the_Corner1.pdf.

47. Maria Dziembowska, "NDLON and the history of day labor organizing in L.A.," *Social Policy* 40, no. 3 (2010): 27–33.

48. P. Hondagneu-Sotelo, *God's Heart Has No Borders: How Religious Activists Are Working for Immigrant Rights* (Berkeley: University of California Press. 2010).

49. Ruth Milkman, "New workers, new labor, and the new Los Angeles," in *Unions in a Globalized Environment: Changing Borders, Organizational Boundaries, and Social Roles,* ed. Bruce Nissen, 103–129 (Armonk, NY: M. E. Sharpe, 2002).

50. For example, see Pulido, *Black, Brown, Yellow, and Left.*

51. David Hesmondhalgh, *The Cultural Industries,* 2nd ed. (London: Sage, 2007); Toby Miller, Nitin Govia, John McMurria, et al., *Global Hollywood 2* (London: British Film Institute; Berkeley: University of California Press, 2005).

52. See Tarrow, *Power in Movement.*

53. Henry Jenkins, "Transmedia storytelling," *MIT Technology Review,* January 15, 2003, http://www.technologyreview.com/Biotech/13052.

54. See http://transmediaactivism.wordpress.com.

55. Vincent Mosco, *The Political Economy of Communication: Rethinking and Renewal* (Thousand Oaks, CA: Sage, 1996).

Chapter 1

1. Jesse Díaz, "Organizing the brown tide: *La gran epoca primavera* 2006, an insiders' story," PhD diss., University of California, 2010, http://www.escholarship.org/uc/item/3m92x4nb (retrieved August 1, 2013).

2. Communication scholars have long used the term "media ecology" to examine the relationship between media technologies, media content, and social structure. In this book I use the term in its more popular sense, as a synonym for "media system" or "media across all channels and platforms." This is how the term is usually deployed by the activists and organizers I interviewed. I use it to highlight flows of information across multiple channels, including mass, community, and social media. Readers interested in the scholarly literature on media ecology should explore Harold Adams Innis, *The Bias of Communication* (Toronto: University of Toronto Press, 2008); Neil Postman, "The humanism of media ecology," *Proceedings of the Media Ecology Association* 1 (2000): 10–16; and Lance Strate, *Echoes and Reflections: On Media Ecology as a Field of Study* (Creskill, NJ: Hampton Press, 2006).

3. Robert W. McChesney and John Nichols, *Our Media, Not Theirs: The Democratic Struggle against Corporate Media* (New York: Seven Stories Press, 2011).

4. Arlene Dávila, *Latinos, Inc.: The Marketing and Making of a People: Updated Edition with a New Preface* (Berkeley: University of California Press, 2012).

5. Erika Lee, "The Chinese exclusion example: Race, immigration, and American gatekeeping, 1882–1924," *Journal of American Ethnic History* 21, no. 3 (2002): 36–62.

6. Andreas Peter, *Border Games: Policing the US-Mexico Divide* (Ithaca, NY: Cornell University Press, 2000).

7. For more on heteropatriarchy, see Andrea Smith, "Heteropatriarchy and the three pillars of white supremacy," in *Color of Violence: INCITE! Women of Color Against Violence,* ed. Andrea Smith, Beth E. Richie, and Julia Sudbury, 66–73 (Cambridge, MA: South End Press, 2006).

8. Ibid.

9. Wahab Twibell and Ty Shawn, "The road to internment: Special registration and other human rights violations of Arabs and Muslims in the United States," *Vermont Law Review* 29, no. 2 (2005): 407–553; Rachel Ida Buff, "The deportation terror," *American Quarterly* 60, no. 3 (2008): 523–551.

10. Immigration and Customs Enforcement, "Fact Sheet: ICE Office of Detention and Removal," Washington, D.C., ICE, 2006. http://www.ice.gov/pi/news/factsheets/dro110206.htm (retrieved August 20, 2007).

11. Immigrant Legal Resource Center, "Dangerous immigration legislation pending in Congress," Immigrant Legal Resource Center, San Francisco, December 23, 2005.

12. Peter B. Dixon and Maureen T Rimmer, *Restriction or Legalization? Measuring the Economic Benefits of Immigration Reform,* Trade Policy Analysis 40, Cato Institute, Washington, D.C., August 13, 2009, http://www.cato.org/publications/trade-policy-analysis/restriction-or-legalization-measuring-economic-benefits-immigration-reform (Retrieved April 7, 2014).

13. Otto Santa Ana, Sandra L. Treviño, Michael J. Bailey, Kristen Bodossian, and Antonio De Necochea, "A May to remember: Adversarial images of immigrants in U.S. newspapers during the 2006 policy debate," *Du Bois Review: Social Science and Research on Race* 4, no. 1 (2007): 207–232.

14. Laura Pulido, "A Day Without Immigrants: The racial and class politics of immigrant exclusion," *Antipode* 39, no. 1 (2007): 1–7.

15. Díaz, "Organizing the brown tide."

16. Suzanne Staggenborg, "Can feminist organizations be effective?," in *Feminist Organizations: Harvest of the New Women's Movement,* ed. Myra Marx Ferree and Patricia Yancey Martin, 339–355 (Philadelphia: Temple University Press, 1995).

17. Adrián Félix, Carmen González, and Ricardo Ramírez, "Political protest, ethnic media, and Latino naturalization," *American Behavioral Scientist* 52, no. 4 (2008): 618–634.

18. Mandalit Del Barco, "Spanish-language DJ turns out the crowds in LA," National Public Radio, April 12, 2006, http://www.npr.org/templates/story/story.php?storyId=5337941 (retrieved September 1, 2007).

19. Carmen Gonzalez, "Latino mobilization: Emergent Latino mobilization via communication networks," Unpublished paper, Annenberg School for Communication & Journalism, University of Southern California, Los Angeles, 2006.

20. Ibid.

21. Interview, NB.

22. Interviews, NB, XD, KB, BH, DH, CX.

23. Wayne Yang, "Organizing MySpace: Youth walkouts, pleasure, politics, and new media," *Educational Foundations* 21, nos. 1–2 (2007): 9–28.

24. Interviews, BH, XD, NB.

25. Interview, EN.

26. Ibid.

27. *Source Code*, "Students Unite in LA," Season 3, Episode 10: "Immigration emergency?," 2006, video, http://www.archive.org/details/freespeechtv_sourcecode3_10 (Retrieved April 6, 2014).

28. Knud Larsen, Krum Krumov, Hao Van Le, Reidar Ommundsen, and Kees van der Veer, "Threat perception and attitudes toward documented and undocumented immigrants in the United States: Framing the debate and conflict resolution," *European Journal of Social Sciences* 7, no. 4 (2009): 115–134.

29. A letter signed by more than one hundred psychologists in support of the Drop the I-Word campaign and the AP changes describes in detail the way this term functions on a cognitive level to dehumanize those it is applied to.

30. Emily Guskin, "'Illegal,' 'undocumented,' 'unauthorized': News media shift language on immigration," FactTank, Pew Research Center, Washington, D.C., June 17, 2013, http://www.pewresearch.org/fact-tank/2013/06/17/illegal-undocumented -unauthorized-news-media-shift-language-on-immigration (retrieved October 13, 2013).

31. Santa Ana et al., "A May to remember."

32. Interview, PS.

33. Interview, NB.

34. Interview, XD.

35. Interview, TX.

36. Interview, KB.

37. Ibid.

38. Interview, RF.

39. Interview, LC, online organizer.

40. Elena Shore, "What is the role of Hispanic media in immigrant activism?," *Social Policy* 36, no. 3 (2006): 8.

41. Juan González and Joseph Torres, *News for All the People: The Epic Story of Race and the American Media* (New York: Verso Books, 2011).

42. Interview, LC.

43. Interviews, DH, PS, LC, BH, EQ.

44. Interview, PS.

45. Ibid.

46. Interview, LC.

47. Interview, EQ.

48. William A. Gamson and Gadi Wolfsfeld, "Movements and media as interacting systems," *Annals of the American Academy of Political and Social Science* 528 (July 1993): 114–125.

49. Interview, EQ.

50. Dávila, *Latinos, Inc.*

51. Interview, CY.

52. Beth Baker-Cristales, "Mediated resistance: The construction of neoliberal citizenship in the immigrant rights movement," *Latino Studies* 7, no. 1 (Spring 2009): 60–82.

53. Ibid.

54. Ibid.; Alvaro Lima, "Transnationalism: What it means to local communities," Boston Redevelopment Authority, Boston, Winter 2010. http://www.bostonre developmentauthority.org/getattachment/40c9373f-d170-4ed7-91bf-300f2b7 daeb9/ (Retrieved April 6, 2014).

55. Alan O'Connor, *Community Radio in Bolivia: The Miners' Radio Stations* (Lewiston, NY: Edwin Mellen Press, 2004).

56. Timothy B. Tyson, *Radio Free Dixie: Robert F. Williams & the Roots of Black Power* (Chapel Hill: University of North Carolina Press, 1999).

57. Brian Ward, *Radio and the Struggle for Civil Rights in the South* (Gainesville: University Press of Florida, 2004).

58. Lawrence Soley, *Free Radio: Electronic Civil Disobedience* (Boulder: Westview, 1999).

59. Frantz Fanon, "This is the Voice of Algeria," in *Studies in a Dying Colonialism,* trans. Haakon Chevalier, 69–98 (New York: Monthly Review Press, 1965). First published 1959, in French.

60. John Downing, *Radical Media: Rebellious Communication and Social Movements* (Mountain View, CA: Sage, 2001).

61. See the website of the World Association of Community Radio Broadcasters (AMARC), an international nongovernmental organization serving community radio, at http://amarc.org.

62. Andy Opel, *Micro Radio and the FCC: Media Activism and the Struggle over Broadcast Policy* (Westport, CT: Praeger, 2004).

63. Kevin Howley, "Remaking public service broadcasting: Lessons from Allston-Brighton free radio," *Social Movement Studies* 3, no. 2 (2004): 221–240.

64. For examples, see Alfonso Gumucio Dragon and Thomas Tufte, *Communication for Social Change: Anthology: Historical and Contemporary Readings* (South Orange, NJ: CFSC Consortium, 2006).

65. Graciela Orozco, "Understanding the May 1st immigrant rights mobilizations." (New York: Social Science Research Council, 2007).

66. The FIOB coordinator in Santa Maria, Jesus Estrada, was also able to secure a regular TV show on Telemundo at one point (interview, PS).

67. Interview, KZ.

68. Ibid.

69. Interview, KB.

70. See DIYMedia.net's FCC Enforcement Action Database at http://www.diymedia.net/fccwatch/ead.htm.

71. See the website of Free Speech Radio News, at http://fsrn.org.

72. Simon Cottle, *Ethnic Minorities and the Media: Changing Cultural Boundaries* (Philadelphia, PA: Open University Press, 2000).

73. Interview, SU.

74. Ibid.

75. Interview, LC.

76. Ibid.

77. Interview, TX.

78. Ibid.

79. To be explored in more depth in chapter 5.

80. danah boyd, "Why youth (heart) social network sites: The role of networked publics in teenage social life," in *Youth, Identity, and Digital Media,* ed. D. Buckingham, 119–142 (Cambridge, MA: MIT Press, 2007).

81. See http://myspace.com/infoshopdotorg (anarchist infoshop), http://myspace.com/gpus (Greenpeace), and http://www.myspace.com/feminists for examples.

82. Kara Jesella, "The friendster effect," AlterNet, January 29, 2006, http://www.alternet.org/story/31103 (retrieved June 29, 2010).

83. Araba Sey and Manuel Castells, "From media politics to networked politics: The Internet and the political process," in *The Network Society: A Cross-Cultural Perspective,* ed. M. Castells, 363-384 (Cheltenham, UK / Northampton, MA: Edward Elgar, 2004).

84. Joe Trippi, *The Revolution Will Not Be Televised* (New York: HarperCollins, 2009).

85. danah boyd, "White flight in networked publics? How race and class shaped American teen engagement with MySpace and Facebook," in *Race After the Internet,* Eds. Lisa Nakamura and Peter Chow-White, 203–222 (New York: Routledge, 2011); boyd, "Why youth (heart) social network sites."

86. Jenna M. Loyd and Andrew Burridge. "La Gran Marcha: Anti-racism and immigrants' rights in Southern California," *ACME: An International E-Journal for Critical Geographies* 6, no. 1 (2007): 1–35.

87. Interviews, SU, MO.

88. Interview, ON.

89. Interviews, BH, LC, QK.

90. Interview, LC.

91. Interview, XD.

92. Sasha Costanza-Chock, "Mic check! Media cultures and the Occupy movement," *Social Movement Studies* 11, nos. 3–4 (2012): 375–385.

93. Interview, LC.

94. Ibid.

95. Interviews, LC, ZD, LN.

96. Interview, LC.

97. Ibid.

98. Ibid.

99. Otto Santa Ana, "'Like an animal I was treated': Anti-immigrant metaphor in US public discourse," *Discourse & Society* 10, no. 2 (1999): 191–224.

100. Interview, LC.

Chapter 2

1. Donald P. Ranly, "Action for children's television," Action for Children's Television, Newton, MA, 1976.

2. Marsha Kinder, *Playing with Power in Movies, Television, and Video Games: from Muppet Babies to Teenage Mutant Ninja Turtles* (Berkeley: University of California Press, 1993).

3. Henry Jenkins, "Transmedia storytelling," *MIT Technology Review,* January 15, 2003. http://www.technologyreview.com/news/401760/transmedia-storytelling (retrieved May 19, 2007).

4. Ibid.

5. For example, see Google Books Ngram viewer visualization of the increasingly frequent appearance of the term "transmedia" from 1960 to 2008, http://bit.ly/10IB6aF.

6. Producers Guild of America, "PGA Board of Directors approves addition of transmedia producer to Guild's Producers Code of Credits," Producers Guild of America, Los Angeles, April 6, 2010, http://www.producersguild.org/news/39637 (retrieved May 2, 2013).

7. Amanda Lin Costa, "At Tribeca Film Festival, 'Storyscapes' brings transmedia projects into real life," PBS MediaShift, May 1, 2013, http://www.pbs.org/mediashift/2013/05/digital-storytelling-up-close-in-person114 (retrieved May 3, 2013).

8. Lina Srivastava, "Transmedia activism: Telling your story across media platforms to create effective social change," National Alliance for Media Arts and Culture, San Francisco, March 4, 2009, http://www.namac.org/node/6925 (retrieved November 1, 2013).

9. See http://resistnetwork.com.

10. For examples, see the blog transmedia-activism.com, maintained by Srivastava and the feminist media scholar Vicki Callahan.

11. Soraya Hernandez, "Watsonville High walk out," Bay Area Indymedia, San Francisco, March 28, 2006. http://www.indybay.org/newsitems/2006/03/28/18118141.php (retrieved August 10, 2009)

12. This text was widely reposted across MySpace, as well as to bulletin boards, blogs, and in comments to news articles. For example, it can be found in the comments section of the Free Republic page "Live thread: Some students walk out despite lockdown (Day 3 of LAUSD walkouts)," http://www.freerepublic.com/focus/news/1604770/posts?page=203 (retrieved November 1, 2013). The first two ellipses are in the original text; the third was introduced in editing for this book.

13. Wall post by anonymous MySpace user. All ellipses are in the original post except that after "immigrated."

14. Transcribed from a screenshot of a chat session posted to a MySpace group dedicated to student actions against H.R. 4437. Usernames have been changed to preserve privacy.

15. Interviews, TH, BH, EN.

16. Interview, TH.

17. Judith Donath and danah boyd, "Public displays of connection," *BT Technology Journal* 22, no. 4 (2004): 71–82.

18. Doug McAdam, Sidney Tarrow, and Charles Tilly, "Dynamics of contention," *Social Movement Studies* 2, no. 1 (2003): 99–102.

19. Paula Crisostomo, "Ethnic pride, civil rights and young people: Parallels between the Chicano walkout of 1968 and the Latino demonstrations of 2006," The Lavin Agency, New York, October 2006; Dolores Delgado Bernal, "Grassroots leadership reconceptualized: Chicana oral histories and the 1968 East Los Angeles school blowouts," *Frontiers: A Journal of Women Studies* 19 (1998): 113–142.

20. Mario T. García and Sal Castro, *Blowout! Sal Castro and the Chicano Struggle for Educational Justice* (Chapel Hill: University of North Carolina Press, 2011).

21. Lisa Garcia Bedolla, *Fluid Borders: Latino Power, Identity, and Politics in Los Angeles* (Berkeley: University of California Press, 2005); Hinda Seif, "Wise up!' Undocumented Latino youth, Mexican-American legislators, and the struggle for higher education access," *Latino Studies* 2, no. 2 (2004): 210–230.

22. Michelle A. Holling, "Forming oppositional social concord to California's Proposition 187 and squelching social discord in the vernacular space of CHICLE," *Communication and Critical/Cultural Studies* 3, no. 3 (2006): 202–222.

23. Agustin Gurza, "Reborn in East L.A.: An HBO film by Edward James Olmos resurrects a 1968 L.A. Chicano student walkout that roused an activist spirit," *Los Angeles Times*, December 25, 2005, E1, http://blogs.myspace.com/index.cfm?fuseaction=blog.view&friendId=38303221&blogId=72823076 (retrieved September 10, 2008).

24. Ibid.

25. Post on anonymized MySpace user's wall, 2006.

26. Jesse Díaz and Javier Rodríguez, "Undocumented in America," *New Left Review* 47 (2007), http://newleftreview.org/II/47/jesse-diaz-javier-rodriguez-undocumented -in-america (retrieved November 1, 2013).

27. Interviews, BH, XD.

28. Interview, LN.

29. Ibid.

30. Ibid.

31. Interview, ON.

32. Interviews, BE1, BE2.

33. Interviews, BE1, BE2.

34. Interview, LC.

35. Ethan Zuckerman, "Meet the bridgebloggers," *Public Choice* 134, nos. 1–2 (2008): 47–65.

36. Interview, CX.

37. Henry Jenkins, Sam Ford, Joshua Green, et al., *Spreadable Media: Creating Value and Meaning in a Networked Culture* (New York: New York University Press, 2012).

38. Interview, TH.

39. Charlotte Ryan, *Prime Time Activism: Media Strategies for Grassroots Organizing* (Cambridge, MA: South End Press, 1991).

40. Interview, LC.

41. Interview, ON.

42. Interview, ON.

43. Interview, NM.

44. Interview, LC.

45. Interviews, BE1, BE2.

46. Interviews, BE1, BE2.

Chapter 3

1. Bill Ong Hing, "Institutional racism, ICE raids, and immigration reform," *University of San Francisco Law Review* 44 (2009): 307.

2. Jesús Velasco Grajales, *Lou Dobbs and the Rise of Modern Nativism* (Mexico City: Centro de Investigación y Docencia Económicas [CIDE], 2008).

3. James Strawn, "Whose park: An architectural history of Westlake-MacArthur Park," master's thesis, University of Southern California, 2008.

4. Interview, CZ.

5. Gerardo Sandoval, *Immigrants and the Revitalization of Los Angeles: Development and Change in MacArthur Park* (New York: Cambria Press, 2010).

6. Erwin Chemerinsky, "An Independent analysis of the Los Angeles Police Department's Board of Inquiry Report on the Rampart Scandal, " *Loyola of Los Angeles Law Review* 34 (2001): 545–656. http://digitalcommons.lmu.edu/llr/vol34/iss2/4 (Retrieved April 6, 2014).

7. Sandoval, *Immigrants and the Revitalization of Los Angeles.*

8. William H. Sousa and George L Kelling, "Police and the reclamation of public places: A study of MacArthur Park in Los Angeles," *International Journal of Police Science & Management* 12, no. 1 (2010): 41–54.

9. Including Dr. Larry Gross, director of the Annenberg School for Communication & Journalism, University of Southern California, Los Angeles.

10. A video of Fosforo performing at this event, intercut later with footage of the police attack, is available at http://www.youtube.com/watch?v=FfkoULiI8N0. The track "Guerra," from the EP *Macondo*, can be found at https://myspace.com/fosforo.

11. Los Angeles Police Department, "An examination of May Day 2007," Los Angeles Police Department Report to the Board of Police Commissioners, 2007, http://www.lapdonline.org/assets/pdf/Final_Report.pdf (retrieved October 10, 2007).

12. Amy Goodman, "L.A. immigration protest: The police 'were relentless. They were merciless,'" *Alternet,* May 4, 2007. http://www.alternet.org/story/51454/l.a._immigration_protest%3A_the_police_%22were_relentless._they_were_merciless.%22 (retrieved August 25, 2007).

13. William Bratton, "May 2, 2007 media brief on MacArthur Park disturbance," Los Angeles Police Department, May 2, 2007, http://lapdblog.typepad.com/lapd_blog/2007/05/chief_bratton_b.html (retrieved July 10, 2008).

14. Los Angeles Police Department, "An examination of May Day 2007."

15. Ibid.

16. Interviews, ND, WO.

17. Sandoval, *Immigrants and the Revitalization of Los Angeles.*

18. Otto Santa Ana, with Layza López and Edgar Munguía, "Framing peace as violence: U.S. television news depictions of the 2007 Los Angeles police attack on immigrant rights marchers," *Aztlán* 35, no. 1 (2010): 69–101.

19. Ibid.

20. Interview, KB.

21. Ibid.

22. Ibid.

23. Interview, RF.

24. Ibid.

25. Excerpted from a public, televised statement by the Executive Director of the immigrant rights nonprofit. The transcript from this statement was widely posted and debated in movement forums and online Bulletin Board Systems (BBS).

26. See http://www.miwon.org/mayday2007page.html.

27. Ibid.

28. Sasha Costanza-Chock, "*Se ve, se siente:* Transmedia mobilization in the Los Angeles immigrant rights movement," PhD diss., University of Southern California, 2011. http://pqdtopen.proquest.com/pqdtopen/doc/751220571.html?FMT=ABS.

29. From a televised statement by the communications director for the immigrant rights nonprofit.

30. Maeve Reston and Joel Rubin, "Los Angeles to pay $13 million to settle May Day melee lawsuits," *Los Angeles Times*, February 5, 2009, http://articles.latimes.com/2009/feb/05/local/me-lapd-settlement5 (retrieved November 5, 2013).

31. Interview, NB.

32. Interview, CX.

33. Interview, KB.

34. Interview, OE.

35. Ibid.

36. Judy Richardson, "The mission of media makers," speech, MIT Center for Civic Media, Cambridge, MA, March 15, 2012. A summary of the presentation and discussion is available at http://civic.mit.edu/blog/mstem/judy-richardson. (Retrieved April 6, 2014).

37. Interview, XD.

38. Interview, EQ.

39. Ibid.

40. Nicole Gaouette, "Senate gets tougher on the border," *Los Angeles Times*, May 24, 2007, A16.

41. S. A. Miller and Stephen Dinan, "Senate OKs $3 billion to guard border," *Washington Times*, July 27, 2007, http://www.washingtontimes.com/apps/pbcs.dll/article?AID=/20070727/NATION/107270098/1001 (retrieved September 1, 2007).

42. Detention Watch Network, "Year one report card: Human rights & the Obama administration's immigration detention reforms, October 6, 2010," in *Citing ICE Detention Reform Accomplishments*, Detention Watch Network. See also Presente.org's Deportation Clock project at http://presente.org/deportations.

43. Teóphyllo Reyes, "New path to citizenship looks more like an obstacle course," Labor Notes, May 17, 2013, http://www.labornotes.org/2013/05/new-path-citizenship-looks-more-obstacle-course (retrieved November 2, 2013).

Chapter 4

1. For example, Jesús Martín-Barbero, Elizabeth Fox, and Robert A. White, *Communication, Culture and Hegemony: From the Media to Mediations* (London: Sage, 1993).

2. Jonathan Fox and Gaspar Rivera-Salgado, *Indigenous Mexican Migrants in the United States* (San Diego: Center for US-Mexican Studies, UCSD / Center for Comparative Immigration Studies, 2004).

3. Personal communication, Berta Rodríguez Santos, 2009.

4. Fox and Rivera-Salgado, *Indigenous Mexican Migrants in the United States*, 22.

5. Ibid., 22.

6. Ibid., 27.

7. Alvaro Lima, "Transnationalism: What it means to local communities," Boston Redevelopment Authority, Boston, Winter 2010. http://www.bostonredevelopmentauthority.org/getattachment/40c9373f-d170-4ed7-91bf-300f2b7daeb9 (Retrieved April 6, 2014).

8. Peggy Levitt, *The Transnational Villagers* (Berkeley: University of California Press, 2001).

9. Rafael Alarcón, "The development of home town associations in the United States and the use of social remittances in Mexico," in *Sending Money Home: Hispanic Remittances and Community Development*, ed. Rodolfo O. de la Garza and Briant Lindsay Lowell (Lanham, MD: Rowman & Littlefield, 2002).

10. Interview, PS.

11. Interview, LC.

12. Fox and Rivera-Salgado, *Indigenous Mexican Migrants in the United States;* Lima, "Transnationalism."

13. Fox and Rivera-Salgado, *Indigenous Mexican Migrants in the United States,* 29.

14. Interviews, PS, CS.

15. Interview, PS.

16. Lynn Stephen, "Indigenous transborder ethnic identity construction in life and on the Net: The Frente Indígena de Organizaciones Binacionales (FIOB)," paper presented at the Rockefeller Conference, "Poverty and Community in Latin America," Evanston, IL, May 24–25, 2007, http://csws.uoregon.edu/wp-content/docs/Initiative Articles/ImmigrationPDFs/NWFIOBInternetPaper.pdf.

17. Interview, PS.

18. Ibid.

19. Interviews, PS, DS, and CS; Rodríguez Santos, personal communication, 2009.

20. Rodríguez Santos, personal communication, 2009.

21. Interview, PS.

22. Ibid.

23. James C. Scott, *Domination and the Arts of Resistance: Hidden Transcripts* (New Haven, CT: Yale University Press, 1990).

24. Marina Sitrin, *Everyday Revolutions: Horizontalism and Autonomy in Argentina* (London: Zed Books, 2012).

25. Interview, PS.

26. Ibid.

27. Ibid.

28. Kristin Norget, "Convergences and complicities: Local-National Interactions in the 2006 Movement of the APPO," Center for International Policy, Americas Program, Mexico City, July 14, 2008, http://www.cipamericas.org/archives/1447 (Retrieved April 11, 2014).

29. Ibid.

30. Tami Gold and Gerardo Renique, "A rainbow in the midst of a hurricane: Alternative media and the popular struggle in Oaxaca, Mexico," *Radical Teacher* 81, no. 8 (2008), http://muse.jhu.edu/demo/radical_teacher/v081/81.1gold.pdf.

31. Joel Simon, "CPJ calls for federal probe into killing of U.S. journalist in Mexico," Committee to Protect Journalists, October 30, 2006, http://cpj.org/2006/10/cpj-calls-for-federal-probe-into-killing-of-us-jou.php.

32. Physicians for Human Rights, "Canadians' report leaves more questions than answers in death of US reporter in Mexico," Physicians for Human Rights International Forensic Program, August 5, 2009, http://physiciansforhumanrights.org/library/news-2009-08-05.html; and see Diana Denham, ed. *Teaching Rebellion: Stories from the Grassroots Mobilization in Oaxaca* (Oakland, CA: PM Press, 2008).

33. This film is freely available for download from the Internet Archive: https://archive.org/details/miamimodel.

34. Interview, PS.

35. Monica Wooters, "Mexican Supreme Court finds Oaxaca governor responsible for human rights violations," Center for International Policy, Americas Program, Mexico City, November 17, 2009, http://www.cipamericas.org/archives/1910 (retrieved November 3, 2013).

36. Interviews, CS, PS, DM, BH.

Chapter 5

1. See VozMob.net, and more about IDEPSCA and VozMob later in this chapter.

2. See alliedmedia.org.

3. See several posts about VozMob at http://www.hastac.org/tag/vozmob.

4. Sasha Costanza-Chock, "*Se ve, se siente:* Transmedia mobilization in the Los Angeles immigrant rights movement," PhD diss., University of Southern California, 2011.

5. Raúl Añorve and IDEPSCA Staff, "Queremos vivir sin miedo [We want to live without fear]," in *Globalisation, Knowledge and Labor*, ed. Mario Novelli and Anibel Ferus-Comelo (London: Routledge, 2009), 206.

6. Paolo Freire, *Pedagogy of the Oppressed* (New York: Seabury Press, 1970), 36.

7. Liam Kane, *Popular Education and Social Change in Latin America* (London: Latin American Bureau, 2001).

8. Interviews, NR, SB.

9. John M. Glen, *Highlander: No Ordinary School* (Knoxville: University of Tennessee Press, 1996); and see Highlander Center, *Highlander: An Approach to Education Presented through a Collection of Writings* (New Market, TN: Highlander Center, 1989).

10. See projectsouth.org.

11. Interview, NQ.

12. Manuel Castells, *Communication Power* (New York: Oxford University Press, 2009).

13. Raymond Williams marshals yearly book sales figures, newspaper and magazine circulation data, information about the technological evolution of the printing press, changes in publishing law, taxation, and licensing, quotations from contemporary authors, and other sources to trace the evolution of print literacy. He follows the long trajectory from the Roman system of slave dictation to the creation of the printing press, the rise of penny dreadfuls and radical texts in the 1800s, the emergence of public education, the creation of circulating library systems, and the availability of mass market paperbacks. See Raymond Williams, *The Long Revolution* (New York: Columbia University Press; London: Chatto & Windus, 1961).

14. Nick Dyer-Witheford, *Cyber-Marx: Cycles and Circuits of Struggle in High-technology Capitalism* (Urbana: University of Illinois Press, 1999).

15. For more on the concept of the 1/3 World, see Chandra Mohanty, *Feminism Without Borders: Decolonizing Theory, Practicing Solidarity* (Durham: Duke University Press, 2003).

16. Vincent Mosco, *The Political Economy of Communication: Rethinking and Renewal* (London: Sage, 1996).

17. Manuel Castells, "Communication, power and counter-power in the network society," *International Journal of Communication* 1, no. 1 (2007): 238–266.

18. Tiziana Terranova, "Free labor: Producing culture for the digital economy," *Social Text* 18, no. 2 (2000): 33–58.

19. Siva Vaidhyanathan, *The Googlization of Everything* (Berkeley: University of California Press, 2012); Evgeny Morozov, *The Net Delusion: How Not to Liberate the World* (New York: Penguin, 2011).

20. Ward Churchill and Jim Vander Wall, *The COINTELPRO Papers: Documents from the FBI's Secret Wars against Dissent in the United States* (Cambridge, MA: South End Press, 2002).

21. Glenn Greenwald and Ewen MacAskill, "NSA PRISM program taps in to user data of Apple, Google and others," *Guardian*, June 6, 2013, http://www.theguardian .com/world/2013/jun/06/us-tech-giants-nsa-data.

22. For example, VozMob workshops often start with the example of daylaborers. org, a hate site maintained by an anti-immigrant group that travels to day labor corners, yells racist insults at those waiting for work, then snaps pictures of workers' angry responses and posts them to the web, along with captions like "Some of the most violent murderers and rapists are illegal immigrants who work as day laborers."

23. Henry Jenkins, Katherine Clinton, Ravi Purushotma, Alice J. Robinson, and Margaret Weigel, *Confronting the Challenges of Participatory Culture: Media Education for the 21st Century* (Chicago: MacArthur Foundation, 2006).

24. Mizuko Ito, Sonja Baumer, Matteo Bittanti, et al., *Hanging Out, Messing Around, and Geeking Out: Kids Living and Learning with New Media* (Cambridge, MA: MIT Press, 2010).

25. Samuel Craig Watkins, *The Young and the Digital: What the Migration to Social Network Sites, Games, and Anytime, Anywhere Media Means for Our Future* (Boston: Beacon Press, 2009).

26. Although see the Youth and Participatory Politics series. See also Sasha Costanza-Chock, "Youth and social movements: Key lessons for allies," Berkman Center Research Publication 2013-13, Berkman Center for Internet and Society, Harvard University, Cambridge, MA, 2012, http://cyber.law.harvard.edu/node/8096.

27. Raúl Zibechi, *Autonomías y emancipaciones: América Latina en movimiento.* (Lima: Universidad Nacional Mayor de San Marcos, Fondo Editorial de la Facultad de Ciencias Sociales, 2007).

28. Vanessa Tait, *Poor Workers' Unions: Rebuilding Labor from Below* (Cambridge, MA: South End Press, 2005); Janice Ruth Fine, *Worker Centers: Organizing Communities at the Edge of the Dream* (Ithaca, NY: Cornell University Press, 2006).

29. Victor Narro, "Impacting next wave organizing: Creative campaign strategies of the Los Angeles worker centers," *New York Law School Law Review* 50 (2005): 465.

30. Ruth Milkman and Kent Wong, *Voices from the Front Lines: Organizing Immigrant Workers in Los Angeles* (Los Angeles: UCLA Center for Labor Research and Education, 2000).

31. KIWA, "Toward a community agenda: A survey of workers and residents in Koreatown," Koreatown Immigrant Workers Alliance & Data Center, Los Angeles, 2007, http://www.datacenter.org/wp-content/uploads/towardscommunity .pdf (retrieved March 4, 2010); idem, "Reclaiming Koreatown," Koreatown Immigrant Workers Alliance & Data Center, Los Angeles, 2009, http://www.datacenter .org/wp-content/uploads/KIWA_Report.pdf (retrieved March 4, 2010).

32. Interview, NQ.

33. See *Neidi's Story* (IDEPSCA), http://www.youtube.com/watch?v=XNPd9o2Cazc.

34. Interview, NQ.

35. VozMob project, "Mobile Voices: Projecting the voices of immigrant workers by appropriating mobile phones for popular communication," in *Communications*

Research in Action: Scholar-Activist Collaborations for a Democratic Public Sphere, ed. P. M. Napoli and M. Aslama (New York: Fordham University Press, 2010).

36. See VozMob.net for more information.

37. Interview with VozMob project coordinator, conducted by Cara Wallis.

38. Garment Worker Center, *Crisis or Opportunity? The Future of Los Angeles' Garment Workers, the Apparel Industry, and the Local Economy* (Los Angeles: Garment Worker Center and Sweatshop Watch, 2004).

39. Richard Sullivan and Kimi Lee. "Organizing immigrant women in America's sweatshops: Lessons from the Los Angeles Garment Worker Center," *Signs* 33, no. 3 (2008): 527–532. See also garmentworkercenter.org.

40. Interview, TH.

41. Interview, TH; personal communication, GWC member.

42. A play on words. The term means "flying saucers" in Spanish, but it also means "CD flyers."

43. Interview, TH; personal communications, GWC members.

44. Maegan Ortiz, "Fast for our future: Stand up for immigrant rights!," VivirLatino, Los Angeles, October 14, 2008, http://vivirlatino.com/2008/10/14/fast-for-our-future-stand-up-for-immigrant-rights.php (retrieved August 14, 2013).

45. *Nuestra Voz*, "Garment workers take the radio in their own hands: Radio Tijera in the studio," *Nuestra Voz*, KPFK, April 9, 2009, http://www.kpfk.org/index.php/programs/132-nuestra-voz/1899-499nuestravozdream-act-puede-ser-cultura-gransilencio-documental-eljardin-garifunas (retrieved April 11, 2014).

46. Ito et al., *Hanging Out, Messing Around, and Geeking Out.*

47. Interview, OE.

48. Interview, OE.

49. Interview, BH.

50. Interview, NM.

51. Shelley Goldman, Angela Booker, and Meghan McDermott, "Mixing the digital, social, and cultural: Learning, identity, and agency in youth participation," in *Youth, Identity, and Digital Media,* ed. David Buckingham, 185–206 (Cambridge, MA: MIT Press, 2008).

52. Interview, OE.

53. Ibid.

54. Interview, TH.

55. Interview, BH.

56. Interview, TH; Virginia Eubanks, personal communication, August 2013.

57. For more on media work by the Frente Indígena de Organizaciones Binacionales, see chapter 4.

58. Interview, PS.

59. Interview, EQ.

60. Interview, KZ.

61. Interview, TX.

62. Virginia Eubanks, *Digital Dead End: Fighting for Social Justice in the Information Age* (Cambridge, MA: MIT Press, 2011).

63. Interview, EQ.

64. Marc Prensky, "Digital natives, digital immigrants part 1," *On the horizon* 9, no. 5 (2001): 1–6.

65. Interview, EQ.

66. Interview, OE.

67. Wade Roush, "The moral panic over social-networking sites," *MIT Technology Review*, August 7, 2006, http://www.technologyreview.com/read_article.aspx?id= 17266&ch=infotech.

68. Interview, TH.

69. danah boyd. *It's Complicated: The Social Lives of Networked Teens* (New Haven: Yale University Press, 2014).

70. D. T. Scott, *Killer Apps and Sick Users: Pathological Technoculture in Old and New Media* (New York: New York University Press, in press).

71. Eubanks, personal communication, 2013.

72. Ito et al., *Hanging Out, Messing Around, and Geeking Out.*

73. Interview, OE.

74. Ibid.

75. Interview, DH.

76. Interview, NB.

77. Interviews, NB, BH, LN.

Chapter 6

1. See http://thedreamwalk.org/denver-videos.

2. Julianne Hing, "DREAMers stage sit-in at Obama office to force deportation standoff," *Colorlines,* June 13, 2012, http://archive.is/u6S3R (retrieved October 12, 2013).

3. Arely M. Zimmerman, "Documenting DREAMs: New media, undocumented youth and the immigrant rights movement," University of Southern California Annenberg School for Communication & Journalism, Civic Paths' Media, Activism, and Participatory Politics Project, Los Angeles, June 6, 2012, http://ypp.dmlcentral .net/sites/default/files/publications/Documenting_DREAMs.pdf (retrieved April 11, 2014).

4. White House Press Office, *Remarks by the President on Immigration,* press release, White House, June 15, 2012, http://www.whitehouse.gov/the-press-office/2012/ 06/15/remarks-president-immigration.

5. Interview, LN.

6. Prerna Lal, "How queer undocumented youth built the immigrant rights movement," *Huffington Post,* March 28, 2013, http://archive.is/5ULwu (retrieved October 12, 2013).

7. Jeffrey Passel and Mark Hugo Lopez, "Up to 1.7 million unauthorized immigrant youth may benefit from new deportation rules," Pew Hispanic Center, Washington, D.C., August 14, 2012, http://www.pewhispanic.org/2012/08/14/up-to-1-7-million -unauthorizedimmigrant-youth-may-benefit-from-new-deportation-rules.

8. Lisette Amaya, Wendy Escobar, Monique Gonzales, Heather Henderson, Angelo Mathay, Marla Ramirez, Michael Viola, and Negin Yamini, "Undocumented students, unfulfilled dreams," UCLA Center for Labor Research and Education, Los Angeles, CA, March 26, 2008, http://labor.ucla.edu/publications/reports/ Undocumented-Students.pdf (retrieved April 12, 2014).

9. Michael A. Olivas, "Political economy of the Dream Act and the legislative process: A case study of comprehensive immigration reform," *Wayne Law Review* 55 (2009): 1757.

10. Interview, BH.

11. Margaret D. Stock, "The DREAM Act: Tapping an overlooked pool of home-grown talent to meet military enlistment needs," *Bender's Immigration Bulletin,* January 15, 2006, 63.

12. Interviews, BH, XD, OE; Elvira J. Rodriguez, "Yo Soy El Army: United States military recruitment of low-income Latino youth, strategies and implications," Graduate College at Illinois, 2006, http://web.archive.org/web/

20100617124553/http://www.grad.illinois.edu/content/yo-soy-el-army-united
-states-military-recruitment-low-income-latino-youth-strategies-and-imp (retrieved
November 3, 2013).

13. Michelle Chen, "Is the DREAM Act a military recruiter's dream, too?,"
Huffington Post, May 27, 2010, http://www.huffingtonpost.com/michelle-chen/is
-the-dream-act-a-milita_b_585875.html. Interview, BH.

14. Big Noise Films and Producciones Cimmaron, 2010. See http://bignoisefilms.
org/videowire/38-latest/111-ysea.

15. Presentation by Pedro Paredes, UCLA Center for Labor Research and Education,
Los Angles, April 19, 2013.

16. See DREAMers Adrift, for example, at http://dreamersadrift.com/newest-vid/
01-military-recruitment-the-dream-act.

17. By August 2013, more than 400,000 people had been granted DACA status. See
Roberto G. Gonzales and Veronica Terriquez, "How DACA is impacting the lives of
those who are now DACAmented: Preliminary findings from the National UnDACA-
mented Research Project," Center for the Study of Immigrant Integration, University
of Southern California, Los Angeles, April 15, 2013, http://csii.usc.edu/DACA.html
(retrieved August 15, 2013).

18. Laura Sullivan, "Prison economics help drive Ariz. immigration law," National
Public Radio, October 28, 2010, http://www.npr.org/2010/10/28/130833741/prison
-economics-help-drive-ariz-immigration-law.

19. Immigration and Customs Enforcement, "ICE total removals, through August
25th, 2012," ICE, Washington, D.C., August 27, 2012, http://www.ice.gov/doclib/
about/offices/ero/pdf/ero-removals1.pdf (retrieved October 12, 2013).

20. Politifact, "Has Barack Obama deported more people than any other president?,"
Politifact, August 10, 2012. http://www.politifact.com/truth-o-meter/statements/
2012/aug/10/american-principles-action/has-barack-obama-deported-more-people
-any-other-pr (retrieved October 12, 2013).

21. See http://notonemoredeportation.com.

22. See "Gang of Eight (immigration)," *Wikipedia,* http://en.wikipedia.org/wiki/
Gang_of_Eight_(immigration) (retrieved November 3, 2013).

23. Prerna Lal, "How queer undocumented youth built the immigrant rights movement," *Huffington Post,* March 28, 2013, http://archive.is/5ULwu (retrieved October
12, 2013).

24. Rogelio Alejandro López, "From huelga! to undocumented and unafraid! A
comparative study of media strategies in the farm worker movement of the 1960s

and the immigrant youth movement of the 2000s," master's thesis, MIT, 2013, http://hdl.handle.net/1721.1/81056.

25. Lal, "How queer undocumented youth built the immigrant rights movement."

26. Interview, LM.

27. Interview, KT.

28. Interview with Salgado, conducted by Rogelio Alejandro López.

29. Interview, OE.

30. Jonathan Alexander, with Elizabeth Losh, "A YouTube of one's own: Coming out as rhetorical action," in *LGBT Identity and Online New Media*, ed. Christopher Pullen and Margaret Cooper, 37–50 (New York: Routledge, 2010).

31. Laura E. Enriquez, "Researching and learning from undocumented young adults," *CSW Update Newsletter,* UCLA Center for the Study of Women, Los Angeles, November 1, 2012, http://escholarship.org/uc/item/44q809d7 (retrieved October 13, 2013).

32. See http://juliosalgado83.tumblr.com.

33. See http://DREAMersadrift.com.

34. See http://papersthemovie.com.

35. For scholarly accounts, see López, "From huelga! to undocumented and unafraid!," and Jacob Eric Prendez, "The art of rebellion: Social justice and Chicano visual arts," master's thesis, California State University, 2012.

36. Underground Undergrads, *Underground Undergrads: UCLA Undocumented Immigrant Students Speak Out,* ed. Gabriela Madera (Los Angeles: UCLA Center for Labor Research and Education, 2012); and see http://undergroundundergrads.com.

37. UCLA Center for Labor Research and Education, *Undocumented and Unafraid: Tam Tran, Cinthya Felix, and the Immigrant Youth Movement* (Los Angeles: UCLA Center for Labor Research and Education, Dream Resource Center, 2012).

38. López, "From huelga! to undocumented and unafraid!"

39. Ibid.

40. John Gorham Palfrey and Urs Gasser, *Born Digital: Understanding the First Generation of Digital Natives* (New York: Basic Books, 2008).

41. Interview, DH.

42. Ibid.

43. Interview, TH.

44. Interview, KZ.

45. Interview with Julio Salgado, conducted by Rogelio Alejandro López.

46. Doug McAdam, "The biographical impact of activism," in *How Social Movements Matter*, ed. Marco Giugni, Doug McAdam, and Charles Tilly, 119–146 (Minneapolis: University of Minnesota Press, 1999).

47. Donatella Della Porta, *Life Histories in the Analysis of Social Movement Activists* (London: Sage, 1992).

48. Silke Roth, "Developing working class feminism: A biographical approach to social movement participation in the Coalition of Labor Union Women," in *Self, Identity, and Social Movements*, ed. Sheldon Stryker, Timothy J. Owens, and Robert W. White, 300–323 (Minneapolis: University of Minnesota Press, 1997).

49. Manuel Castells, *The Information Age: Economy, Society and Culture, Vol. 2: The Power of Identity* (Blackwell, 1997).

50. Verta Taylor and Nancy E Whittier. "Collective identity in social movement communities: Lesbian feminist mobilization," in *Waves of Protest: Social Movements since the Sixties,* ed. Jo Freeman and Victoria Johnson (New York: Rowman & Littlefield, 1999), 169.

51. James M. Jasper, *The Art of Moral Protest: Culture, Biography, and Creativity in Social Movements* (Chicago: University of Chicago Press, 2008).

52. Interview, ON.

53. Interview, LC.

54. Interview, LC.

55. Interviews, LC, QK.

56. Interview, TH.

57. Interview, SIM.

58. Interview, SIM.

59. John Downing, *Radical Media: Rebellious Communication and Social Movements* (Thousand Oaks, CA: Sage, 2001).

60. Zimmerman, "Documenting DREAMs."

61. Interview, TH

62. Interview, XD.

63. Interview, SM.

64. Claudia Alejandra Anguiano, *Undocumented, Unapologetic, and Unafraid: Discursive Strategies of the Immigrant Youth DREAM Social Movement* PhD diss., University of New Mexico, 2011 (ProQuest, UMI Dissertations Publishing, 2011).

65. Ibid.

66. Marshall Ganz, "Leading change: leadership, organization, and social movements," in *Handbook of Leadership Theory and Practice*, ed. Nitin Nohria and Rakesh Khurana, 509–550 (Cambridge, MA: Harvard Business School Press, 2010).

67. Julia Preston, "Young immigrants want 'Dream Warrior' army," *New York Times*, December 6, 2012, http://www.nytimes.com/2012/12/06/us/young-immigrants -want-dream-warrior-army.html (retrieved May 22, 2013).

68. Interview, ON.

69. Ibid.

70. Ibid.

71. Ibid.

72. Interview, DH.

73. Interview, SS.

74. Mawish Khan, "CNN polls: Voters strongly support pro-immigrant policies; Obama leading Romney among Latinos 70%-24%," AmericasVoice.org, October 2, 2012, http://americasvoiceonline.org/blog/cnn-polls-voters-strongly-support-pro -immigrant-policies-obama-leading-romney-among-latinos-70-24 (retrieved October 12, 2013).

75. Interview, LC.

Chapter 7

1. Mike Bostock, Shan Carter, Amanda Cox, Tom Giratikanon, Alicia Parlapiano, Kevin Quealy, Amy Schoenfeld, and Lisa Waananen, "How Obama won re-election," *New York Times* Interactive Feature, November 7, 2012, http://www.nytimes.com/ interactive/2012/11/07/us/politics/obamas-diverse-base-of-support.html?_r=0 (retrieved November 3, 2013).

2. Paul Taylor, Ana Gonzalez-Barrera, Jeffrey S. Passel, and Mark Hugo Lopez, "An awakened giant: The Hispanic electorate is likely to double by 2030," Pew Research Hispanic Trends Project, Pew Research Center, Washington, D.C., November 14, 2012, http://www.pewhispanic.org/2012/11/14/an-awakened-giant -the-hispanic-electorate-is-likely-to-double-by-2030 (retrieved November 3, 2103).

3. Jose Antonio Vargas, "My life as an undocumented immigrant," *New York Times,* June 22, 2011, http://www.nytimes.com/2011/06/26/magazine/my-life-as-an-undocumented-immigrant.html (retrieved April 12, 2014).

4. Carolina Valdivia Ordorica, "DREAM ACTivism: College students' offline and online activism for undocumented immigrant youth rights," master's thesis, San Diego State University, 2013; and see http://trail2010.org.

5. Ibid.

6. Jose Antonio Vargas, "Not legal, not leaving," *Time,* June 25, 2012, 34–44.

7. Henry Jenkins, "'Cultural acupuncture': Fan activism and the Harry Potter Alliance," in "Transformative Works and Fan Activism," ed. Henry Jenkins and Sangita Shresthova, *Transformative Works and Cultures* 10 (2011), doi:10.3983/twc.2012.0305.

8. Personal communication, anonymous media activist, May 10, 2013.

9. Interview, SIM.

10. Personal communication, anonymous community organizer.

11. Julia Preston, "Young immigrants want 'Dream Warrior' army," *New York Times,* December 6, 2012, http://www.nytimes.com/2012/12/06/us/young-immigrants-want-dream-warrior-army.html?hp&_r=0 (retrieved June 5, 2013).

12. See http://FWD.us.

13. U.S. Citizenship and Immigration Services, "Westat evaluation of the E-Verify program," USCIS, U.S. Department of Homeland Security, Washington, D.C., January 28, 2010, http://www.uscis.gov/sites/default/files/USCIS/Native%20Docs/Westat%20Evaluation%20of%20the%20E-Verify%20Program.pdf (retrieved November 4, 2013).

14. Somini Sengupta and Eric Lipton, "Fwd.Us raises uproar with advocacy tactics," *New York Times,* May 8, 2013, http://www.nytimes.com/2013/05/09/technology/fwdus-raises-uproar-with-advocacy-tactics.html (retrieved November 4, 2013).

15. John D. McCarthy and Mayer N. Zald, *The Trend of Social Movements in America: Professionalization and Resource Mobilization* (Morristown, NJ: General Learning Press, 1973); Suzanne Staggenborg, "The consequences of professionalization and formalization in the pro-choice movement," *American Sociological Review* 53 (1988): 585–605.

16. INCITE! Women of Color Against Violence, *The Revolution Will Not Be Funded: Beyond the Non-profit Industrial Complex* (Cambridge, MA: South End Press, 2007).

17. Ibid.; Staggenborg, "The consequences of professionalization and formalization in the pro-choice movement."

18. Daniel Faber and Deborah McCarthy, *Foundations for Social Change: Critical Perspectives on Philanthropy and Popular Movements* (Lanham, MD: Rowman & Littlefield, 2005).

19. INCITE!, Women of Color Against Violence, *The Revolution Will Not be Funded.*

20. Data Center and the National Organizers Alliance, "Sustaining organizing: A survey of organizations during the economic downturn," DataCenter.org, June 2010, http://www.datacenter.org/wp-content/uploads/SOS-report.pdf (retrieved November 4, 2013).

21. Interview, PS.

22. Interviews, BH, LN, TH, DM, OE, TX, NB.

23. Interviews, NB, BH, TH, DH, KB.

24. Interview, NB.

25. Ibid.

26. Alberto Melucci, *Challenging Codes: Collective Action in the Information Age* (Cambridge: Cambridge University Press, 1996).

27. Interviews, DH, KZ, EQ, BH.

28. Interviews, LN, XD.

29. Interviews, LN, XD, OE, BH.

30. Interviews, LN, XD, OE.

31. Interviews, XD, LN.

32. Interview, XD.

33. Interview, NB.

34. Jeffrey Juris, *Networking Futures* (Durham, NC: Duke University Press, 2008).

35. Interview, NB.

36. Francesca Polletta, *Freedom Is an Endless Meeting: Democracy in American Social Movements* (Chicago: University of Chicago Press, 2004); Tim Bartley, "How foundations shape social movements: The construction of an organizational field and the rise of forest certification," *Social Problems* 54 (2007): 229–255.

37. Interviews, OE, LN, NB, TH, XD.

38. Interview, XD.

39. Ibid.

40. Ibid.

41. Interview, OE.

42. Interviews, OE, XD, TH, KZ.

43. Interview, OE.

44. Interview, DH.

45. Ibid.

46. Interview, XD.

47. Interviews, NB, LN.

48. Interview, NB.

49. Interviews XD, LN.

50. Personal communication, anonymous scholar/activist, August 5, 2013.

Conclusions

1. Maria Camila Bernal, "Immigrants around the country unite for National Day for Dignity and Respect," *NBC Latino,* October 4, 2013, http://nbclatino.com/2013/10/04/immigrants-around-the-country-unite-for-national-day-for-dignity-and-respect (retrieved October 5, 2013).

2. Yunuen Rodriguez, "Challenging our ideas of home and belonging: The importance of the Dream 9 and Dream 30 actions," *Huffington Post,* October 1, 2013, http://www.huffingtonpost.com/yunuen-rodriguez/dream-30_b_4023478.html (retrieved October 6, 2013).

3. Roberto G. Gonzales and Veronica Terriquez, "Preliminary findings from the National UnDACAmented Research Project," Immigration Policy Center, Washington, DC, 2013, http://www.immigrationpolicy.org/just-facts/how-daca-impacting-lives-those-who-are-now-dacamented (retrieved October 28, 2013).

4. See https://www.dmv.ca.gov/pubs/newsrel/newsrel13/2013_29.htm.

5. Anil Kalhan, "Immigration policing and federalism through the lens of technology, surveillance, and privacy," *Ohio State Law Journal* 74, no. 6 (2013), http://ssrn.com/abstract=2316327 (retrieved April 13, 2014).

6. Juan Gonzalez, "President Obama heads toward deportation milestone as immigration reform flounders," *New York Daily News,* October 4, 2013, http://www.nydailynews.com/news/politics/obama-heads-deportation-milestone-article-1.1476073 (retrieved October 5, 2013).

7. Joanna Zuckerman Bernstein, "Immigration reform 2013: Millions of people could get cut out of the pathway to citizenship," PolicyMic.com, http://www

.policymic.com/articles/27002/immigration-reform-2013-millions-of-people-could
-get-cut-out-of-the-pathway-to-citizenship (retrieved October 6, 2013).

8. See Julio Salgado and Favianna Rodriguez. "5 Easy art projects for your October 5th event: A how-to guide," CultureStrike.net, http://www.youtube.com/watch?v =vmxr1mGeSpk (retrieved October 5, 2013).

9. Manuel Castells, *Communication Power* (Cambridge: Oxford University Press, 2013).

10. Subbiah Arunachalam, "Public access to the Internet," in Alain Ambrosi, Valérie Peugot, and Daniel Pimienta, eds., *Word Matters: Multicultural Perspectives on Information Societies* (Paris: C & F Éditions, 2005). http://vecam.org/article.php3?id_article =557 (retrieved April 13, 2014).

11. Esmeralda Bermudez, "Giving immigrant laborers an online voice: A new program teaches workers to use cellphones to tell their own stories and to document their lives and work," *Los Angeles Times*, September 19, 2010, http://articles .latimes.com/2010/sep/19/local/la-me-laborer-blogs-20100919 (retrieved October 27, 2013).

12. Jeffrey Passel and Mark Hugo Lopez, "Up to 1.7 million unauthorized immigrant youth may benefit from new deportation rules," Pew Hispanic Center, Washington, D.C., August 14, 2012, http://www. pewhispanic.org/2012/08/14/up-to-1-7-million -unauthorizedimmigrant-youth-may-benefit-from-new-deportation-rules (retrieved September 10, 2013).

13. See Chris Peterson, "User-generated censorship," master's thesis, MIT, 2013. http://cmsw.mit.edu/user-generated-censorship (retrieved April 13, 2014).

14. Tiziana Terranova, "Free labor: Producing culture for the digital economy," *Social Text* 18, no. 2 (2000): 33–58.

15. William A. Gamson and Gadi Wolfsfeld, "Movements and media as interacting systems," *Annals of the American Academy of Political and Social Science* 528 (July 1993): 114–125.

16. Ernest L. Boyer, "The scholarship of engagement," *Bulletin of the American Academy of Arts and Sciences* 49, no. 7 (1996): 18–33.

17. See chapter 1 for more on the history of radio as a key platform for social movements; and see the Detroit Digital Stewards and commotionwireless.net for more on community mesh networks.

Appendix A

1. William Foote Whyte, ed., *Participatory Action Research* (Newbury Park, CA: Sage, 1991).

2. See my Civic Media: Collaborative Design Studio course at http://codesign .mit.edu.

3. See "Participatory action research" resource page by INCITE! Women of Color Against Violence (2014), at http://www.incite-national.org/page/participatory -action-research.

4. Andrea Hricko, "Global trade comes home: Community impacts of goods movement," *Environmental Health Perspectives* 116, no. 2 (2008): A78.

5. Gary Blasi and Jacqueline Leavitt, "Driving poor: Taxi drivers and the regulation of the taxi industry in Los Angeles," report prepared for the UCLA Institute of Labor and Employment, 2006.

6. Victor Narro, "Impacting next wave organizing: Creative campaign strategies of the Los Angeles worker centers," *New York Law School Law Review* 50 (2005): 465.

7. Alfonso Gumucio Dagron and Thomas Tufte, *Communication for Social Change Anthology: Historical and Contemporary Readings* (South Orange, NJ: CFSC Consortium, 2006).

8. Paulo Freire, *Pedagogy of the Oppressed* (New York: Continuum, 2000).

9. Ibid.

10. Gumucio Dagron and Tufte, *Communication for Social Change.*

11. John Downing, *Radical Media: Rebellious Communication and Social Movements* (Thousand Oaks, CA: Sage, 2001).

12. Cees J. Hamelink, *The Politics of World Communication* (London: Sage, 1995).

13. Clemencia Rodriguez, *Fissures in the Mediascape: An International Study of Citizens' Media* (Cresskill, NJ: Hampton Press, 2001).

14. Maria Elena Figueroa, D. Lawrence Kincaid, Namju Rani, and Gary Lewis, "Communication for social change: An integrated model for measuring the process and its outcomes," Communication for Social Change Paper 1 (Baltimore: Johns Hopkins University Center for Communication Programs, for the Rockefeller Foundation, 2002), 50 pp.

15. Ibid.

16. See http://garmentworkercenter.org/media/radiotijera.

17. See http://vozmob.net.

18. The complete transcriptions follow the oral history guidelines, available at http://www.slq.qld.gov.au/__data/assets/pdf_file/0010/174574/SLQ_-_Transcript _std_1.01.pdf. Quotations in the main body of the book also follow these guidelines. In some cases, bridge words ("um," "uh") and crutch words ("like," "you know") have been removed to improve sentence clarity.

19. Sharan B. Merriam, *Qualitative Research: A Guide to Design and Implementation* (New York: John Wiley & Sons, 2009).

20. Kimberlé Crenshaw, "Mapping the margins: Intersectionality, identity politics, and violence against women of color," *Stanford Law Review* 43, no. 6 (1991): 1241–1299.

21. Judith Butler, "Performative acts and gender constitution: An essay in phenomenology and feminist theory," *Theater Journal* 40, no. 4 (1988): 519–531; Craig Calhoun, ed., *Social Theory and the Politics of Identity* (New York: Wiley-Blackwell, 1994).

22. Sandra Harding, *The "Racial" Economy of Science: Toward a Democratic Future* (Bloomington: Indiana University Press, 1993).

23. Patricia Hill Collins, "Toward a new vision: Race, class, and gender as categories of analysis and connection," *Race, Sex & Class* 1, no. 1 (1993): 25–45.

Index